CRIME IN AMERICA

CRIME IN AMERICA

CONTROVERSIAL ISSUES

IN TWENTIETH CENTURY CRIMINOLOGY

Edited with an Introduction
and Critical Comments

BY

HERBERT A BLOCH, Ph.D.

Professor of Sociology and Anthropology, Brooklyn College;
Coordinator of Police Science Program,
Brooklyn College;
Graduate School, New York University

PHILOSOPHICAL LIBRARY

New York

Printed in the United States of America

CONTENTS

CRIME IN AMERICA

INTRODUCTION

Herbert A. Bloch

To the man on the street, the subject of crime has always constituted a source of endless fascination. There are undoubtedly many reasons for this which the social philosopher in the past and today's modern psychiatrist have both frequently attempted to explore. It is possible, in the claim so commonly advanced by psychiatrists, that a good deal of what appears to be a morbid curiosity about crime and criminals stems from the compelling need which men so frequently experience to repress impulses towards lawlessness and violence of a greater or lesser degree. It appears reasonable to believe, likewise, that modern man especially, living in the steel and concrete rabbit-warrens of our huge metropolitan enclaves, going about his mechanized daily routines in an industrial civilization which tends to grow increasingly impersonal, and subject to the countless frustrations which our abnormally incentive-laden society fosters, develops self-discipline and control at considerable cost to himself. Under such auspices, in the common recital of man's woes by the psychiatrist, man's self-discipline becomes an easy prey to his longings and his imagination, and to his personal concern—frequently an uneasy concern—about the potential lawlessness of others. When we begin to consider not only the psychiatrist's horribilia in the form of the minor tensions and irritants which beset our daily lives, unrelieved by the ameliorating influence which past institutional outlets provided, but the ever present fear of international catastrophe which pervades our daily lives as well, it is probably equally impressive that Western men are as law-abiding as they are.

Our concern with crime, therefore, may very well represent a vicarious interest in the wide-ranging motivations which actuate us all. The much abused aphorism—that there but for the grace of God go I—may be construed not merely as an acknowledgement of the fact that human life is all too frequently conditioned by factors beyond our personal control but, even more, a tacit recognition that the motivations which impel some men towards lawless behavior are not much different than the urges which we too so frequently experience. This interest in crime and criminals by the public is not the first time in human history that the sinner has been confused with the saint. If this interest in human behavior, thus, is as widespread as it would appear, as may be evidenced in countless details of public taste, morality, curiosity and behavior—not the least of which perhaps is the soaring sales of paper-backed crime thrillers—then it may suggest quite forcibly that the motivations we examine in the criminal may very well lurk within ourselves.

If this interest of the public in some of the more sensational aspects of criminal activity, irrespective of how derived, was simply an expression of curiosity, the issue in itself might not be of undue significance, as much as the moralist might have occasion to deplore it. But with this curiosity to know frequently goes the attitude to punish. One does not have to be a Freudian to sense the profound impulsions towards punishment, vengefulness, and crime which pervade in varying degree the consciousness of all men, as Alexander and Staub indicated a quarter of a century ago in their small volume, *The Judge, The Criminal and the Public*, which has now become almost a minor classic. It is perhaps this sense of potential destruction of conventional standards and legal barriers, as well as the lurking sense of punitive disaster which lies within us, that makes the criminal such an object of baleful fascination. If civilization is the sum total of our painfully acquired social inhibitions, then the criminal, in his act of social defiance, opens up new vistas of behavior—strange, ominous, and sometimes frightening—which fall beyond the narrow grooves of our commonplace and routinized lives. The stark novelty of the unaccustomed behavior—as novelty always will—provides its own sublimated thrill and quickened sense of excitement.

Although the historian of legal jurisprudence may make out an excellent case, on purely rationalistic grounds, for the development of criminal codes as a means of anti-social deterrence and social redress, there would appear to be a sound psychological basis as well. From the psychological standpoint, it is reasonable to assume that the public hue and cry to punish the offender in part betokens far more a deeply sensed resentment of the need to maintain one's own precarious state of social balance than sympathy for the victim of the criminal act. Hans von Hentig, in his analysis of the economic conditions which tend to induce crime, has suggested that each one of us may be vulnerable to the commission of criminal acts if the pressure of events becomes sufficiently great. The doctrine of *temptation* which he formulates assumes that the motivations towards lawlessness are invariably present in even the most law-abiding men. That they do not manifest themselves, according to this doctrine, is due to the fact that in the ordinary course of events the adverse pressures of circumstance do not press upon us with sufficient intensity. Similarly, the French psychiatrist, Lucien Bovet, in an international report on the causes of delinquency prepared for the United Nations a few years ago, speaks of the "shock troops of delinquency"—those youths who, while not presently committing delinquent acts, may do so when social pressures become more intense and extensive.

Irrespective, however, of the public's peculiar and long standing interest in the criminal and his ways, to the hard-working practitioner in any one of the several areas of criminology, law enforcement and penology, his task appears mundane enough. Although it might reasonably be argued that those professionally concerned with the criminal may have motivations even more suspect than those of the unsophisticated layman—and the claim, unfortunately, has been made—the professional performance and activity of the practitioner in these fields are a far cry from what the public conceives them to be in its sensational curiosity. Indeed, to the often hard-bitten practitioner in any one of the several fields of criminology, whether it be the arduous and difficult field of law enforcement or one of the special branches of correction, the public's attitude of sensationalism is a source of amused tolerance or annoyance, depending upon the pressures of the moment to which he may be subject. The police official, the prison warden, the probation or parole officer knows that his client is all too human and not very much different, if different at all, from the citizen he meets on the street. All criminals are not motivated by dark and sinister passions or strange quirks of the mind. Indeed, only a very small percentage may be said to be motivated by pathological or abnormal traits of mind. From bitter experience and through many years of laborious and accumulated research into the various aspects of the offender's personality and environment, the criminologist has learned that in mentality, physical and even psychological constitution, the offender is not far removed from his law-abiding compatriots. Further, in the more recent forays into the realms of so-called "white collar crime," it is apparent that the divisions between law-abiding and illegal behavior are so faint as to appear indistinguishable, upon occasion, to the trained observer.

To the professional who is devoted to the task of identifying and apprehending the lawbreakers, as much as to those eventually charged with what frequently appears to be the hopeless task of reformation of the habitual offender, the task becomes one of exercising infinite patience and painstaking detail in carrying out routine responsibilities. Such tasks, however, are based upon a considerable substratum of carefully tested experience and research knowledge. Of these hard-won gains, the public is apt to know little, if anything at all. This is not to say that, upon rare occasion, remarkable feats of deduction in the apprehension of a skilled criminal are not exercised. There may be, and upon occasion, striking feats of deductive intelligence are displayed by well-trained and competent law enforcement officers. The use of the disciplined imagination and deductive logic is not a sphere of activity restricted only to science and the learned professions. The penologist, too, has his share of these virtues. For the greater part, however, the apprehension of an offender is brought about by endless questioning, detailed examination of both the injured person and the suspect's associates, and a knowledge based upon experience of how certain types of criminals operate. The intellectual *tours de force* of some fictitious Hercule Poirot or the aggressive bravado of the so-called "private eye"—how the jargon of the police and the underworld has crept into our common speech!—and publicized so widely today through television and the other mass media, are hardly ever found in the routines of law enforcement. The same painstaking detail and attention to routine tasks apply to any one of the several branches of practical penology and correction.

There are, however, remarkable developments in the fields of criminology and law enforcement, of which the public is all too frequently completely oblivious. Much has transpired since the days of the great 18th Century humanitarian and prison reformer, John Howard. The great scientific dispensation of the 19th Century and the growth of the behavioral sciences in our own have begun to penetrate deeply into our consciousness and our thinking concerning the treatment of life's derelicts. Not only has the scientific perspective in criminology, brought into being in the 19th Century by the work of the positivist philosophers of jurisprudence and the demonstrated convictions of Lombroso that criminals could be studied scientifically, enabled us to draw closer to the endless reasons for man's preying upon his neighbors but our value-perspectives have changed. Our attitudes concerning treatment and care, while not changing proportionately, have nevertheless shown considerable signs of modification. Further, it is possible, on the basis of many of our new insights and new methodological presuppositions and research techniques, that we may actually be on the threshold of invigorating new developments in the field of penology. In a world which is continually trembling on the brink of new scientific "breakthroughs," it is not inconceivable that some of our most significant "breakthroughs" in this century may occur in the human field, of which the understanding and treatment of the offender is a significant phase.

Indeed, it can be readily argued that in relation to how a society views its mentally ill and its prisoners—categories, ironically, which history has so frequently linked together—

can it best be judged in terms of its moral character and social advance. Certainly, in the laborious history of man's slow progress, the development of new penal insights seems to have been closely associated with significant new developments in the growing horizons of man's social vision. Historians of penology are constantly being astounded at the novelty of penal insights and methods of periods long past, in which the concern with the treatment of social offenders was closely linked to revolutionary new advances in man's social thinking.

It is true, nevertheless, that the significant changes in penal and criminological research since the 19th Century has been slow in bringing about the public awakening and penal reform which its protagonists hoped for. As the writer has so frequently remarked and written, the reasons for this slow lag in the adoption of improved techniques, on the part of the public generally and responsible government officials in particular, constitutes an area of research which itself has been seriously neglected. We know far more about the causes and treatment of crime than the public knows or appreciates, and than the functioning leadership of society is willing to accept. Nevertheless, effective inroads upon traditional and time-worn concepts are being made—and we do not mean by this the pampering and indulgence of society's recalcitrants and lawbreakers. Reforms must not always be judged in terms of some vague and sentimental humanitarian philosophy, but rather in terms of their capacity to deter what is conceived as socially evil and to reform its practitioners. In this light, reforms leading to the deterrence of crime and the more successful treatment of offenders are being effectively accomplished, even though the rate of progress may be more slow than the progressive penologist would like to see. The salvaging of human outcasts in the struggle against crime, however, is a continuous process and a far more hopeful one than the uninformed imagine.

The reforms which will eventually make the endeavors in crime control and the social rehabilitation of offenders far more effective is drawn from several fields. The field of criminology is no longer a single field if, in truth, it ever was. Penology and criminology have become highly subdivided into specialized fields, in keeping with the growth of our knowledge and the dictum of the late nineteenth century philosopher of science, Poincaré, that the solution of any limited problem in science immediately raises a number of new queries which clamor for attention. In penology and criminology, this has been particularly true; with the new queries have come new inquiries and new research methods which, upon occasion, have tended to engender new specialized areas of criminological investigation.

For our purposes, we may regard our field of study as consisting of law enforcement and its specialized branch of *criminalistics* (the development of scientific techniques of detection, investigation, collection and preservation of legal evidence, and the use of the natural sciences in identifying individuals and episodes associated with a given crime); *jurisprudence* and the development of criminal statutes; *criminology proper*, the sociological, social psychological and psychological conditions associated with the causes of crime and crime conditions; and *penology*, the vast areas encompassing the detention, imprisonment, treatment and rehabilitation of offenders, in which probation and parole are conspicuous parts.

Today, the unifying theme which brings the several branches of criminology together is the belief in the efficacy of the scientific method and a conviction that the use of science is itself an ennobling practise. There is, however, a qualification to such a conviction which is becoming widely accepted. Whereas the use of the scientific method may instill a deep respect for facts and the ability to test our experience on the basis of controlled comparisons so that we can predict and control, there is a more fundamental conviction involved. This conviction—and it may be more true of criminologists than many other professions—is a belief in the worth of the human individual and a sense of humanitarian purpose which is allied to the scientific spirit. We are learning a bitter lesson today, a lesson which states that science, devoid of human compassion and purpose, may not only be sterile but destructive of mankind's best interests. It is apparently no accident, historically, that the awakening of man's deepest liberal and humanitarian convictions appears to have been stirred by his growing reliance upon dispassionate and objective inquiry.

Although it may be true that there is considerable agreement upon the use of scientific method, especially when informed with the conviction of humanitarian purpose, there are nevertheless serious controversies in the field of criminology. Many of these differences emerge as a result of special spheres of interest which appear contradictory. For example, the concern of the law enforcement official to apprehend and gain the conviction of a proven offender appears to come into direct conflict with the view of the probation and parole officer, whose major concern is one of rehabilitation and restoration to society of the offender. Such conflicts can be bitter, frequently leading to confusion of understanding and purpose, and which, perhaps, can only be reconciled in the long run by the emergence of a new philosophy within the entire field of corrections. Such a philosophy is beginning to take shape and is based upon the premise that most, if not all, offenders can be rehabilitated and that the techniques for such reclamation lie only partially in compulsive detention and punishment. Punitive measures, for example, are only effective if integrated within an entire program of rehabilitation.

However, there are more fundamental differences than such common conflicts of interest. It should be added, as well, that such conflicts of interest are, more often than not, deceptive. Frequently, they are more apparent than real and rarely, if ever, mutually exclusive. There are differences, however, which exist largely because of the imperfections of our methods of approach and treatment, and the almost unavoidable intellectual biases which spring to life because of overspecialization of our professional concerns. Such differences, frequently, encourage and are accompanied by lack of clarification of the several professional objectives in criminology and the failure to articulate with precision our specialized and partial interests. Although frequently founded on intellectual predilections, such controversies, nevertheless, can be vitriolic. What remains to be done is not only to specify the distinctive areas and the limited objectives with which the specialized fields of criminology must concern themselves, but to recognize those vital and inseminating areas which impinge upon each other. The intellectual controversies which exist in the field of criminology are, to a considerable degree, brought about by the failure to recognize the different levels upon which science operates. The concern of the sociologist, for example, is not that of the psychiatrist, even though the two scientific interests may overlap at several crucial points. Further, the historic development of one field tends to emphasize approaches and interests quite unique and different from the points of view of others. For example, the social sciences have been concerned since their inception—possibly overconcerned—with the development of scientific method. Psychiatry, on the other hand, has from the outset been a method of therapy and only very recently has embarked upon the field of research in a truly scientific sense.

The result of these differences has produced a number of variations in point of view concerning the apprehension, treatment, identification and rehabilitation of the offender, which still await effective reconciliation. This book frankly acknowledges such differences of view and attempts to present some of them in their broad diversity. Eventually, it will be possible to reconcile such divergent views but the moment is not yet at hand. Although the answers to the complexities extant in the several fields of criminology do not lie in the mere pooling of our several intellectual resources, it constitutes, nevertheless, an essential first step in this direction. The development of new conceptual approaches must also take place but it is dubious whether such concepts may be developed unless we first begin to understand each other. This we are slowly, but with increasing effectiveness, beginning to do.

Most of the contributions in this volume were first read as papers before the annual meetings of the American Society of Criminology. It is a tribute to this enterprising organization that it has encouraged differences of opinion and view as a means towards the attainment of coherence of purpose and clarification of objectives for the practising criminologist. The first section of this book deals with certain aspects of the difficult problem of treatment of the criminal offender, ranging from contradictions in correctional administration to the much-debated problem of capital punishment. The second section deals with some of the more specialized concerns of modern criminology which do not always find themselves in our standard reference books. The third section concerns itself with some of the most pressing issues which appear in the field of modern penology, a consideration of those problems of sex and sanity which touch upon some of the most vital moral issues in contemporary society. The last section deals with some of the more recent methodological interests in approach to the study of crime and delinquency, including some observations of the American penchant for ascribing illegality to certain matters of a private and moral concern.

In the preparation of this book, considerable gratitude must be extended to Donal E. J. MacNamara, Dean of the New York Institute of Criminology and President of the American League to Abolish Capital Punishment—veritably a stormy petrel in the field of practising criminology. His active interest, enlivening intelligence, and profound concern with the several problems discussed in this volume is a tribute to his unflagging zeal and devotion to the furtherance of progressive thinking in criminology. Grateful acknowledgement must likewise be made to the members of the American Society of Criminology who have developed such a stimulating forum for the discussion of vital criminological issues and who have contributed to this volume. Our gratitude is likewise extended to Susan Bloch and to David Duvall, whose sacrifice of bright and sunny afternoons in Ceylon in undertaking the laborious task of proofreading is deeply appreciated. Finally, as always, special tribute must be paid to my wife, Adeline S. Bloch, without whose generous sacrifice of time and self, and her unstinting effort, the bringing of this book to completion would have been far more difficult.

Although the contributors to this volume might cavil on a number of vital intellectual and moral issues dealing with any one of the numerous special aspects of crime and criminology, they would all, it appears likely, agree on certain fundamentals in the development of modern scientific criminology. These fundamentals stipulate that human behavior is adaptive behavior, and that criminal behavior constitutes a special type of adaptation. Secondly, if criminality is the result of external environment and internal adaptation, then it can only be removed by modification of external circumstance or internal conditioning. Lastly, since men are capable of an endless variety of adaptations and susceptible to an infinite variety of learning processes, the redemption of men rests with our imaginative insight, intellectual ingenuity, and moral courage.

Herbert A. Bloch

Colombo, Ceylon
November, 1959.

Part I
Crime and Punishment in Twentieth Century America

Twentieth century criminology includes the whole social process of crime control. This process begins even before a crime has been committed with the concept of prevention and continues in the work of detection and apprehension, the trial and disposition of the offender by the court, as well as the supervision of the convicted person under imprisonment, probation, or parole. In the evolution of this process over the past two hundred years, there have developed certain notions which are often taken for granted by the average citizen, regarded as sacrosanct by those engaged in the process, and accepted with little question by those who purport to speak professionally for criminology in the reference volumes. These are correction's "sacred cows." There are certain conclusions concerning them which we can draw.

1. That crime prevention is primarily the function of the police is not only unrealistic but it is dangerous in that those other agencies in society, whose job prevention really is and who are especially trained and qualified for it, are inclined to impose their responsibilities upon the police.

2. That the "broadened social concept" of police work results in the police giving less and less attention to crime and criminals and more and more attention to non-criminal activities, until in some areas a vast amount of the time and energy of police are devoted to such activities.

3. The concept of "deterrence" embodied in the criminal law, and the notion that criminality is an entity in itself which can be curbed or controlled by will-power or by force, are basic concepts which require serious reappraisal.

4. That the housing of convicts in massive, monastic, medieval, monolithic, monumental monstrosities is not only a "sacred cow," but plain "monkey-cage" penology; future construction of such institutions, both Federal and State, is both unnecessary and unsound.

5. That making rehabilitation a "sacred cow" of prisons has resulted in omitting from parole one of the essentials for success, namely, the intermediate plan used by the founders of the Irish System. Rehabilitation occurs only under normal conditions in the normal society to which the offender belongs. To meet these and other problems at this mid-century point in American correctional administration, a three-point program is suggested.

Chapter 1

CORRECTION'S SACRED COWS

Howard B. Gill

Director, Institute of Correctional Administration
The American University, Washington, D. C.

The general theme of this volume, dealing with "Controversial issues in Twentieth Century Criminology," is a refreshing departure from the usual smugness to which we are accustomed in this field. What we consider modern in criminology is hardly two hundred years old. To be sure there were experiments in better ways of dealing with offenders as early as 1682 in Penn's Great Experiment which lasted until 1719, and in the program of Pope Clement in Rome in 1704. But it was not until Cesare Becarria in 1763 and John Howard in 1777 penned their famous statements on *Crime and Punishment* and *The State of The Prisons* that criminology began the era which has continued down to our times. This era is one in which treatment of the individual offender for the better protection of society has become the central thesis of all criminology.

When I speak of "Criminology," I am not speaking only of the process usually associated with prisons, but rather of the whole social process of crime control. This process begins even before a crime has been committed, with the concept of prevention, and continues in the work of detection and apprehension by the police, the trial and disposition of the offender by the court, as well as the supervision of the convicted person under imprisonment, probation, and parole.

It may even extend to the exercise of clemency and pardon by the legislature and the executive. In the evolution of this process over the past two hundred years, there have developed certain notions which are often taken for granted by the average citizen, regarded as sacrosanct by those engaged in the process, and accepted with little question by those who purport to speak professionally for criminology in the texts. It is to some of these notions that I wish to call your attention.

Crime Prevention

The first "sacred cow" which I believe we should send to the slaughter house is the notion that crime prevention is primarily the function of the police. O. W. Wilson, Dean of the School of Criminology at the University of California, says quite simply in his notable text on *Police Administration*,[1] "Police duties may be classified . . . as the prevention of the development of criminal and antisocial tendencies in individuals. . . ." (p. 2). And again, "The police department is created to prevent the commission of crimes, and no other agency has been created for this primary purpose." (p. 204). In an entire chapter devoted to "The Prevention of Criminality," Wilson enlarges on this thesis to set up the police as the initiators, coordinators, and operators of a widespread program of crime prevention dealing almost exclusively with juveniles and ignoring the potential adult criminal. He proposes that the police shall "deal directly with problem children" (p. 206), "impose on offenders who are not persistent criminals requirements of conduct in lieu of prosecution"— a course which he admits is "pre-judicial action," and he labels as erroneous the contention that "the police are not qualified, that their performance of these tasks results in an unwholesome experience for children, and that other social agencies are designed for this purpose." Authorities such as Paul Tappan, Pauline Young, Herbert Bloch and the late Edwin Sutherland, as well as the National Conference on Prevention and Control of Juvenile Delinquency and the International Chiefs of Police Association, are extremely cau-

tious and often forthright in opposition to these broad assertions that prevention is a police function. Certainly an examination of actual police programs shows that these broad
claims are not supported by the facts.

However, without going into the unrealistic aspects of
this presentation, there is another phase of it which is far more
significant and dangerous, namely, that when the police assume
and persist in their claims to such wide functions, those
other agencies in society, who have a specific stake in prevention, are all inclined to "let George do it." The results are
that this "sacred cow," to which such respect is paid, too
often successfully forestalls an intelligent and organized program of crime prevention—both juvenile and adult. Such preventive programs are the responsibility of the home, the
school, the church, and those other character-building organizations of society which are especially trained and qualified (as the police notoriously are not) to undertake the work
of "prevention of the development of criminal and anti-social
tendencies in individuals."

In passing, it should be noted that, without doubt, the
police have an important part to play in such a program, one
which involves the discovery, and the referral of crime hazards and potential criminality to the proper authorities, and
cooperation with such authorities for the eradication of such
evils. But let us not saddle the police with responsibility for
"the prevention of the development of criminal and anti-
social tendencies in individuals"—a responsibility which calls
for the training, wisdom, and experience of parents, teachers,
ministers, psychologists and many others not to be found in
the police forces of our nation.

The Police

Increasingly in the United States, the police are giving less
and less attention to crime and criminals and more and more
attention to what may be called non-criminal activities. These
include duties having to do with inspections of buildings,
services and utilities, attendance at parades, weddings, dances,

funerals, and other social activities, the operation of boys' clubs and camps, traffic control including giving drivers' tests, inspecting motor vehicles, lecturing on safety at schools, investigating accidents, as well as directing traffic, operating ambulances and delivering babies, conducting lost and found departments, acting as centers of information, and, in general, performing what a manual issued by the Los Angeles Police Department describes as "controlling the conduct of society." To these, O. W. Wilson adds: "protection . . . against harmful acts, both willful and inadvertent, of the non-criminal as well as the criminal class," "protection against immoral conduct," and "the regulation of people in their non-criminal activities," all of which he includes under "the broadened social concept" of police work. (pp. 2, 3). In one mid-western city of approximately 100,000 population, the Chief of Police estimated that 90 per cent of the time and energy of his police department was devoted to such non-criminal activities.

As the result of some well organized "public relations" on the part of numerous police departments, such activities are looming larger and larger as the principal function of the police. In contrast, the detection and apprehension of criminals gets less and less attention. The American people are being taught that "police service has been broadened to include certain aspects of social service for which the police are particularly well suited" (p. 3), including "cases (of) more than ordinary social-welfare significance, notably those involving the mentally defective, the very young, the very old, and family relationships." (Wilson, p. 3). It is difficult to combat so plausible an appeal at making the policeman a big friendly fellow who loves everybody; but if the correctional process is to function properly, some one must concentrate on the work of detecting and apprehending criminals which is in itself a full-time job. Since our police are not doing too good a job at these primary functions, perhaps we should avoid this big, gentle, cow-like concept of police work in favor of the stern, firm and authoritarian figure who is supposed to be the terror of the wrong-doer. This turning of the bull into another Elsie is a feat of endocrinology which can have only the direst consequences for the correctional process.

The Courts

Of all the sacred cows in the correctional field, perhaps the most obdurate is the one known as the Criminal Law. For nearly seventy-five years, the notion that the practise of criminal law is a dirty, sordid business has become ingrained in the mores of our society and in the curricula of our law schools. Nearly fifty years ago, William Howard Taft, who later became Chief Justice of the Supreme Court, referred to criminal law in the United States as a "disgrace." Most law schools in this country recognize this point of view by offering no programs of specialization in this field of training, and few if any students with a background in psychology, sociology, criminology, and human relations are encouraged to enter our law schools with a view to becoming specialists in the criminal law. Why is this so?

Chiefly because the criminal law has made a sacred cow of a concept which emerged in the dark ages,—a concept called "deterrence"—and has insisted upon regarding criminality as an entity in itself. According to this archaic view, criminality can be curbed or controlled by will-power or by force rather than viewing such behavior as the quality of an act determined by many factors, of which choice and force are only minor. No one except policemen, lawyers and judges believes in deterrence as a major factor in controlling crime. (And here I do not mean repression when I speak of deterrence.) As a result, we still sentence convicts for crimes committed rather than for the fundamental maladjustments under which they operate; we deal with symptoms instead of causes or basic problems involved. In spite of the fact that Dr. Benjamin Rush in 1787 suggested the way out of this ignorance and Enrico Ferri, the great Italian criminal lawyer and teacher, reinforced this point of view in 1881 and again in 1921 in the proposed Italian Criminal Code, American jurists with few exceptions continue to operate as though one could measure the pain to be inflicted on a criminal by the pleasure he is supposed to have derived from his criminal act. To shatter this sacred cow is one of the first requisites of an intelligent correctional process.

The Prisons

Of all the areas of criminology, perhaps the prisons possess the biggest herd of sacred cows. Their names are legion. Let me list a few.

First, there is the concept of "prison discipline." Beginning about 1830, this sacred cow grew to such proportions that it became synonymous with penology, and in some quarters it is still regarded as such. This disciplinary type of penology was composed of many facets. It began with non-communication, sometimes known as the silent or the solitary system, and while the system has long been discredited, it still survives in many limitations on prisoner visiting, mail, and contacts with the community. It included degradation and deprivation, and while the shaved head and the striped suit are no longer fashionable in most prisons, the attitude adopted toward any person unlucky enough to land in prison is to regard him *ipso facto* as a pariah in society. "Treat 'em rough and give 'em hell" may be popular today only in Marine brigs—and even there this philosophy has been having a difficult time of late; but the more subtle cruelty, by which society pins the label, "ex-con," on everyone who is unlucky enough to get caught, is even more degrading and lasts longer.

The traditional concept of prison discipline also stood for "hard labor," until "teaching a convict an honest trade" has been accepted by a great many people as the end-all and be-all of imprisonment. Our laws state the form of punishment in terms of "hard labor" and our judges solemnly intone the sentence in terms of "hard labor," and thus obeissance to this sacred cow having been given, we send the convicted man to prison to rot in stultifying idleness. This is a form of painful self-deception which verges on the nonsensical. It is true that except for the youthful criminal who is still in need of vocational training, the problem involved in criminality in perhaps 75 per cent of cases is not related to the work problem. So it does not matter too much. The chief damage done is that the public, fed on this sort of false premise, fails to grasp the true significance of treatment for offenders.

This prison discipline also proudly boasted that it treated every prisoner alike—it played no favorites. Such simple justice appealed to simple-minded folk—even to prisoners sometimes. But it is one of the sacred cows that has begun to languish only within the past twenty-five years and only among a limited number of professionals who dare to defy tradition.

The list of paradoxes could go on indefinitely. Subservience to rules—the petty whims of petty men. The prohibition against "fraternization," which in some prisons goes so far as to state, "Employees and foremen are strictly prohibited from holding conversation with convicts upon any subject disconnected with their duty or labor . . . nor shall they listen to any convict history, or to the history of his crime and case on which he was convicted." We accept without question the injunction that "no prisoner is going to tell us how to run our prisons," while on every side the prisoners *are* running the prisons. Indeed, it is doubtful whether they could be operated without their help and cooperation. It almost seems as though progress in penology—progress through chaos—is only possible due to their determined opposition. It is probably not too bold to claim that, in certain states, the only progress made in penology in the last one hundred years has been made as a result of prison riots.

There still lingers, however, one sacred cow to which I should like to draw special attention. It is a sturdy animal kept fat and sleek by the prison construction companies, among others, who would have us believe that prisons must be built of tool-proof steel, with inside cells and all the clanging mechanisms that go with them. Like our automobiles, the belief is fostered that our prisons must be bigger and broader, and longer and more powerful, lest we be overwhelmed by the wild men incarcerated in them.

In 1823, Elam Lynds and John Cray completed a prison at Auburn, New York, which was modelled after a punishment building in which escaped convicts had been housed in inside cells. The cellular idea had been inherited from the church whose notion of penitence was to remand the guilty to mediaeval monasticism. In America, the inside cell was an invention of Lynds and Cray to prevent prisoners from escape. It consisted of rooms within a larger room, with no access to the outer wall. In time, this concept has become refined until now we have as many as three to five hundred such rooms with conventional steel-barred fronts in a single enormous shell for housing prisoners. These massive "monkey-cages" have become symbols of modern imprisonment as the movies, T.V., cartoons, and standard publications depicting prison life all testify. "No other single factor," states the *Federal Handbook of Correctional Institution Design and Construction*, "has so retarded the development and success of rehabilitative programs as has the lag in correctional architecture." [2] (p. 2). Yet in this same text, Chapter V, entitled "Planning a Model Super-Security Institution," presents a design which outdistances any prison built to date as an example of man's inhumanity to man. It is an inside-cell block type of prison lighted only by sky-lights. It too finds its prototype in a punishment block. At the State Prison at old Charlestown, Massachusetts, the punishment cells were lighted only by sky-lights in the roof. Apparently there is nothing new under the sun.

Of this structure, Harry Elmer Barnes wrote in the second edition of *New Horizons in Criminology*: [3] "This design is well-nigh perfect for a maximum security institution." (p. 498). Fortunately, in the third edition, published recently, Professor Negley Teeters has deleted this chapter. Is it too much to hope that the Federal Bureau of Prisons will follow suit and delete Chapter V from their *Handbook*, publishing instead the more modern concepts of therapeutic community prisons to be found now both in this country and abroad?

Unfortunately, some local and state agencies, assuming that they were following the most modern plans, have erected sky-light prisons for maximum security prisoners. The new state prison at Walpole, Massachusetts, is such a structure. They got their plans from the construction offices of the Federal Bureau of Prisons, with or without the blessing of the Bureau. If the opinions of the men who are trying to operate this monstrosity are any criterion, the Commonwealth of Massachusetts is already heartily sick of its bargain.

At the present time, plans are under consideration for the abandonment of the Federal Prison at Alcatraz and the construction of another super-security prison somewhere else. With the abandonment of Alcatraz, everyone agrees; it has proved uneconomical, cruel, brutal, and, in the last resort, unprofessional. But with approximately 4,500 to 5,000 maximum security cells in existing Federal prisons—most of them of the inside, animal-cage variety—the Federal Bureau does not need more maximum security cells. Barnes and Teeters, for example, have indicated that "not over 20 per cent of convicts require maximum security custodial provisions." And they also state that "to erect a super-maximum-security prison in its (Alcatraz's) place is highly debatable." Better to make such use as we can of those ancient bastilles at Leavenworth, Atlanta, McNeil Island and elsewhere for intractables, and devote the development of new prisons to the type of therapeutic communities which will serve the future of penology instead of its past.

No one is going to deny the necessity for keeping prisoners securely. This is the first duty of every prison official. Nor am I so naive as to believe that we are going to tear down these massive, monastic, mediaeval, monolithic, monumental monstrosities—even if they are unsound both custodially and otherwise. These sacred cows are with us to stay for a long time. It is urgent, however, to know them for what they are—representatives of an outworn penology—and deal with them accordingly. Further, since they are unnecessary and unsound, we should build no more of them.

But lest one thinks that sacred cows in our prison system are all of ancient vintage, attention should be drawn to two golden calves which we have been erecting in the name of modern penology. One is called "classification" and the other is the assumption that every member of the prison staff is a correctional worker trained and devoted to rehabilitation.

Thirty-five years ago, there developed in some of our more progressive prisons a procedure which became known as "classification." It consisted mainly of gathering a case history about each prisoner and setting up a program for him approved by a board of specialists. These three elements—the case history, the program, and the classification board—have become crystallized into a system which is almost a fundamental tenet of progressive penology today. As a result, we are becoming overwhelmed with files of information about prisoners, so much so that we have no time or energy for treatment. In this welter of information, the significant problems of prisoners are often lost sight of, and the programs which are designed for rehabilitation are little more than conventional routine assignments to activities available in a particular institution without regard to the individual prisoner's criminal tendencies. And all of this is meticulously gathered for and solemnly reviewed by high-paid specialists sitting on Classification Boards. The results are that often considerable high-flown effort is devoted to relatively minor problems, and not enough pertinent effort is expended on really serious cases. Programs, rather than problems, have become the center of attention. The whole business is a survival from the days when history-taking was the end-all and the be-all of social work, and while it did much to establish individualized treatment as part of the prison program, it has long since outlived its usefulness.

Dr. Ralph Brancale, a penal psychiatrist of considerable experience, says of classification:

"The average classification process . . . consists of little more than a check list of the inmate's deficiencies and assets, with specific recommendations for rectifying or exploiting each specific finding. The assumption behind this approach seems to be that an atomistically constructed picture of the patient's assets and liabilities, followed by a forced cementing of this into a hodgepodge semblance of personality structure, will automatically provide the basis for a prescription of treatment which is expected to solve all of the offender's problems.

This segmental approach to classification which is so prevalent in correctional institutions should be recognized for what it is: a superficial, impractical, nonintegrative approach which ignores the core of the problem of offenders and their personality structure." [4]

To meet this problem, it is time that the field of corrections adopted a more professional approach to individual adjustment through well-recognized clinical procedures. Such procedures do not ignore case histories but they do make them secondary to the establishment of inter-personal relationships between clients and therapists, and they rank problem-solving above programs as a means of treating specific criminal tendencies in prisoners.

The notion that every member of the prison personnel is a correctional officer is so unrealistic as to fall of its own weight. However, this cliché is being preached in such high places that few dare oppose it. Some prisons, as just stated, prohibit any conversation between a guard and a prisoner relative to the latter's problems; other so-called progressive prisons enjoin the guard to be both a security officer and a treatment officer. In these prisons, the prison officer has a wide range of duties, mostly of a security nature, but with some vague responsibility for treatment. As a result, neither security nor treatment is handled adequately. While it is true that all prison workers need to understand the nature of corrections to be effective team-workers, it is equally true that when good officers specialize in security and other equally good officers are properly directed to specialize in treatment, the best procedures for both will be developed. As it is, either we are producing a sickly sentimentalism which is fundamentally unrealistic or we are giving only lip service to treatment.

Probation and Parole

Finally in the correctional process we come to probation and parole. Being the latest innovations in two hundred years of progress, we find fewer sacred cows in these fields than elsewhere. Although serious efforts have recently been made to limit the fields of probation and parole to a select few with professional social work certification, there is a growing resistance to this tendency.

Recently I received a letter from the judge of a Juvenile Court in a mid-western state who was looking for a probation officer; he ended his letter by stating—"And don't send me one of those social workers!" The Director of Social Work in another juvenile court, herself a member in good standing of her professional group, complained to me that the graduates of schools of social work who were applying for positions in her court knew a great deal about social work but nothing about crime and delinquency. Our concern here should not be an attitude of resistance to social workers but rather an effort to prevent the deification of social work.

In the field of parole, we have never had enough success to develop any very sturdy sacred cows. Perhaps the blind faith which is reposed in the traditional conditions of parole, which set forth *what a parolee may not do* to solve his problems, comes closest to becoming a fetish. I have examined the official conditions of parole in many states. They deal mostly with rules against changing one's job, home, or marital status without permission of the authorities, and against associating with evil companions, getting drunk, or committing crimes. These are no doubt important for an orderly supervision of parolees. However, I have yet to see a single official presentation of "Conditions of Parole" which states that the parolee must try to carry out the program which has been set up to solve his particular problems and thus reduce his tendency to crime. In view of the recidivism among parolees, estimated at over sixty percent, it almost seems as though some attention should be paid to problem-solving and treatment. When Gaylord Hubbell, the warden of Sing Sing prison, went to Europe in 1869 and came back to report enthusiastically on the so-called "Irish System" at the first meeting of the American Prison Association in 1870, he apparently emphasized only two phases of the new system of parole, namely penal servitude and parole; he left out the so-called Intermediate Plan. The result has been that for over fifty years we, in the United States, have sought to establish a parole program in which one of the essential factors is missing. This, combined with the sacred cow called "Rehabilitation," which assumes that prisons accomplish results which no prison ever has or ever can accomplish, has had a most disastrous effect on parole in the United States.

Decidedly limited as to personnel and facilities, prisons by their very nature, can perform only a limited service; they can keep, observe, diagnose, plan, and train a little; they can not rehabilitate. Rehabilitation occurs only under normal conditions in the normal society to which the offender belongs. The founders of the Irish System, Sir Walter Crofton and Sir Joshua Jebb, apparently recognized this. Following a period of penal servitude, a period of social servitude had to be served before a prisoner was placed on parole. This social servitude consisted of a period of service in the community under the close supervision of prison officials. The significance of this Intermediate Plan (as they called it) was that it gave prison officials the opportunity to help an offender really make good in society before releasing him on his own under parole. It was a wise provision.

Recently, the military services have adopted a similar procedure in their "Installation Parole"; the state of Wisconsin has been experimenting with its Huber Law for misdemeanants; and Sweden, Norway, Denmark, Holland and other European countries have been using a method called Private Pre-Release, which is based on much the same principles as the Intermediate Plan of the Irish System.[5] If the United States is ever to halt the extravagant and useless addition of more and more costly institutions for offenders, we must first trim the prison system down to size, and then supplement it with a program of servitude in the community under strict and continuous supervision just as soon as the offender and society are ready for it. This is the next step in the evolution of 20th Century penology. Thus, we shall slaughter two sacred cows with one blow: more monumental monstrosities and prison rehabilitation—the one a menace, the other a myth.

The correctional process is not made up of five or six separate constellations—prevention, police, courts, prisons, probation, and parole—each whirling in space in its own orbit, and occasionally colliding one with another. It is a single process and demands an integrated and coordinated program under the unified command of a professional leader of the highest calibre on at least three levels—federal, state, and city. Because of the lack of such coordination and such high professional leadership, we may be losing the war on crime in the United States.

REFERENCES

1. Wilson, O. W., *Police Administration* (McGraw-Hill, New York, 1950), p. 2.

2. U.S. Bureau of Prisons *Handbook of Correctional Institution Design and Construction* (Federal Prison Industries, Inc., Leavenworth, Kansas, 1949).

3. Barnes and Teeters, *New Horizons in Criminology* (Prentice-Hall Inc., New York, 1959).

4. Tappan, Paul W. (Editor), *Contemporary Correction* (McGraw-Hill, New York, 1951), p. 193.

5. United Nations, Department of Economic and Social Affairs, *Prison Labour* (Publication ST/SOA/SD/5, June 1955, New York).

There is considerable interest today in the pressing problem of making criminology a genuine profession. But the field of criminology is not a single, unitary enterprise but a variety of different fields, each with its own traditional techniques, procedures, predilections and biases. These biases stem from different sources historically, but primarily they emerge from the fields of law enforcement, the courts, the prisons, and the academic world. The objective and scientific view of the academic criminologist has frequently come into direct clash with the more pragmatic considerations of the other fields. In the hope of developing a comprehensive and integrated view, Dr. Jameson suggests what might profitably be done and anticipated in the effort to reconcile the divergent views springing from these several fields as well as the so-called "common sense" approach.

Chapter 2

SOME CONTRADICTIONS IN
CRIMINOLOGICAL TRAINING

SAMUEL HAIG JAMESON, PH. D.

I. *Introduction*

Those accustomed to worship at the altar of statistics contend that the rate of crime in the United States is still on the rise. Apparently we have become a nation of thieves and robbers, rapists and addicts. Our jails are packed, courts are behind in their calendar, prisons overcrowded, probation and parole officers overloaded, and the public overawed. Meanwhile the rest of the world looks to us wth expectations as the leaders of "modern penology." Our prisons set the pace for the humane treatment of their wards; our probation and parole workers probe into overt life histories; and the psychiatrists penetrate behind the concrete walls of the mind into the realm of the unconscious. Our ingenuity, to turn the inside out and the outside in again, is matchless.

Today we are somewhat confused, frustrated, groping and, at times, irrational. True, the old trigger-happy gun-guard in the tower has been displaced by the trained "sociologist" at the Guidance Centers; the chain-gangs are transformed into industrial and trade trainees within the prison walls; and the re-conditioned erring culprits released into this blooming and buzzing world for rehabilitation. We have traveled a long and rough road because of that glimmering faith in daring to do something against the custodial collective psychosis. But all this only *after* the commission of the anti-social act. Meanwhile, religious, political, economic, even educational vested interests have militated against efforts to show "our faith through our works."

Undoubtedly our views are colored by our milieu. As an academic trainer in this process of enlightenment, let me be blunt. As yet we do not have a *profession* of criminology at the grass roots level; what we pride ourselves in is a galaxy of *competitive occupations* with conflicting and hostile ideologies. Yet we would not share this common concern without a belief common to all, namely, the restorability of society's erring members, nor could we entertain any hope unless convinced of the probability of preventing potential anti-social behavior.

Early criminology and penology, imbued with the custodial psychosis, and the modern era intoxicated with the reform virus, approached their subject matter *after* the criminal act was committed. The Geneva Conference on Crime is a living witness. Its concern with the six areas in the handling of the crime situation so familiar to many of us were: minimum rules for treatment of prisoners; open institutions; prison labor; personnel; juvenile delinquency; and the sentencing methods. Each one of these deals with situations after the commission of the anti-social act. They are valid facets of the total crime picture but not quite inclusive of *all* the facets. What is missing? Investigations of the criminogenic factors and their control. This means that attention should be focused upon the process *before* the act instead of the current practise of *after* the act. What to do to *prevent* the occurrence of the undesirable act and not only how to deal with the actor after he has committed the act should constitute our principal concern.

II. *Meanderings in Criminology*

The future path of Criminology is bent by its past and the present. One cannot say that criminology's meandering scenery has been uninteresting or totally barren. Religious, legalistic, reformistic, heuristic explanations and remedies expounded in literature from the Code of Hammurabi to the current legislation recommending the abolition of capital punishment, offer hair-raising, artful and shifty documentaries. But none of the past attitudes equal the handicap which the paradox of our contemporary American John Q. Public displays.

The nostrum of well-meaning citizens' choruses echo throughout the land: "Why doesn't government do something"? "What are these scientists doing about crime"? "How long will this mollycoddling of criminals by the probation and parole officers continue"? "What has come upon our judges? Don't they believe in protecting society's Rights"? "What's this indeterminate sentence which makes imprisonment a joke"? "Why have the prisons become social clubs"? "How long will the taxpayers be expected to bear the burden"? "It is time that somebody did something instead of talking about it." "Let's do something. . . ."

"Let's do something." But we are accustomed to delegate functions to other agencies. We expect the fire department to put out the fire; the police to apprehend the arsonist, the judge to sentence him, the custodial institutions to punish him, the parole officer to supervise his behavior for a while, etc., etc. These are necessary because John, Dick and Harry, Jane, Helen and Mary have neither the time nor the equipment to do anything with and for the arsonist. All they can do is scream against the arsonist and get assurance from the law enforcement agencies that he is "locked up" and that the public is safe for the time being.

"Let's do something"? Something was done. What did the screaming citizens do? An apathetic, uninformed, agitated citizenry fanned the fires of hostility against the arsonist while fearing arson in the future. It asked severe punishment for the act; the judge's severe sentence evened the score. There stopped the public's interest. Whether the firebug commits suicide in prison because of guilt feeling, or the institution, after administering psychiatric treatment, "cures" and returns him to society, is no concern of the average citizen. The paradox may be spelled out: People are interested in the *act* and not in the *actor*. In depraved cases, interest in the actor ends with his probable liquidation or permanent incarceration in a penal institution. Our unholy fear of convicts contributes to the stabilization of the heightened hostility. A public with such retributive philosophy and punishment cannot offer much help to those suffering from a guilt complex. And our law enforcement and correctional personnel are recruited from the rank and file of such a public.

III. *Evidences of Forward March*

To the chorus of "let's do something," our choir responds: "We have done much, and are doing more."

Remember the abolition of the lash in Florida, control by terror and beatings in Montana, emergence of the mobile county circuit courts, detention homes, youth aid divisions of police departments, juvenile courts, minimum security prisons, reception and guidance centers, probation and parole, special treatment of sex psychopaths and the emotionally disturbed, inmate education, group therapy, forestry camps, indefinite sentence, residential treatment, and a host of others now so familiar to us.

Whereas the objective of these constructive measures is the restoration of the offender to respectability in his civilian milieu, still they are geared to the grinding concept of punishment and retribution. Apparently faith in complete redemption is to be found only in the religious sphere! Maximum security remains the fundamental concern of our prisons, and those of us who peddle rehabilitation in the name of the "New Criminology," do so with tongue in cheek. Key to resolute faith is self-discipline which can be induced only through the creation of insight into the role which self plays in the social milieu.

IV. *Looking Ahead*

Avoiding the administration of potent "shots in the arm" and the prescription of a wonder drug, let me stress the necessity of a balanced nutritional diet in criminological training.

Without an analysis of the job to be done it would be superfluous to talk about training. Assuming that our ultimate

objective is to socialize the anti-social, to adjust the maladjusted, and to alter potent liabilities into actual assets (thus
preventing the recurrence of noxious social behavior), criminological training has been following two courses: *common
sense* and *scientific objectivity*. In the future it is *not* going to
carve a new path.

1. Common Sense Channels

Social action enthusiasts are pushing criminological training into practical channels. Businessmen, housewives, school
teachers, lawyers, physicians, ministers, laborers and politicians, with an eye on quick results, have compromised with
the facts of life and their conscience. While professing the
sacredness of the human life, they have hanged and electro-
cuted; while preaching forgiveness, hysterically they have
objected to pardons; while advocating reformation, they
have persecuted and punished; while vociferous against petty
crimes, they have closed their eyes to gigantic frauds; while
the judges order social investigations, they keep on sentencing
with their preconceived personal biases; and whereas the efficacy of extra-mural treatment is acknowledged, both the
public and the correctional administrators still plan for bigger
maximum security institutions!

These current compromises strengthen the belief in the
efficacy of the trial-and-error methods of training. Experience is taken as the supreme teacher in which the "do-good-
ers," "know-not-howers," and the "breast-beaters" find solace.
Training-on-the-job and in-service methods help the situation
somewhat, but, all in all, action is slanted by wishful thinking. Hence, criminological training is moving more and more
in the direction of *skills* and *social fads* rather than knowledge
and social control.

2. Scientific Objectivity

In contrast with the massive action-manic segment of our
society, there is a small, cautious, but persistent band of
tested knowledge addicts. By tested knowledge we do not

mean theoretical speculation; it is empirical as well. The utilization of atomic energy emerged from a fund of previously proven knowledge. Hypotheses became concrete applications both in academic and non-academic circles. Thus our program is geared to academic and pragmatic techniques of training and our speakers and panelists will herald their convictions based on observation and knowledge.

Increased and sound scientific orientation of those engaged in the professional handling of criminals is a *"must."* Academic inculcation of some principles as a first step in training is taken for granted. Like the pre-medical or the pre-law student, engineering or education majors, each is expected to be grounded in basic principles. Although the knowledge of principles is essential, no principle *per se* has healed the suffering sick, built bridges or transferred wisdom to the uninitiated students. Principles become concrete acts only when human beings apply them to specific situations. Formal training may sharpen the insight, but a single bitter experience in the university of hard knocks may dull it permanently. Current watertight intellectual compartmentalism in institutions of higher learning encourages insulation, causing thought stagnation. Premature specialization, so common in secondary schools, junior and four year colleges, accentuates the processes of this insulation. These practices may teach technical skills, but they increase mental astigmatism blurring the vision because of limited horizons.

Workers in the correctional field, in any capacity, are expected to be *human engineers*. The edifices they build are men and women within their social frame of reference. Theirs is the task of molding and remolding personalities acceptable by the standards of the dominant groups. But how would one dare to reshape a deviant personality unless he knows the image of his society? And if the image of his society itself is distorted, what is the worker's role? Is it to redistort the deviant? Such questions shall constitute the essence of the training programs of the future.

As an academician it would be treason not to advocate grounding of all workers in the basic contributions of the physical and the social sciences. In spite of overspecialization, the age of interdisciplinary orientation is upon us, and to ignore its beckoning would ultimately destroy the delusively self-confident specialists. The wider the range of knowledge, the greater the prospect of tested principles and sound applications in the fields of crime and corrections. Our workers need orientation in genetics and psychology, physiology and economics, anthropology and political science, statistics and, I might add, sociology, to become effective human engineers. These are academic vested interests—and there are many others—guarding their respective citadels zealously, every day and in devious ways building barriers against possible encroachments by others, wasting resources on testing knowledge which has been already tested and proven by others, and dubbing it "research"! Our future successes lie in co-ordination, in integration of any and every proven principle in the handling of man whether they come from the ivory towers or the gutter colleges.

I should not labor the implications of this simple yet crucial issue. There has been, and will continue to be, ample discussion of this point for some time. Therefore, let us pass on to the consideration of a hitherto neglected area of criminological training: the orientation of the public.

V. *Training of the Masses*

The education of "cops," probation and parole workers, district attorneys, judges, prosecutors, chiefs of police, wardens, supervisors, guidance center technicians, clinicians, guards, and counsellors, even that of the executioners, have absorbed most of the attention of the academicians and on-the-job trainers. Criminology would have made no strides without due emphasis upon the preparation of these "professionals" who constitute the core of our crimino-penal system and in whose work large numbers of individuals are involved. Our concern is the orientation of the vast public on the periphery whose unavoidable impacts either stimulate or curb our cherished programs.

In our democratic social structure voters are kings. Their verdict at the ballot box, and subsequently the acts of their representatives, determine the rules of the social game. The future of crimino-penal trends is bound up with the climate of public opinion.

Housewives with their beliefs in old tales; businessmen with their blind or enlightened selfish interests; men of the cloth wrapped up in their heuristic beliefs: school teachers confined to the rote of the three Rs; journalists and other operators of media of mass communication with their drive for the spectacular; lawyers with the urge to settle disputes (right or wrong); psychologists, psychoanalysts and psychiatrists with their personalized conjectures; incensed taxpayers, power-infatuated labor organizers, charlatans and scientists alike dictate, directly or subtly, social values, and shape attitudes which insure their perpetuation. Through political representatives in local, state and national government levels, these color, to say the least, and set the tone and the pace of criminological thinking. Irrespective of all the tested knowledge by students in the field, a tentative and at times a raw statement by J. Edgar Hoover in the *Reader's Digest* carries more weight than one hundred research articles in the *Journal of Criminal Law, Criminology and Police Science*.

Who trains these helpless souls who, prompted by marked curiosity, devour the pages of daily newspapers with sordid accounts of crime? Who is educating the millions in our midst seeking vicarious satisfactions through the "two-bit" novels? Who is imparting instruction to men and women who make a business of frauds, bankruptcies, vice and depravities? These organized and inchoate interests exert their pressures in ingenious ways to dispirit and dissuade realistic attacks upon criminal behavior and penology. Some because of ignorance, others by design, encourage anti-social acts. These too need training, perhaps not within the walls of ivy leagues, but in the highways and the byways of daily mass media orientation.

Who is bringing the results of tested knowledge to people's attention regarding the concept of multiple causation of crime; the reasons for high rate of recidivism; the ineffectiveness of severity of punishment; the irrationality of penitentiary treatment; the savagery of retribution; the innocuousness of capital punishment, etc., etc.? We talk about these seamy facets of our profession among ourselves—the believers. Even if there be a consensus of opinion within our sacrosanct circles, who is preaching the gospel to the infidels? How are we endeavoring to change the deeply ingrained retributive complex to a socially enlightened view and turn people from the punishment craze to sober prevention? The public's orientation in these areas may create a duller social climate for us to work in, but it promises some reduction in the rate of anti-social behavior and sadistic vengeance.

Here is a long overlooked task for those engaged in law enforcement who deal with the offenders and the public. People watch our utterances and movements with suspicion. A knock at the door by the police, sheriff's car in the street, probation officer's untimely visit, a phone call from the jail, a letter from the warden inspire fear. The newspapers fan these smouldering feelings to the extent of creating hostilities against the law enforcement personnel. Hence opportunity for the emergence of a new breed of workers, *social lubricants,* to allay the fears and sell law enforcement and corrections to the public. You call this "Public Relations." Under any name this is a "*must.*" If we have anything to brag about because of the demonstrable salutary results we have achieved, it is high time to publish them, otherwise we shall perish from the wear and tear of constant social friction.

All is not well when some irresponsible officer or an agency behaves unprofessionally; neither is it at all well when a new idea, technique or law is advanced against the outworn beliefs. The education of the masses calls for the work of skilled technicians in human engineering. Who and where are we training these social engineers? Who and how are they influencing public opinion?

VI. *Observations and Admonitions*

No matter through what medium, learning is a great adventure. The ventilation of watertight intellectual and behavioral compartments comes through new exposures. It is apparent that, traditionally, skills imparted to the practitioners are fixed. Repetition is expected to increase efficiency. This is true in a static social structure. Unfortunately we live in a dynamic milieu and we take pride in it. Spelled out, we have either to sharpen our dulled tools or else acquire new tools.

Whether these tools in dealing with the anti-social segments of our society come from the academic circles or through the in-service and on-the-job training quarters, the "old order passeth away and the new is ushered in." That both the academician and practitioner are inclined to stratification is a matter of record. Therefore, just as collegiate faculties are granted sabbaticals to get out of their cocoons and see the bright sun for a spell, so do the correctional workers and the law enforcement personnel of every grade and description *need* the opportunity to see the other side. Should a periodic three, or six, or nine months of academic atmosphere to the practitioner be mandatory? Should a similar chance be given to the academician in reverse? Such experiences might have some chastening effects. Our current concern with "short-cut" methods of training should confirm the rationale of this issue. Assuming that some opportunity for the balancing of the academic and the pragmatic training is made available to the personnel, the question as to the content of training becomes of paramount importance.

Imitating the laboratory technique of the physical sciences, certain social scientists have resorted to the use of the "clinical" method. Hypotheses are spurned unless they are clinically tested. Some possessed by the clinic-craze, have popularized the "couch" technique in the revered sanctum of the analyst. Do behavior explosions in private repeat themselves in public? Can criminal behavior, controlled in a clinical setting, be expected to become a constant pattern in a nonclinical milieu? Would the composure and insight gained on the couch withstand the stresses and the strains imposed upon the compulsive criminal by a heartless and hostile public? How is the released offender's self-confidence, while leaning upon the sympathetic, understanding and helpful approach of the parole officer, going to fare in the midst of perpetual surveillance of the suspicious law enforcement officers? Would the authority-mad and status-hungry officials exploit the predicament of the "ex-con" for personal gain? Where and how are these officers being taught impartial and dignified performance of their tasks?

As we search the fields we operate in, one observes the prevalence of status-starvation. Desirable status, the most cherished possession of every human being living in an organized society, if denied, causes frustration beyond measure; therefore it is fraught with disaster. How much awareness of this socially-imposed compulsive drive is being imparted to those handling their wards? How do we equip our officers on the beat and the workers in correctional institutions to ascertain the nature and the degree of group affiliations and identifications in the incidence of anti-social behavior? Are the skills gained in detection, apprehension, submission, incarceration and liquidation of offenders related to the control and prediction of future behavior? What type and intensity of knowledge is to be infused into the life of practitioners? What tools are to be devised by the theoretician for pragmatic application? What systems of fluid communication lines could we initiate to get quick results? Or are we going to keep on deluding ourselves by finding refuge behind incompatible statistical charts and tables? We need objective answers to these questions to combat the "do-gooder" detergents in our social washtub.

Obviously the criminological training program of the future will emphasize some division of labor among its advocates: 1) *diagnosticians* to delve into the causative factors in anti-social behavior. These are the "research" people whose hunches are to be verified for consumption by the rest of us. 2) *Practitioners* to execute the revelations of the researchers. These constitute a heterogeneous mass, ranging from the fingerprinting specialists to the vice squad personnel, from the traffic officer to the chief of police, from the probation and parole workers to wardens and superintendents of correctional institutions. 3) *Prognosticians* and *therapists* to attend to the needs of individuals who display symptoms of anti-social behavior. These range from counselling pastors to the "super-snooping" analysts and from social surveyors to political planners.

For the conditioning of this extensive galaxy of personnel the existing channels are bound to continue. These include formal academic courses with specific objectives; in-service indoctrinations; on-the-job apprenticeships; brief institutes; instructive and constructive public lectures; and similar procedures.

These techniques will prevail with one overall emphasis: widened mental horizons for each and every person engaged in law enforcement and correctional fields. Since a man's judgment is never better than his information, the more catholic the orientation, the greater is the prospect for balanced judgment. Whatever the source of information (particularly verified information), the airing of the mind and the cleansing of personal biases are indispensable requisites in criminological training.

Finally, do we need to be reminded that, according to reports released by the Federal Bureau of Investigation, over 60 percent of criminals had previous records? If this is true, every phase of law enforcement and corrections has to re-deal with these repeaters. Is their *modus operandi* information in the files revealing enough to offer an adequate profile of character analysis? Do we dare "underwrite character"? Of course. But should we in our attempts to recondition, stress character-building? If character underwriting is a post-crime phenomenon, could we develop character to obviate the commission of the crime? Who is going to open our sails in this unchartered realm, and how?

VII. *Conclusion*

Today, criminological training is headed in one direction with two separate rails of the track. On the academic level it aspires to become objective in analyzing the criminal as a person and ascertaining the contributing factors to his anti-social behavior. Daily its probings are becoming more and more intricate and the findings less and less definitive. On the practitioner's level, grassroot resistance to humane treatment of the offender and insistence upon retribution, contribute to the mounting confusions and frustrations. Under these circumstances no great forward leap in criminology should be expected.

Our knowledge is widening as well as deepening, but the diffusion of this knowledge among the regimented practitioners and traditionally disaffected public is only dribbling. *Quo vadimus?* We are moving towards the promised land, but still sojourning in the wilderness of fear and clouds of aspiration. We are still the cave-men in a technological civilization. Our past record in dealing with the criminal is shrouded with compromises. The sacred and the secular have exerted their impacts upon each other, modifying beliefs and behavior here and there. Old superstitions linger. Neither the academicians nor the practitioners seem capable of shaking off outworn notions. And so long as the materialistic success goal is overemphasized, irrespective of the means employed in reaching that goal, personal and collective anti-social behavior will thrive.

An overhauling of our current way of life in dealing with the anti-social elements of our system is in order. This is a task for the academic criminologists. We look to them for direction and guidance.

With proper channels of communication, the law enforcement agencies, because of their direct contact with the offenders, will serve as social lubricants between the experimenting academicians and the expectant public.

When we turn the searchlight upon our doings in the academic halls, in periodic institutes, in the in-service and on-the-job orientational pursuits, we shall be able to discern our goals and methods with greater clarity. Then we shall know whither we are going. We may be headed towards the promised land. Who knows? Perhaps none of us; yet all of us do care.

In the first chapter, Howard Gill presented some of the traditional concepts of repression in the prisons and the conditions associated with them as part of penology's long history of the need to maintain "discipline." In this chapter, Dr. Fox reveals the contradictions which exist between the traditional concepts of maintaining order and the principle of therapy which has come to the fore. The high percentage of recidivism in our prisons, and the even higher percentages of prisoners who do not respond to disciplinary measures once they are confined, places the problem within realistic focus. The effort to rehabilitate and to punish becomes even more complex in the light of the several sanctions to which the prisoner is asked to respond—that of the custodial staff, the prison program itself, and the standards of the inmates. Dr. Fox, who played a significant role in quelling the serious riots at the State Prison of Southern Michigan in 1952, writes with considerable understanding of the tensions existing in prison life and as one profoundly conversant with the inmates' outlook.

Chapter 3

THE PROBLEMS OF PRISON DISCIPLINE

VERNON FOX

Chairman of the Department of Criminology and Corrections at the Florida State University, Tallahassee. Formerly Psychologist and Assistant Deputy Warden in charge of individual treatment at the State Prison of Southern Michigan.

Nearly two thirds (63-65 percent) of the inmates entering American prisons each year have been in prison before.[1] An even higher proportion, approximately four out of five (80 percent) of the prisoners who are sent to solitary confinement—the jail within the prison—it has been estimated by prison administrators, have been in solitary confinement or punishment status before.[2] This high proportion of failure indicates that the problem of inducing conforming behavior from persons exposed to our punishment programs remains unsolved. It is difficult to solve because of conflicting needs on the part of administrative personnel and on the part of the non-conforming personality. On the one hand, the authority of society must be maintained and, on the other, the permissive therapeutic atmosphere is necessary to effect spontaneous and genuine personality changes. This interdependent major dilemma in handling prison disciplinary problems renders their analysis most difficult. The analysis of prison disciplinary problems must include the non-conforming behavior of the individual as well as the countering behavior of the prison administration which cures, intensifies, or fails to affect the objectionable behavior of the individual.

The disciplinary problems in a prison constitute the manifest culmination of all the problems faced by the inmates and the administration of the institution. Disciplinary problems constitute a threat to an administration because they disrupt the order, tranquility, and security of the institution. In many prisons, the reaction to this threat is immediate and drastic. In the majority of adult penal institutions in the United States, psychological and social treatment ceases when rules are violated, and the offenders are placed in solitary confinement or in other punishment status. Upon violation of rules, then, prisons are faced with a policy dilemma in their withdrawing treatment facilities from those who, by their behavior, have demonstrated that they need treatment most.

Many prison personnel and even parole boards have displayed a tendency to evaluate the prospects of successful adjustment outside the prison on the basis of an inmate's lack of misconduct reports in the prison. Many wardens regard the institution as a small community which gives practice to prisoners in getting along with others, the effect of which can be transferred to the larger community. There is, too frequently, no suspicion that the ability to adjust to institutional controls is little assurance that adjustment can be made as easily when those institutional controls are removed. That discipline is necessary for the treatment process, however, is obvious.[3] The problem is in determining how much, how little, and how the best discipline is achieved to accomplish optimum results.

The analysis of prison disciplinary problems, then, is a highly significant project, but it is most controversial. The practical implications of such an analysis may threaten and question many practices that are customary, almost traditional, in present American penology.

Prison Discipline

The term, "discipline," has frequently been confused with some of the techniques by which it is achieved. "Discipline" is group order. Traditionally, the prison is characterized by exaggerated discipline.[4] There are many techniques by which group order may be achieved. Practices vary widely from institution to institution, from philosophy to philosophy, and from administrator to administrator.[5] Punishment is the technique most frequently resorted to in many institutions, without much understanding as to how best to use it. Punishment techniques have a constructive function in prison discipline, but they have to be applied in a carefully diagnostic and well-chosen manner or they can cause more damage than they ameliorate.[6] The most desirable motivation for group order lies in good morale, good food, a challenging and interesting program, and excellent spontaneous communication and relations between all individuals and sub-groups of which the total group is comprised. When communication, morale, and other relationships break down, some type of force is administered by the administration to maintain group cohesion. The types of force most frequently used in the prison are, in decreasing order of their incidence:

1. Solitary confinement, frequently with dietary restrictions.
2. Locking-in own cell with loss of yard privileges.
3. Loss of visiting, correspondence, canteen, and/or other privileges.
4. Transfer to another institution.
5. Assignment to a "discipline squad" for menial labor.
6. Down-grading in a grading system and/or forfeiture of earned good time.
7. Corporal punishment, formal in some southern prisons, informal in several others.

The introduction of drastic measures into the maintenance of group order creates conflict and generates anxieties which have distracting overtones on total group cohesiveness. As soon as any force needs be used, then, group order must suffer. Because all prisons resort to some sort of force in order to cope with deviant behavior among inmates, even if this force is only to transfer the inmate to another institution, the beginning of the analysis of prison disciplinary problems becomes one of determining the level at which group order is to be maintained by good communications, program, and relationships, and at what point force must be employed.

Level of Custodial Control

The problem faced by many custodial departments in American prisons is the level at which custodial control can be established. In 1957, there were wide variations in American prisons in the ratio of officers and employees to inmates, but the average was about one officer to six inmates. In those few institutions with almost a one-to-one relationship between officers and inmates, a high level of custodial control can be achieved because there are enough officers to enforce whatever regulations are made. In institutions where the ratio of officers to inmates is about one officer to twelve, fifteen, or more inmates, however, the officers have to "get along" with the inmates. In such prisons, many officers have developed convenient blindness unless inmate behavior so flagrantly violates the rules that the presence of other inmates forces him to act. Many officers in overcrowded and undermanned prisons have indicated that there was no point in giving an inmate an order which could not be enforced, anyway. As a consequence, many prisons operate with the assistance of inmates and at a low level of custodial control, thereby complicating the role of the custodial officer. At the same time, the professional personnel who agree with the inmates that imprisonment, in and of itself, is enough punishment, constitute another position that complicates further the already complicated officer-inmate relationship.[7]

While extreme examples of inmate participation in custodial control can be observed in two or three Southern states in which trusted inmates carry rifles and shotguns to guard other inmates, the type of inmate control is generally informal and with the approval and periodic check of the administration. This informal control usually takes the form of the deputy warden's appointment of certain capable inmates to clerical jobs in his office, the cell block officer having a "runner," "bolter," and clerk selected from the inmate body. Most work supervisors and other responsible personnel in the prison will have also selected inmate clerks. By default and disuse, some of the routine responsibilities of prison administrators at different levels come to be performed routinely by the selected inmate clerks. Consequently, much of the group order or "discipline" in most prisons is accomplished by an informal type of self-government among the inmates, themselves. Whether this type of informal control is effective or impeding to the primary treatment objectives of the prison is dependent upon how the inmates are selected and how they are used. There is some evidence to support the contention that group living is therapeutic, but it has to be in a therapeutic milieu.[8] In a small institution, this type of system can be beneficial to the administration and to the inmates, alike, but the risk increases as the prison grows in size to a large, cumbersome, complex institution in which administrative control is practically impossible.

An informal type of self-government by inmates can reduce the number of disciplinary problems brought to the attention of the administration. The effect of this type of inmate control, however, may be quite undesirable and harmful to the less capable inmates who are "being controlled" and, perhaps, "exploited" by the other more capable inmates who have a vested interest in the *status quo*. Therefore, another problem in the analysis of prison disciplinary situations is what the type of custodial control is doing to the inmates who are subjected to it.

Quality of Custodial Control

Custodial control can be conveniently divided into the social sanctions by which it is achieved. Custodial control can be motivated by (1) guards, (2) the institutional program, and (3) the inmates, themselves. The guards are generally interested in the enforcement of prison regulations that are designed to foster discipline. The program, including athletic events, psychological services, food, religion, school, industry, farms, radio and TV, library, recreation, and other facilities are all designed to achieve total group order. The informal type of self-government that appears in all institutions to some degree is geared toward the maintenance of discipline. Whether the desire for discipline among inmates results from an effort to maintain the *status quo*, to avoid anxiety and seek tranquility, or to avoid administrative reprisals does not alter the fact that inmate sanctions are toward self-discipline.

The proportion of disciplinary problems to total prison population is roughly dependent upon the level of custodial control and its oppressiveness. A strong custodial force can be discreet in its handling of inmates or it can be oppressive. The most oppressive custodial situations, however, can result in the driving inward of aggression, so that, rather than expressing aggression overtly, inmates may modify the aggression and break their own legs, cut their heel tendons, go on sit-down and slow-down strikes, or other means to thwart their captors without running as great a personal risk as open rebellion. On the other hand, a more permissive or free custodial atmosphere may permit whatever aggression is generated to be expressed outwardly.

Students of human behavior, particularly those engaged in therapy, are vitally concerned as to whether the aggressions generated by anxiety are driven inward by strong external forces or are permitted some sort of expression. Herein lies the crux of the institutional disciplinary program in a prison. Essentially, the achievement of group order is always at balance between the guards, the program, and the inmates. When this balance permits channelling of aggressions outwardly through sports events, drama, or, of necessity, overt misconduct in a less exaggerated disciplinary milieu, the chances of a therapeutic program being successful are greater than when the balance is in the direction of custodial control so oppressive that resentments and hostilities have to be internalized.

Individual Misconduct

Controlled movement of inmates and segregation procedures are the two broad classifications of techniques used by custody to maintain order in an institution. Moving lines of prisoners, gate control, and the pass system constitute the controlled movement of prisoners. Segregation includes the prisoners in solitary confinement; in the mental ward, hospital, and other special facilities; and those prisoners held away from the general population because of chronic incorrigibility or safe-keeping. The persons in solitary confinement are those who have been found guilty of violation of the prison rules. It is this group and this relationship, then, to which many people refer as "disciplinary procedures." It is this relationship which is the ultimate manifestation of the general levels and quality of the custodial relationship. Consequently, any analysis of prison disciplinary problems must include an analysis of the specific violations of institutional rules and regulations and how they are handled.

Rules and regulations are drawn by custody in order to set standards of behavior and to define to inmates and to officers the kinds of behavior for which an officer should arrest and report an inmate. The rules are fairly standard in most prisons, although some rule books are thicker than others. The offenses most frequently reported in custodial summary courts are:

Fighting
Gambling
Homosexual Practices
Stealing (from cells, kitchen, library, work assignments, and "high-jacking")
Smuggling in contraband or possession of contraband
Skating (being in an unauthorized area without a pass)
Disobedience
Refusal to work
Making alcoholic beverages (spud-juice, cane-buck, raisin-jack, etc.)

Bartering with other inmates without permission
Escapes, planned escapes, or attempted escapes
Miscellaneous

These offenses appear fairly frequently in all institutions. The types of offenses committed by each individual may be psychiatrically diagnosed according to the area in which the individual finds conformity most difficult. The specific nature of the offenses committed by each individual is partially dependent upon the personality structure of the offender.[9] There is a tendency for each offender, outside prisons and within prisons, to repeat the same types of offenses, some to a greater extent than others.

The motivation for misconduct appears to lie within the personality, since the sanctions in society and prison culture from guards, administration, and inmate colleagues, are to "get along" with a minimum of friction. Further, a relatively small percentage of the inmate body has a record of misconduct reports. The average prison in 1957 had approximately one inmate in punishment status per one hundred prisoners.[10]

Approximately three percent of the inmate population is involved in misconduct reports in any given year. This means that there is a high incidence of repeating, an indication which is confirmed by the observation of experienced prison personnel and an examination of the records of inmates who have accumulated misconduct reports.

The three most common major disciplinary problems in prison are gambling, sex, and fighting. The fighting frequently results from the gambling and sex problems. Inability to pay a gambling debt or disagreement as to the quality and quantity of the debt may lead to fighting, as may also the "eternal triangle" in a homosexual relationship. Consequently, many prison people hold that gambling, fighting, and sex are the three major disciplinary problems.

The causes for individual misconduct would of necessity be in the province of a psychiatric or psychological diagnosis. Many psychiatrists and clinical psychologists have indicated the possibility of social and emotional maturation influencing the type of offense an individual would commit.[11]

In this problem of emotional maturation, one of the difficulties is for the maturing personality to move from operating on the pleasure principle to operating on the reality principle, or the movement from the simple avoiding of pain and seeking pleasure type of functioning to the more mature postponement of immediate gratification for future reward. Many offenses are committed when immediate gratification cannot be postponed.

The psychopath, a concept well known to the penologist but hard to define, has caused considerable difficulty in diagnosis and attempted treatment. It has been called by the term, "psychopath," "sociopath," and has been termed "neurotic" by many writers and even "psychotic." Whatever it is, the clinical group does exist. The American Psychiatric Association has a place for him in their classifications. He has a tendency to verbalize without understanding and will indicate, "I'm crazy as hell, Doc," without the statement having much meaning to him. His superficial transformations and verbalized intentions have frustrated many a prison administrator trying to maintain discipline. The problem of insufficient or delayed maturation has been suggested here, as well as in many other behavioral aberrations.

The Recidivism Cycle

The dynamics of the repeated misconduct appears to be related to the concept of social maturation, the psychopathic condition as it is suspected, and shows some dynamics similar to that of the development of a chronic neurosis. In the first place, the reality principle does not operate. Further, the individual does not "learn by experience" nor is he able to develop "insight" other than superficial verbalizations. Alexander and Ross have indicated the following phases in the development of a chronic neurosis: [12] (1) circumstances that precipitate a situation with which the patient cannot cope, (2) failure in solution of actual problem after unsuccessful attempts, (3) replacement of realistic measures by substitute regressive fantasies or behavior, (4) reactivation of old conflicts in regression, (5) efforts to resolve old conflicts revived by evading actual situations, (6) secondary results of the chronic neurotic state.

Somewhat the same dynamics occur in recidivism, setting up a recidivism cycle. The progression begins with (1) the situation in the institution with which the prisoner cannot cope, (2) failure to solve the problem, followed by (3) replacement of realistic efforts by substitute regressive behavior, (4) an intensification of the original problem by failure of substitute methods, (5) repeatedly grasping for an answer, some answer, any answer and, finally (6) the compulsive repetition of the one answer he has found, whether it works or not. The various combinations of immature, psychopathic, and neurotic dynamics in behavior offer possibilities for an explanation of repeating misconduct in and out of prisons that has more meaning for this writer than have several other similarly hypothetical explanations. Herein, too, lies the crux of the analysis of prison disciplinary problems as far as the individual is concerned.

Handling Disciplinary Problems

It is obvious that individual misconduct in prison is, from the psychological and psychiatric viewpoint, a very complex problem. Because of the traditional absence of psychiatric and psychological help in most prisons, however, a simplified procedure for gaining discipline had to be found. Since the conditioning process in a mature individual who operates on the reality principle appears to function well, it would seem logical to assume that it would work with anybody. That the reality principle did not function for the persons who are in prison, and certainly not for those who have accrued misconduct reports after they have been sentenced, has not seemed to deter the traditional prison administrator from this customary and logical course. It is obvious to the student of human behavior, however, that social and emotional maturation has not taken place in the prisoner and, particularly, the incorrigible prisoner. Yet, the traditional prison summary court, which places prisoners in solitary confinement for misconduct, operates on the assumption that the offender is a free moral agent who chooses to violate rules and can be "conditioned" to behave otherwise. For the psychologist and psychiatrist, this position is not defensible.

The pattern of custodial routine in handling misconduct cases begins with an original demand for compliance and is followed by deprivation or punishment to reinforce the original demand.[13] The increased demand on the emotionally immature individual or the psychopath actually intensifies his problem, setting up the recidivism cycle and resulting in repeated misconduct of the same general type without the ability to appraise himself. The handling of difficult disciplinary cases is a psychological and psychiatric problem which requires more than routine custodial attention. There is no lessening of antagonism and no helpful results from a demonstration of force without any judicial understanding of the problem. The problem is to understand the prisoner's reason for his resistance to authority and to help him move from infantile emotional positions to a mature status in which he can function normally.

Several states have moved away from the routine custodial handling of misconduct and toward a treatment-oriented approach to discipline. The custodial personnel at Folsom and San Quentin, for instance, have said that they experienced some pleasant surprise at the benefits gained by the prison system from this movement in terms of shorter periods of time in the "adjustment centers" for the inmates and less repeating of misconduct within the institutions.[14] Throughout the country, there is a steady movement away from the old solitary confinement with bread and water toward a type of segregation with concentrated treatment facilities for those found guilty of misconduct within the institution.

Analysis

Correctional systems face a dilemma in the handling of misconduct within the institution. Society needs a system of rewards and punishment to promote normal emotional maturation, so that the majority of persons will still learn to postpone immediate gratification for future reward. A system of rewards and punishments is necessary to maintain the *status quo* as far as society's value system is concerned. To accept this system of rewards and punishments and develop the capacity to postpone immediate gratification for future reward, each individual has to have the ability to respond to the punishment-reward system in an acceptable way. A minority of individuals do not have that capacity. This is why punishment is not an effective deterrent. For those people, there is need for a moratorium on the system of rewards and punishments to permit emotional maturation to occur in a controlled environment. This is what the ideal prison attempts to do.

The problem the prison administrator faces is that of knowing when to shift from the pattern of rewards and punishments, which can be used with emotionally mature personalities, to the "moratorium" status of treatment. Within the system of rewards and punishments, the prison administrator must maintain a treatment center or adjustment center, which is a "therapeutic community" without the sanctions of reward and punishment which the incorrigible offenders have already demonstrated by their incorrigibility that they are not prepared to take. This is a difficult concept to accept because, first, it takes more understanding of human behavior than is normally obtained in the work-a-day world, and, secondly, it affords no emotional release of aggression for the prison administrator who considers himself and social authority offended by the offender. Consequently, the custodial personnel who attempt to maintain discipline in a prison must be prepared to understand human behavior, rather than trying to judge the amount of pressure necessary to keep a man in line.

Summary

In summary, the analysis of prison disciplinary problems needs to take into account the sanctions within the prison for conformity as held by the guards, the total prison program, and the inmates, themselves. Variations in the balance of quality and quantity of sanctions in the interrelationships between these three conceptual units will cause to vary widely the level of custodial control extant in any given institution. Further, the individual offender who builds up a series of misconduct reports within the prison is a seriously disturbed individual with complex mental dynamics that seem to combine elements of emotional immaturity, some types of behavior observed in the psychopath, and seems to develop the repetitive compulsion in much the same manner in which a chronic neurosis seems to develop. Yet, for this complex individual, the pattern of custodial routine is an original demand for compliance and subsequent deprivation and punishment to reinforce the original demand, which intensifies the problems by imposing more pressures upon already existing pressures without providing any solution to the original problem.

It is obvious that the handling of disciplinary cases is a psychological and psychiatric problem requiring more than routine custodial attention. Recognition that prison disciplinary problems are in need of more judicious attention than that ordinarily found in a traditional reward-punishment system is demonstrated by the fact that several prison systems have already moved from the traditional solitary confinement idea toward the "therapeutic community" and "adjustment center" idea. Several of these facilities are already in operation and the trend in American penology is definitely in the treatment direction.

REFERENCES

1. Unpublished survey of 48 States by the author in 1953 and in 1957. Also, see *Federal Prisons—1955* (U. S. Department of Justice, 1956), p. 48.

2. Unpublished survey of 48 States by the author in 1953. Observation in State Prison of Southern Michigan, 1950-51.

3. Wilson, J. G. and Pescor, M. J., *Problems in Prison Psychiatry* (Caldwell, Idaho, 1939), p. 34-35.

4. See "Prison Systems" in Branham, Vernon C. and

Kutash, Samuel B., *Encyclopedia of Criminology* (New York, 1949), p. 383.

5. Teeters, Negley K., "A Limited Survey of Some Prison Practises and Policies," (*Prison World*, May-June, 1952), pp. 5-8, 29.

6. Knight, Robert P., "The Meaning of Punishment," Lindner, Robert M., and Seliger, Robert V., in *Handbook of Correctional Psychology* (New York, 1947), pp. 667-677.

7. See Pescor, M. J., "Interpersonal Relationships Among Inmates and Personnel," Lindner, Robert M., and Seliger, Robert V., *Handbook of Correctional Psychology* (New York, 1947), pp. 440-451.

8. Fox, Vernon, "Frustration-Aggression Hypothesis in Corrections," *The Quarterly Journal of The Florida Academy of Sciences*, Vol. 17, No. 3, (September, 1954), pp. 140-146.

9. Fox, Vernon, "The Influence of Personality on Social Non-Conformity," *Journal of Criminal Law, Criminology and Police Science*. Vol. 42, No. 6 (March-April, 1952).

10. Unpublished survey by the author in 1957.

11. Saul, L. J., *Emotional Maturity* (New York, 1941). Banay, Ralph S., "Immaturity and Crime," *American Journal of Psychiatry* (September, 1943). Bromberg, Walter, *Crime and the Mind* (Philadelphia, 1948).

12. Alexander, Franz and Ross, Helen, *Dynamic Psychiatry* (Chicago, 1952), p. 121.

13. Bromberg, Walter, "Antagonism to Authority Among Young Offenders" in Lindner, Robert M., and Seliger, Robert V., *Handbook of Correctional Psychology* (New York, 1947), pp. 452-462.

14. Conversations with correctional officers during the author's visit there in 1956.

A sentence of "hard labor," a shibboleth of traditional penology, has become virtually meaningless in many segments of America's huge prison establishment. With the growing emphasis upon rehabilitation in modern correction, it is recognized that successful readaptation to society cannot be accomplished unless the prison inmate masters certain fundamental and enduring vocational skills during the period of his incarceration. It has constantly been demonstrated that in the development of patterns of social adjustment, the capability of maintaining employment at some satisfying and useful occupation provides one of the most basic elements. The prisons, however, are actually attempting to serve a dual purpose— that of providing some basic job skills which the inmate can carry into society upon his release, and the need to maintain an industrial plant which can function efficiently. How to maintain such a dual purpose, especially in the face of historic opposition from the public, industry, employers and the labor unions, poses a classic dilemma in prison administration. Donal MacNamara, an earnest student of penology's many-sided problems and a forthright exponent of his carefully considered convictions, traces the historic background of the problems of prison industries and recommends policies which may reconcile some of the current differences of view existing in the field.

Chapter 4

PRISON LABOR AND EMPLOYMENT

DONAL E. J. MacNAMARA

Dean, New York Institute of Criminology; President, American League to Abolish Capital Punishment

Penology's "Four Horsemen of the Apocalypse" may rightly be regarded as despair, perversion, overcrowding, and idleness. Each is a major problem, but unless we can in some manner find meaningful employment for a far larger proportion of our prisoners than we are presently doing, we must abandon the idea that we are operating institutions of correction and reform. Some of our most recent figures disclose that more than fifty percent of prisoners in federal institutions are not productively employed, and that those who are, rarely work a full work week or produce at levels commensurate with the man-hour production levels of free labor. "Hard labor" has become a meaningless component of the modern prison sentence; idleness with its resultant boredom, attempted escapes, rioting, planning of future crimes, and general deterioration of the human personality is, for the greater part, the rule. Since 95 percent of our prisoners eventually return to a society in which good work habits and job skills comprise one of the most significant bases for social adjustment, the failure to develop adequate work patterns in our prisons is of utmost importance in effective rehabilitation.

This situation has not always existed. It is the result, paradoxically, of social pressures and conditions of a diametric sort, in which exploitation of the prisoner's labor was the centuries' old rule. This tradition of the use of prisoners as impressed labor gradually took a different form in the need to adapt this usage to the considerations of a free and competitive economy. Prisoners in ancient times served as galley-slaves and performed heavy labor for the benefit of the state. During the 17th and 18th centuries, convicts worked in mines, developed new areas in the form of penal colonies, and were indentured to private employers, largely as agricultural laborers. In England, non-productive drudgery on the tread-wheel and crank was for a time the rule. American prisoners, however, after some experimentation with a solitary work program, in which each prisoner worked alone in his own cell, had settled down by the early 1830s to the Auburn congregate system, sometimes known as the prison-factory, with a few prisons in the South emphasizing the prison-plantation production of cotton, tobacco, sugar and other regional crops. The objective was to make the prisons self-supporting and, if possible, profitable to the state—an objective which, interestingly enough, was upon occasion impressively achieved. In 1825, for example, Massachusetts' prisons earned ten thousand dollars above operating costs; in 1851, fifteen American state penitentiaries earned a total of three hundred and twenty-five thousand dollars above expenses; and the Connecticut Penitentiary, over an eighteen year period (1833-1850), earned a profit of more than ninety thousand dollars.

During the nineteenth century, three closely related open-market systems of convict employment prevailed: the *piece-price* system under which a contractor furnished the raw material and received the finished product, paying the prison a fixed sum for each unit accepted by him; the *contract* system, in which the contractor furnished the raw material, the machinery, the supervisory personnel, and paid the state a stipulated daily sum for the labor of each prisoner; and the *lease* system, extended after the Civil War, under which the entire responsibility for the housing, clothing, feeding, working as well as the guarding and disciplining of prisoners, was turned over to private contractors for stipulated sums. In the State of Georgia, for example, in the year of 1867, the sum of twenty-five hundred dollars was paid for the labor of one hundred convicts for the period of one year.

That these systems were profitable to the contractors, there can be little doubt. Further, they relieved the states of the burden of supporting their prisoners. However, the abuses and vicious practises they brought in their wake were glaring, and demoralizing to all concerned. Exploitation of the convicts was the rule. There was virtually no interest whatsoever in physical, mental or moral rehabilitation. Corruption in the letting of contracts and in the settling of accounts cheated the states out of much of their rightful earnings. Employers of free labor complained of unfair competition; labor unions decried the effects of cheap prison labor upon wage standards, particularly during depression periods. Finally prison reform elements, concerned about the emphasis on profits rather than on the rehabilitation of human beings, publicized the abuses with such good effect that, by the latter part of the nineteenth century, six states (California, New York, Massachusetts, New Jersey, Ohio and Pennsylvania) had already legislated the contract system and its variants out of existence. By 1936, every state had enacted legislation abolishing these systems, although some local jails still cling to certain forms of these convict labor practices, particularly to the lease system.

Three substitute systems have been developed in the past decades to meet some of the difficulties and objections enumerated above. The *state account* system represents a new attempt, in which the state enters the open market as an entrepreneur selling prison-made products for its own profit. The Minnesota and Wisconsin prison systems, for example, have almost a monopoly on binder-twine and San Quentin manufactures jute bags cheaply for California's farmers. The *state-use* system has also come into existence, under which the various departments and sub-divisions of the state are either required or encouraged to buy prison manufactured school and office furniture, clothing and shoes, canned foods, brooms, license plates, and a variety of other items. Among other administrations, Maryland and the Federal Prison Industries, Incorporated, have adapted phases of this system.

Finally, there is the *public works and ways* system in which prisoners, working directly under state supervisors, do highway construction and maintenance, reforestation, parasite control, and construction and repair of public buildings, particularly prisons. None of these has been either profitable or wholly successful, except for during brief periods of World War II. The state account system is opposed by both business and labor, and, at best, gives little trade training of value to the convict which he can use upon his release. The state-use system has not developed enough markets for its products to keep any significant number of convicts working full-time at maximum efficiency. The public works and ways system is opposed by contractors and construction workers and has recently led to serious abuses at Rock Quarry Prison in Georgia, although it is seemingly working well in the California Honor Camp system.

A separate form of prison labor, agriculture, presents real possibilities as a vocational and rehabilitative agency. At the present time, some 250,000 acres are under cultivation on prison farms, contributing to better prison fare, reduction in operating costs, saleable surpluses, and healthful out-door work for a large number of convicts. Prison maintenance work (food preparation and service, cleaning, clerical duties, etc.) accounts for perhaps one-third of the labor of the convict population but because of chronic over-assignment neither job skills nor good work habits result.

The opposition of employers and labor unions to prison labor has resulted in legislation, notably the Hawes-Cooper Act of 1929, the Ashhurst-Sumners Act of 1935, and supporting state and Federal enactments, which effectively limit the open-market distribution of prison-made products. The development of the state-use system however, while slow, has increased prison production from less than ten millions in 1940 to more than eighty millions during the present decade. This production can be further increased if sound business principles and practises are introduced, such as, for example, the introduction of incentives, especially wage incentives. Present wage scales range from no payment in some sixteen states, through token payments of two cents in Washington, four cents in Kansas, and eight cents in Kentucky per diem, to maximum payments of one dollar a day in Oregon and seventeen and a half cents an hour in the Federal System.

Considerable attention must likewise be given to proper industrial planning in relation to prison population patterns, potential markets, and competition from free industry. Until very recently, problems of diversification of products, and the planning of production in relation to buildings and equipment available, have not figured prominently, if at all, in overall planning of prison industry. If prison industry is to serve its dual purpose of training in job skills for rehabilitation and meeting the market demands of outside industry, modern personnel methods in job classification and assignment, constantly improved vocational training and superior supervision must be seriously and actively incorporated within present planning. Further, the more aggressive marketing of products must be acknowledged as essential in the promotion of any continuing industry, prison or not. Opposition from employers is being reduced by diversification of output, thus reducing the impact upon any one industry. In the case of labor unions, objections are being met by staying out of overcrowded fields and concentrating apprenticeship training programs and prison industry production in areas of known labor shortage and with the active cooperation of labor unions at all stages.

It is now recognized that "teaching the prisoner a trade" is no longer in itself a valid objective and that the prison labor system must be integrated with the entire rehabilitative program; that the prison labor system should be neither punitive nor profit-motivated; that idleness, made-work, and inefficient methods contribute to disciplinary problems within the prison and recidivism or poor adjustment after release; and that the annual loss of the productive capacity of 180,000 prisoners is too heavy a burden even to America's strong economy.

A program of correction, to be truly effective, must be deeply cognizant of the individual's own capacity for growth and self-direction as well as the need to impose external controls upon the antisocial person, frequently of a rigorous and severe nature. The modern psychotherapeutic point of view has tended increasingly to stress the need for permissiveness in the development of the individual's own sense of responsibility and the need for the exercise of that inner control without which any form of correction is frequently a painful delusion. To the professional psychotherapist, however, permissiveness —contrary to the opinion of the untrained layman—is neither complete freedom to act as one chooses, nor license, which is tantamount to the same thing. The therapist in correction is acutely aware of the need to curb dangerous impulses in his client, impulses not only dangerous to society but also dangerous to himself. The growth of the therapeutic instrumentalities in correction, however, has not been orderly nor has there developed an integrated point of view on the basis of which principles of treatment may be employed which will enable the therapist to recognize the point at which external controls must be imposed. Dr. Jacob Chwast, a lieutenant in the Police Department of the City of New York and with extensive practical experience in its Youth Division as a practising psychologist, deals with this difficult problem in attempting to formulate certain guide-lines for reconciling permissiveness with the use of authority in the treatment of the antisocial person.

Chapter 5

THE SIGNIFICANCE OF CONTROL IN THE TREATMENT OF THE ANTISOCIAL PERSON

JACOB CHWAST, PH.D.

Youth Division, New York City Police Department

To say that treatment services—casework, counseling or phychotherapy—for the antisocial person have been put together rather haphazardly is probably a charitable understatement at best. Each time a void in such services has been discovered, the attempt has been made, sometimes rather crudely, to fill it in by creating a new agency or by stretching awkwardly the capacities of an already existing agency. It seems quite apparent that expediency has too often dictated what new or substitutive resources would be feasible to meet unmet needs. Admittedly, the helping professions have not typically been so advantageously situated in our power structure to determine solely by themselves, on the basis of their considered professional judgment, what social machinery should be constructed to meet emerging social problems. The role of boards, budget makers and the various special interest groups are sufficiently familiar to all of us in demonstrating, if such proof is necessary, how social change is so frequently the end-product of political compromise. This statement, however, should not be construed as minimizing the positive aspects of such non-professional influences in shaping social policy. But expediency and compromise alone are not entirely to blame for the state of our treatment services. It also seems evident that the conceptual framework for the treatment of the antisocial individual has not been outlined with sufficient clarity by professional theoreticians and practitioners to help the community most effectively fashion its therapeutic armamentarium.

Perhaps the failure to develop an adequate frame of theoretical reference, as well as the many conspicuous failures in the actual treatment of antisocial persons, can be attributed in part to a misconception of the usefulness of permissiveness as a therapeutic agent which has led to its being used inappropriately. While the writer fully appreciates the value of the caseworker's or therapist's democratic acceptance of the right to self-determination of the client, some adaptation of this principle which emphasizes the helpful role of control and authority with antisocial clients or patients requires consideration.

An awareness of this deficiency in our understanding has unfortunately not been sufficiently clear to enough authorities in the fields of delinquency and treatment, although there are some significant stirrings to repair the situation.[1]

In surveying current programs for the treatment of antisocial individuals and the philosophies from which they are derived, one detects the common assumption underlying them that a systematic array of social, protective and correctional agencies are required which are geared to meet the antisocial person at his particular level of social and psychological need. This analysis will attempt to examine some of the theoretical considerations which appear to underly this assumption.

It is, of course, recognized that there is no single etiological basis for antisocial behavior. Nosologically, different types of antisocial individuals are distinguishable such as the "neurotic" or "psychotic" offender, the "normal" delinquent and the psychopathic personality. Furthermore, it is quite clear that specific treatment techniques vary considerably for such diagnostically different groups. For present purposes, however, it is believed that the view of antisocial phenomena as existing on a continuum will prove helpful.

Treatment Objectives

At the outset, it might be well for us to arrive at some understanding of what is entailed in the treatment of the antisocial person. Obviously, although some overlap is inevitable in comparing the techniques of treatment of the antisocial person with the treatment of the usual neurotic or psychotic patient, important differences do occur. Chiefly, these differences are in the extent to which social difficulties must be dealt with. Indeed, this should hardly surprise anybody since, if the circularity might be forgiven, the antisocial person's difficulties are social in nature. This fact, however, should not, on the other hand, as has sometimes happened, obscure the frequent concomitance of intrapsychic difficulties with those of a primarily social nature. The failure on the part of many otherwise professionally astute observers to take these simple facts into account has led to a number of unnecessary and possibly avoidable therapeutic impasses.

From this, it would seem quite clear that the basic task in treating the antisocial individual, regardless of what his diagnosis might be, is that of bringing his social activities into greater harmony with those of the community at large. To express the matter in another way, success in treating the antisocial person is very much contingent upon the extent to which his antisocial activities—aggressive most often—are curbed. Insofar as the larger community can perceive it, the delinquent or criminal cannot be deemed to have been rehabilitated if he continues to injure others in their person or possessions, despite the strides he may have made in dealing with his inner problems as the result of some form of therapy. For example, a man who learns that he is hostile towards older women, and even understands to some extent why he feels this way, is hardly improved if he persists in acting assaultively against them. In fact, this might become a rather strong argument against attempting primarily to give insight to offenders since, in their case, the threat of insight is frequently accompanied by anxiety which may be easily converted into aggressive "acting-out." Evidently something more has to be added. This is somewhat different from the case of the usual neurotic individual for whom such internal progress is essentially the *sine qua non* as a treatment objective. Unless his outward actions become controlled, i.e., socially adapted, the antisocial person cannot legitimately be considered to have been treated successfully. On the other hand, it is quite obvious that even if this should take place, it also cannot be assumed that he is actually rehabilitated: for the arrival at some state of inner equilibrium is also a prerequisite to successful treatment. Success in treatment requires some resolution of both inner and outer conflict.

The Relationship between "Release" and "Control" Functions

Successful treatment requires the bridging of the dichotomy between the individual's self-expressive activities on one hand, and the necessity to control the degree to which he expresses himself so that others may not be hurt, on the other. For purposes of convenience, the present writer prefers to refer to these processes as they occur intra-personally as the "release" and "control" functions of the individual. Although an excessive amount of either variable may be accompanied by a diminished amount of the other, they are in no sense mutually exclusive.

The release functions, within this context, consist of all those activities in which the individual engages that enable him to gain satisfaction from the exercise of his own powers and capacities, as well as those that enable him to widen his potential for a fuller and more productive life. It might be added that if all of his self-expressive activities were socialized, there would probably be little or no problem for the individual or society. However, for better or worse, some activities are socialized and others destructive to varying degrees.

The control functions refer to the activities whereby the individual keeps his self-expressive activities in check. As far as other people are concerned the release or self-expressive activities of a destructive nature assume a special importance, inasmuch as frequently it is these others who suffer the consequences of such activities.

Since both of these processes characterize all human performances, the extent to which they are displayed will vary from person to person. It will be noted that such persons who exhibit large amounts of either of these intra-personal variables by itself may verge upon the pathological in behavior. In one instance, if the release variable predominates, insupportable impulsivity and utter self-absorption may occur. At the other pole, an excess of control may range in effect from inhibition through emotional flatness and paralyzing rigidity. Characteristically, however, these functions are blended sufficiently well so that the individual is able to live within his milieu without experiencing too much stress, either internally or externally.

Indeed, one finds that the most productive and creative talents in our midst possess a surfeit of both of these variables simultaneously. How this is possible might best be appreciated by taking a look at the nature of control.

Development of Control

Control, as Bettelheim and Janowitz among others have noted, follows an evolutionary course of development within the individual.[2] At first, the young child is directly urged toward socialized behavior by his parents. In essence, since he cannot yet control himself, the actual external pressure of his parents controls him. Later, assuming a normal course of development, the child can keep in mind the parental injunctions and no longer requires their physical presence to refrain from giving free play to unsocial impulses. Yet, even here, it should be observed, it is the remembrance of an external *verbot* that exacts control. That is, the child remembers what his mother and father may have told him and he obeys. Finally, the child, if he feels secure, loved and accepted moves toward a fuller identification with the attitudes, ideals and beliefs of his parents. The controls over his behavior become anchored in his ego structure and eventually are completely internalized. He is now capable of distinguishing for himself what is right and what is wrong. Nobody has to tell him either by physical example or by serving as a controlling mental image. He does not hurt anybody else or disobey the customs, laws and standards of society because to do so would be to do damage to his own picture of himself: his self-concept.

Social Value of Control

For a person like this, control over basic drives, wishes, urges and appetites is ego-syntonic. Doing this does not leave him feeling that he has been cheated and deprived. Since controls for him are truly from within, he does not find it necessary to expend the energy potentially available for creative expression by corrosive hostility and aggression. In addition, he has felt loved by the significant persons in his life and so he has been able to love them freely in return, and to identify more completely with their interests, goals and values. It thus becomes possible for such a person to exercise a reasonable quality of control over his impulses and drives which can thereby be harnessed into the service of ever-growing intellectual, emotional, spiritual and social horizons.

Control Failure

If, on the other hand, the individual has not succeeded in meeting the challenges of life as they have arisen during various stages of development, the probabilities are quite strong that he will remain fixed at the point at which he has failed. This would have very serious consequences for him—among other things very decidedly in the area of control. Of course, a rather similar situation might occur as the result of regression to a simpler level of functioning because a higher level cannot be maintained for one reason or another. In these instances, a more primitive mode of control could well persist or even become reestablished. External force might be necessary to keep such a person from hurting those about him. Since mastery over oneself is a process which is extended in time and does not uniformly apply to all human activities, the need for some amount of external control never disappears entirely. Of and by itself, external control need not *necessarily* be injurious to the individual's development. In making this point, the writer wishes to emphasize that this should not be interpreted as giving aid and comfort to the protagonists of the punitive approach to unsocialized behavior. The helping disciplines often speak of the setting of limits and the constructive use of authority, but we must acknowledge, despite some beginnings, our understanding of these concepts is still *in utero*. This has many unfortunate consequences for until we clarify the dynamic significance of external control, socially and psychologically, and accept our responsibilities in regard to it, we will continue to remain ineffectual within an enormous area of social well-being now served by our immense and relatively unperceptive authoritarian machinery. The public and the mass media of public expression demand that external control be exerted—will we, nil we—over certain types of offenders against the public weal. With society constituted as it is today, pious hopes to the contrary, we must soberly realize that unless the enlightened social scientist becomes capable of moving in on such situations—fraught as they are with discomforts and dangers —the traditional, punishing approach will persist.

To return to the effect of external control, it is rather when such control is inappropriate, when it overlooks the child's developmental needs, or irrational, because it is excessively applied, that it can cause harm. For one thing, external control of this kind blocks the expansion of the self thereby reducing the individual's capacity to more fully participate in life and society. Furthermore, such unattuned outer suppression can cause confusion in the child's mind, and by damming up natural impulses and drives produce wasteful and intense hostility against the frustrating agent. This in turn can lead to further trespasses against the repose, safety and comfort of other members of the social community.

Principle of Graded External Control

If one assumes the foregoing analysis to be valid, it would seem to be a psychologically sound principle that in the curbing of antisocial behavior, only that much and no more outside control—authoritative intervention—is called for in a given instance as will meet the needs of the situation, if the rights of the individual to growth and fulfillment are to be respected.

In action, this principle simply means that a parent does not resort to threats and physical punishment if explanations will do, a teacher does not send a pupil to the principal if she can caution him herself, a policeman does not arrest a boy when an admonition will serve, a judge does not commit a defendant if probation is feasible, and confinement in an institution is reduced if the prisoner can be paroled.

By this means, the intrusion of superior power, invariably experienced by the weaker person as a very real threat to his integrity with quite frequent traumatic repercussions, either flagrant or subtle, is delimited. The concept of authority used as a means of setting limits to deviant behavior seems perfectly consistent with this thesis.

Above all, successful treatment requires the avoidance of any traumatization to the extent that this is possible. Not only is traumatization an affront to the ego, but it also weakens the growth of inner control—a primary treatment objective.

To restate the principle in another way, the relationship between outer control and inner control is inverse. The more inner control the individual possesses, the fewer are the outer sanctions called for; the less the inner, the more the need for outer control. Success in the treatment of each case of antisociality is critically dependent upon the preciseness with which these two control factors can be psychodiagnostically evaluated. The amount of outer pressure exerted must be just sufficient to meet the needs of a situation but never more, lest it hamper the development of inner control so essential to healthy personality development and, *de rigueur*, democratic living.

For the person lacking in inner control, a permissive treatment approach with no realistic setting of limits can be fatal, because of the failure to deal with basic issues. How much the offender asks for outer control has been nowhere more poignantly and tragically expressed than the lip-sticked plea on a mirror by a mentally deranged killer in recent years: "For Heaven's sake—catch me before I kill more—I cannot control myself." [3]

General Treatment Implications

The implications of the foregoing discussion for treatment of the antisocial person within the community appear rather clear.

It is essential to assess carefully the control potential of each agency in terms of meeting the control needs, inner and outer, of each person it services. Just as the individual's control in the population at large ranges along a continuum, the control which our agencies (casework, psychiatric, protective and correctional) offer can also be charted on a continuum. The ideal conditions for treatment occur at the point at which a given agency's control capability intersects with the precise control needs of each individual served.

The "normal" and "neurotic" offender will probably require a minimum of control; indeed for the neurotic, a reduction of excessive inner pressure in certain areas may very well be necessary. The real antisocial, acting-out personalities will probably need considerably more outer control.

Summary

The state of casework, counseling and psychotherapeutic services for the antisocial person seems to be less than orderly. This appears attributable not only to expediency, but also to a failure to make clear a cohesive, theoretical framework to guide in the creation of therapeutic resources. The failure seems to have been especially derived from an inability to reconcile permissiveness with the use of authority and control in the treatment of the antisocial person.

Although antisocial behavior can be manifested by individuals belonging to a diversity of diagnostic groups, it seems quite clear that the primary treatment objective should be to control such antisocial behavior. In addition to this, it would be quite desirable if a reduction of inner conflict, if it is present, could be effected.

It might be fairly stated that the treatment problem for patients of all types is to bring into harmony the individual's needs for self-expression or "release" and those for control. An excess of either the release or the control activities can be indicative of pathology, although ordinarily they are blended well enough to enable the individual to get along without too much trouble to himself or others.

As the child grows, control evolves from the need for external parental pressure upon him for socialization, to a remembered mental image of what has been impressed upon him by significant adults, to, finally, an internalization of values and ideals as part of his ego structure. When the last stage is reached, the individual can reasonably adapt his actions to society's demands because he has not been unduly frustrated and does not feel the need to rebel. If, however, the child feels insecure and unloved, he cannot take on the requirements of social living, and so controls may not become internalized.

In such a case, external controls may be necessary. Such controls need not be damaging unless they are excessively or irrationally applied. The latter eventually would be unfortunate because of the resulting confusion and hostility, and the blocking of growth potential for the child. In view of this, it would seem a valid principle that antisocial behavior should be curbed with only that much and no more outside control as is necessary to meet a given situation. More than this can be traumatic and lead to a further weakening of inner control.

Treatment success depends upon the preciseness with which the individual's inner control capacity and his outer control needs, both of which appear to be inversely related, are assessed. If a person lacks inner control, permissiveness without appropriate limit setting can prove utterly inadequate.

After the assessment has been made, the psychodynamic

meaning of the helping resource, in terms of the amount of outer control it offers, and its ability to enable the building of greater inner control and the realizing of productive self-expressive potential, must be evaluated. Where the resource offers the precise control capability adapted to the individual's control needs, a major hurdle in treating the antisocial person has been surmounted.

REFERENCES

1. For notable exceptions to the general neglect of this area, see the writings of Melitta Schmideberg and Alfred J. Kahn. Also refer to the *Proceedings of the Workshop on Treatment Practice with Delinquents*, Interprofessional Committee on Treatment Practice with Delinquents. This meeting was held at the New York School of Social Work, June, 1957.

2. Bettelheim, Bruno and Janowitz, Morris, *The Dynamics of Prejudice* (Harpers, New York, 1950).

3. Freeman, Lucy, *Before I Kill More* (Crown Publishing Co., New York, 1955).

Very few problems in the entire field of penology excite so profound an emotional reaction as the issue of capital punishment. In one sense, the movement to abolish the death penalty is a logical outcome of the trend towards rehabilitation and reclamation of the offender as opposed to the traditional view of sheer punishment. If we accept the logical implications of the assumption that the criminal act is an aspect of the individual's social maladjustment and that it is reflective of a peculiarly pernicious environment, then the concept of the individual's responsibility for his offense becomes less important, perhaps, than his accountability for the wrong-doing he has perpetrated.

It is within this historic transition from individual responsibility to individual accountability that some of the most serious dilemmas of modern penology lie. In the ultimate sense, this would imply that even the most serious of lawbreakers, those for whom ordinarily the death penalty may be reserved, must be reexamined in the light of their full responsibility for their acts. Seen in this light, the problem of the capital offender is placed within a different focus—a focus implying psychological and medical considerations rather than problems of a juridical and legal nature. It is in this light that the bitter present day controversy concerning the mental state of the offender, as well as the issue of capital punishment, is being waged.

The moral connotations involved in the suspension of capital punishment are even more profoundly affected than the issues of law and criminal deterrence. Towards the end of the last century, the eminent British sociologist and social philosopher, L. T. Hobhouse, expressed the view that the taking of life by process of law weakened the moral fibre of the entire social order. We have tragically witnessed in our own lifetime the establishment of monolithic states where the taking of human life, in the so-called interests of the state, has been pursued with the utmost cynicism and expedience. The conscientious and zealous opponent of this traditional legal right of the state to take human life, even when dignified by judicial procedure, is first of all moved by moral revulsion by what is regarded essentially as a deeply inhuman act, and only secondly, by the need for logical and factual exposition.

Mrs. Ehrmann, long a devoted and tireless worker in the effort to remove what she considers a brutal, senseless, and archaic socal practise, raises an eloquent voice in support of the abolition of capital punishment. In the paper which follows she not only presents the case against the death penalty but gives the reader a valuable survey of the movement toward its abolition in the modern world.

Chapter 6

CAPITAL PUNISHMENT TODAY—WHY?

Mrs. Herbert B. Ehrmann

Director, American League to Abolish Capital Punishment

The infliction of death as a punishment for crimes against the person, property, or public morals has now been dropped in most civilized countries. These include all of the democracies on the western continent of Europe, except France and England, almost all of South and Central America, several Australian and Asiatic states, the U.S.S.R.,* and the state of Israel, totalling about 38 countries.[1]

The United States Territories have abolished capital punishment also—Puerto Rico, Hawaii, the Virgin Islands, and Alaska, the 49th state. But within this country the situation is mixed and unclear. Nevertheless, the trend toward abolition, halted by the first world war, has resumed and, again, public opinion appears to be mounting against capital punishment.

On April 2, 1958, after an educational campaign of high quality, Delaware completely abolished capital punishment, the first state to do so in 43 years.[2] The other abolition states are Maine, Michigan, Minnesota, North Dakota, Rhode Island and Wisconsin. In the past, nine states abolished and later restored the death penalty. In most cases, restoration occurred shortly after World War I and Prohibition, as part of a reaction to what was believed to be a rising tide of

* In the U.S.S.R., capital punishment has been restored for premeditated murder (1957).

violent crime. A subcommittee report of the Commission now investigating capital punishment in Massachusetts, released for publication in December 1958, made the following statement:

"No significant difference between the relative homicide rates in these states before, during and after abolition, is noted. There appears to be no well defined reason or reasons which prompted the restoration of capital punishment in any case, but available information indicates that in several instances restoration followed the commission of a particularly brutal murder."

Since 1949, five states have eliminated mandatory death from their statutes.[3] Where capital punishment is still retained, the alternate penalty of life imprisonment is now permitted by every state and the Federal Government, the sole exception being the District of Columbia.

The Trend Toward Abolition

But even in these retention states, it now seems clear that the public is turning against capital punishment. There has been a decided trend toward less frequent use of the death penalty. Executions rose from 155 in 1930 to 199 in 1935, but fell to 65 in 1956 and in 1957. During the decade, 1930-1939, the average was 167; in 1940-1949, it was 128; and during the period of 1950-1958, it fell to 79—despite the great increases in population of these periods.

Each year only about half of the 44 retention jurisdictions actually carry out any executions. Six states in 1956 [4] and four states in 1957 [5] accounted for more than half of the number of executions for these years. In Delaware and in Massachusetts, no one has been executed since 1947. Other states and jurisdictions have done without executions for long periods, as for example, the states of New Hampshire, Montana, Wyoming, Oregon, Vermont and the District of Columbia.

As the rate of executions has declined, the incidence of homicide in the United States has shown a marked decrease as well, although other major crimes have increased since World War II. In the 10-year period of 1919-1928, homicide rates (per 100,000 of the population) ranged from 1.4 in Vermont to 29.7 in Florida. In 1956 no homicides were reported in Vermont and the highest rate was 15.5 in Georgia. In 1956, the Florida rate dropped to 11.9. Sixty-two persons were executed in 1953, the lowest number recorded. In the following year, murders decreased by 3.8% and the 1954 homicide rate was the lowest for a twenty-year period (4.2%).[6]

The homicide rates of the abolition states have been consistently among the lowest of the states. In all scientific comparisons of the homicide rates in neighboring states of similar character—racial, industrial and social—it is found that those in abolition states are as low, and generally lower, than in the retention states. This fact appears to have been verified in scientific investigations.

Legislative Surveys and Hearings

The United Kingdom, where in the last century over two hundred offenses were punishable by death, has led in world studies of capital punishment.[7] Official commissions and committees have conducted no less than six intensive inquiries since 1819.[8] One of these bodies, the Select Committee (1929-1930), reported as follows:

"Our prolonged examination of the situation in foreign countries has increasingly confirmed us in the assurance that capital punishment may be abolished in this country without endangering life or property, or impairing the security of society."

The most complete investigation, perhaps, was made recently by the British Royal Commission. However, the terms of reference of this report precluded any expression of views about the desirability of abolition itself. The Royal Commission of 1949-1953 reported:

"The general conclusion which we have reached is that there is no clear evidence in any of the figures we have examined that the abolition of capital punishment has led to an increase in the homicide rate, or that its reintroduction has led to a fall."

In this country the extensive report of studies published in the special volume of *The Annals of the American Academy of Political and Social Science*, "Murder and the Penalty of Death" (November 1952), comes to a similar conclusion:

"The presence or absence of the death penalty makes no particular difference in the amount of murder . . . the death penalty is inconsequential as a deterrent."

In Canada and in a number of states in this country there have been a number of recent investigations and studies, and nationally prominent figures have testified at various legislative hearings on the subject. Based upon the evidence presented, the conclusions (except those in the Report of the Canadian Commission [9]) are all the same—that there is no factual basis for the assumption that capital punishment is necessary to protect the community.

The Legislative Research Analyst, in a summary of testimony presented at two recent New Jersey Hearings, went further and stated:

"In fact, the bulk of the evidence points to exactly the opposite conclusion, that executions tend to incite crimes of violence in mentally or emotionally disturbed persons." [10]

Appearing before the *Massachusetts Commission Investigating Capital Punishment* at a public hearing held in Rhode Island, the Governor of Rhode Island, Dennis J. Roberts, said that "the death penalty is no deterrent to a potential murderer," and ". . . The Rhode Island Legislation, combined with a sound program of rehabilitation, is to be preferred over the very questionable policy of capital punishment." His views were supported by the Chief of Police of Providence, John A. Murphy, and other Rhode Island Department of Justice and Correctional Officials, including eminent Supreme Court Judges and the Attorney General.

Some of the additional conclusions which may be drawn from the mass of evidence presented by the legislative surveys and testifying authorities on the subject are that capital punishment is brutalizing; creates morbid sensationalism; is haphazard in its application; creates unnecessary problems of determining "degrees" of murder and mental responsibility; disturbs the course of the administration of justice; has no place in modern penology; obstructs penal progress; and presents the ever-present danger of executing an innocent person.

The Action of Religious, Social and Political Groups

Many religious groups have long been opposed to capital punishment. Now their voices are clearer, and more determined. The Society of Friends has long led the movement in England and in this country. In October of 1958, the Protestant Episcopal Church of the United States, at its 59th General Convention in Miami, passed a resolution stating that the death penalty ought to be abolished. In June of the same year, the Conference of Reform Jewish Rabbis recorded unanimously against capital punishment. Although the Catholic Church has taken no official position on the subject, Catholic prison chaplains in various states have vigorously protested the death penalty. Two priests have served on the Board of the American League to Abolish Capital Punishment. In Massachusetts, prison chaplains have been leaders in the hard fought, annual campaigns. The Catholic Chaplain of the Connecticut State Prison has called capital punishment "absolutely cruel, inhuman and paganistic" and has stated that "it should be abolished."

Groups of social workers and social agencies, civic groups, some labor groups, and even some political organizations are now joining the abolitionists. "Capital Punishment," the October issue of the *Prison Journal* of the Pennsylvania Prison Society, includes a survey and bibliography of basic documents produced during 1948-1958, an important contribution to study on this subject.

In the past year, private citizens have organized Abolition Groups in Connecticut, New Jersey, New York, Tennessee, California, Pennsylvania, and Illinois. Governors, attorneys-general, and other high government officials are now taking an open stand against the penalty of death, among them Governor E. G. Brown of California, who previously served as Attorney General.

The Growth of Interest in the Mass Media of Communication

Unusual increase in public interest is shown, recently, in the vast area of mass communication in this field. Reflecting British sentiment against capital punishment, following the execution of Mrs. Ellis, Bentley, Evans, and Christie, numerous articles and editorials on capital punishment have been published in leading newspapers and periodicals across this country.

Television, radio, dramatic productions and the movies reflect what appears to be a growing opposition to capital punishment. A variety of public hearings, debates and speeches has been televised and broadcast. Within the past year, Donal MacNamara, the president of the American League to Abolish Capital Punishment, discussed capital punishment on the Bennett Cerf program. The Los Angeles Television Station, KNTX, took a strong editorial stand against capital punishment. An hour-long program, "Thou Shalt Not Kill," was presented on which leading penologists spoke, and condemned men were interviewed in the San Quentin death house. In New York, C.B.S. presented the "Sacco-Vanzetti Case" in two television programs during the summer of 1958. The "Omnibus" program of October 26th, 1958, was wholly devoted to the theme of "Capital Punishment," dramatically produced and narrated by the well known Boston attorney, Joseph N. Welch. The moving film, "I Want To Live," starring Susan Hayward, deals a powerful blow against the death penalty. It purports to be the authenticated story of Barbara Graham, who was executed in California in 1955. The grim details involved in the execution of a human being are all too realistically portrayed in this film production. In the case of Barbara Graham's execution, there is some reason to believe that she may have been innocent of the crime for which she was put to death.

Legislative Development

During the past decade, efforts to change the statutes requiring the death penalty for certain capital offenses have increased significantly. Only in Delaware have such efforts been completely successful. Connecticut and Massachusetts, however, ended mandatory capital punishment in 1951, while Vermont took similar action in 1957. It is interesting to note that Vermont has also seriously modified the famous "M'Naghten's Rule" defining "legal sanity." Abolition bills have gained strong support. Bills were filed in eighteen states last year and in the federal government. Moves in this direction have likewise been made in California, Illinois, New Jersey and Tennessee. Legislative debates on capital punishment have continued into 1959 and will become an active part of the legislative calendar for a considerable time to come.

In Oregon, a constitutional amendment to abolish capital punishment lost at the polls during the fall of 1958 by a vote of 10,000 out of a total of over 525,000 votes cast, although an abolition measure had previously been passed by the Oregon Legislature. Another attempt is already scheduled for 1960.

As a counter movement, however, the death penalty has recently been extended to cover additional crimes in certain jurisdictions, as in the case of the recently passed Federal law which permits the sentence of death for selling narcotics to a minor and for certain other offenses.

Growth in Public Awareness of Judicial Miscarriages

The public is also becoming more aware of the danger of executing the innocent. Mistakes in convictions are possible, and it is reasonable to assume that some innocent people are executed upon the evidence at hand at the time of trial. Courts and juries ordinarily do the best they can to protect the accused and the public. But knowledge of the facts may be limited and emotion may cause dangerously faulty evaluation of the evidence. Reversals of verdicts and new trials are common in civil cases, but until recently such reversals have been quite uncommon in capital criminal cases. A number of mistakes, fortunately, have been discovered and corrected. But it is exceedingly difficult to prove innocence after death. Instances of such proof are, of necessity, very rare and usually appear as a result of accident.

It is possible, for example, that Wilbur Coffin, who was hanged in Quebec five years ago, protesting his innocence to the end, may now be proven to have been innocent. On November 29th of this year, it was reported that Francis Gilbert Thompson, a Canadian Indian, confessed that he and a companion did the killing. Some years ago Paul Dwyer [11] was found guilty of murder in Maine, an abolition state. The authorities are only now examining his continued claims of innocence. During the summer of 1958, James Fulton Foster, twice condemned to die in Georgia, was finally freed by the confession of a policeman. In Massachusetts, a young Puerto Rican bus boy, Santos Rodriguez, was freed last year after serving three years of a life sentence, when the true murderer finally confessed.

Recent books, such as *Not Guilty*, by Judge Jerome Frank and Barbara Frank, and *Reflections on Hanging*, by Arthur Koestler, have been widely read and have underscored the danger of convicting the innocent.

A constant flow of press clippings on homicide cases from the various states, received in the office of the American League to Abolish Capital Punishment, report many instances where mistakes have been discovered.

It is also becoming more apparent that the death penalty may function inequitably, discriminating against the poor, and especially against Negroes. Of the 3,504 persons executed during 1930-1956, 1,881 were Negroes, 1,583 were white, and 40 unidentified in the statistics. In executions for rape, 360 were Negroes as compared to 39 white persons. In 1954, ten juveniles were put to death—all Negroes.

Sensational cases involving death sentences continue to shake and stir the public. Among such cases which have captured the attention of the public recently are the following: Jimmy Wilson, condemned to die in Alabama for stealing the sum of one dollar and ninety-five cents (the sentence here was finally commuted); Isaiah Green, fifteen years old, condemned to die in Pennsylvania; Caryl Chessman, sentenced to die in California over ten years ago, and whose recent execution created world-wide protest [Ed.—Occurred after speech]; Burton Abbott, executed at San Quentin minutes before word of reprieve arrived.

Legal Insanity and Capital Punishment

Modern psychiatry has probably produced the greatest change in public attitude toward the death penalty since ancient times by its attack on the archaic judicial rules defining legal sanity. If Massachusetts abolishes or further modifies its death penalty statutes, it may be partly due to the recent suicide of a mentally ill youth, Jack Chester, who killed his sweetheart. He had made several earlier suicide attempts, and had, in fact, pleaded with the jury to be allowed to die in the electric chair. At his trial, defense and prosecution psychiatrists disagreed on his mental state. Chester addressed the jury himself, and said—"It is my opinion that any decision other than guilty of murder in the first degree with no recommendation for clemency is a miscarriage of justice." When he was sentenced to die, he thanked the judge. Chester refused to sign any application to the Governor for commutation.

Before the last execution date of December 15th, further examination made by the Department of Mental Health revealed that Chester had "suicidal tendencies" and could not "appropriately be executed." Commutation was about to be recommended by the Governor on Monday, December 1st, but on November 29th, Chester hanged himself with his sweater in his cell. In Massachusetts this case is commonly regarded in some quarters as the *reductio ad absurdum* of the "M'Naghten's rule" governing legal insanity. The report of the Massachusetts Commission which has been investigating capital punishment during the period of this case will consider the problem of legal sanity as well as the issue of capital punishment.[12]

Opposition and the Future

From what has been said thus far, it is apparent that the movement to end capital punishment in our country is gathering momentum. Probably no other change in the handling of social problems has received such unanimous approval of informed leaders. There is scarcely an outstanding authority in penology, criminology or psychiatry who is not opposed to capital punishment. There is a widespread and firm conviction that capital punishment—with its profound social implications, its undesirable publicity features, its dangers of killing the innocent, its affront to religion and morals, its disrupting influence in the handling of mental responsibility and the administration of justice—should be eliminated from our penal codes. Why, then, is legislative change so long in coming?

The obstacle does not arise from organized opposition. Except for the activities of some police organizations—an opposition, incidentally, by no means negligible—there is little organized support for the death penalty. The real block lies in the natural but massive resistance to changing traditional practices apparently sanctioned by the centuries. Ancient laws die hard. The very fact that a penalty has existed for ages creates a powerful presumption that it must serve some end. Massive inertia can be overcome only by an even more powerful force. The elements of such a force are present, but they have not been unified and directed. The movement lacks effective organization—articulated in terms of constituency, aggressive leadership, and the active backing of scientific bodies embracing the fields of penology, criminology, and psychiatry. Without this support, it need hardly be added, that finances for effective work are also lacking.

There is even lacking a central agency where reliable information and data may be obtained.

Opposition to the death penalty does not arouse a national constituency such as was the case with Woman Suffrage or Prohibition. An occasional execution seems a little too remote to the average citizen to arouse him to crusading action. Even if he is opposed to the death penalty, he is apt to regard it as minor as compared with manslaughter on the highways, or the fatalities brought about by disease or war. The moral and social implications of the problem are not sharp enough to stir him emotionally unless, perhaps, some proven execution of an innocent person should accidentally come to light.

To rouse public opinion to the point of compelling action is the business of leadership. Although capital punishment is opposed by citizens of the highest standing, whose sympathies are profound, in general few have assumed the active role which is necessary to precipitate public sentiment, now so widely diffused throughout the community. The movement to abolish the death penalty needs not only their good will, which it has, but their aggressive and determined leadership.

To be successful, the movement must have the active and continuing support of organizations devoted to the study of penology, criminology, and psychiatry. Strangely enough, although many individual leaders in these fields have left no doubt as to their stand on the death penalty, formal opposition to it has not as yet come from their professional associations. Until recently, the subject of capital punishment did not even have a place on the agenda of meetings of such bodies. Perhaps this is logical, in a sense, because killing a supposed offender is neither penology nor criminology, nor psychiatric treatment. It is, in fact, a repudiation of the basic principles of these sciences, and a reproach to their ideals and the goals which they seek. For this reason alone, they should bring their weight to bear in the struggle to repeal the death penalty, a movement now going on throughout the country. Once the opposition of such informed groups becomes active, capital punishment will begin its unregrettable disappearance, now so long overdue.

REFERENCES

1. Tables I and II of Appendix A to this chapter present some of the most recent evidence concerning the status of capital punishment in various parts of the world and in several jurisdictions of the United States.

2. Bennett, James V., "Delaware Abolishes Capital Punishment," *American Bar Association Journal* (November 1958).

3. Massachusetts, Connecticut, North Carolina, New Mexico, and Vermont (up until June 1, 1957).

4. Mississippi, 8; Florida and Texas, 7 each; Georgia and New York, 6 each; California, 5 (Total 39).

5. Georgia, 14; California, 9; Louisiana, 7; Texas, 5 (Total 35).

6. Federal Bureau of Prisons, Washington, D. C., *National Prisoners Statistics* (Executions 1956).

7. Koestler, Arthur, *Reflections on Hanging,* (Victor Gollancz, Ltd., London, 1957), p. 29.

8. During the following years: 1819; 1829; 1839; 1861; 1866; 1929-30; 1949-53.

9. The Canadian report conceded statistical evidence, but accepted testimony based upon opinion. (House of Commons, No. 115, Wed., 27th June, 1956, p. 800.)

10. Deardoff, J. G., Analyst. Summary of Testimony on A-33 and A-34, *New Jersey Assembly Judicial Commission*, June 5 and 19th, 1958.

11. Unpublished data in the files of the American League to Abolish Capital Punishment for this and other cases mentioned on this and subsequent pages.

12. On December 30, 1958, the fifteen member Massachusetts Commission, appointed to Investigate the Advisability of Abolishing Capital Punishment, reported as follows:

10 in favor of immediate and complete abolition;

3 in opposition to abolition;

1 request for a referendum.

Two members abstained from voting.

Appendix A
COUNTRIES AND STATES WHICH HAVE ABOLISHED CAPITAL PUNISHMENT
(For "Civil" Crimes)

Table I—United States and Territories

Key:
(D) Abrogated by Disuse
(P) Reinstated for Political Crimes

Year Abolished	State or Territory	Year Abolished	State or Territory
1847	Michigan	1911	Minnesota
1852	Rhode Island	1929	Puerto Rico
1853	Wisconsin	1957	Hawaii
1887	Maine	1957	Alaska
1915	North Dakota	1957	Virgin Islands
		1958	Delaware

Table II—Foreign Countries

Year Abolished		Last Execution	Year Abolished		Last Execution
1786	Tuscany		1921	Sweden	1910
	Luxembourg (D)	1822	1922	Argentina	
	Belgium (D)	1866		Lithuania (P)	1911
1863	Venezuela			Queensland	
1865	Roumania (P)	1833	1924	Dominican	
1867	Portugal			Republic	
1870	Holland [1]	1860	1928	Mexico [4]	
1879	Switzerland [1]		1930	Greenland	
1880	Costa Rica		1931	Nepal (India)	
1889	Italy [2] (1948)		1940	Cuba [5]	
1891	Brazil	1946	1944	Iceland	
1892	Denmark [3] (D)	1892		Travencore (India)	
1893	Nicaragua		1947	U.S.S.R. [6] (P)	
1894	Honduras		1949	Finland	1826
1895	Norway (D)-1875	1892		Germany	
1897	Ecuador			(Western)	
1900	Peru		1950	Austria (1781)	
1903	Panama		1954	Israel	
1907	Uruguay			New South Wales	
1910	Colombia			Surinam	

1—Abolished in all cantons in 1942   4—Abolished except 10 states
2—Restored under Mussolini   5—Position not clear
3—Finally abolished by law 1930   6—Restored for certain crimes—1954

Guatemala: Abolition of capital punishment for women and children—1955.
Spain: Abolished 1932; Restored under martial law since 1939.
New Zealand: Abolished 1941; Restored 1950; Last execution, 1935.
England: 1949-1954, Capital Punishment suspended.
         1957—Capital punishment abolished except for killing police, murder with use of guns or bombs, or during robbery.

Appendix B

Table III

HOMICIDE RATES OF STATES IN THE UNITED STATES
(per 100,000 population)

Key:
† Abolished Capital Punishment
* Abolished & Restored

State	1919-1928	1956	State	1919-1928	1956
Vermont	1.4	0.0	Ohio	7.6	5.4
New Hampshire	1.5	.4	Colorado *	8.8	3.5
Maine †	1.7	1.2			
			California	9.2	4.4
Wisconsin †	2.	1.3	North Carolina	9.6	11.5
North Dakota †	2.	1.3	Illinois	9.7	5.9
Massachusetts	2.4	1.4			
Iowa *	2.4	.9	Oklahoma	10.4	4.2
Rhode Island †	2.6	2.2	Virginia	10.5	9.1
Minnesota †	3.1	1.1	Missouri *	11.1	7.8
Connecticut	3.2	2.3			
Idaho	3.5	4.0	Arizona *	12.	7.3
Nebraska	3.9	2.2	Wyoming	12.	4.5
			West Virginia	12.9	3.9
Oregon *	4.7	2.4			
New Jersey	4.8	2.3	South Carolina	13.1	9.0
Utah	4.8	2.5	Kentucky	13.8	8.5
New York	5.	3.2	Arkansas	15.5	8.7
Washington *	5.2	2.5			
Kansas *	5.4	4.5	Tennessee *	17.	14.8
			Georgia	17.7	15.5
Pennsylvania	6.	3.1	Louisiana	19.2	9.9
Indiana	6.1	5.0			
Montana	6.6	2.3	Alabama	20.1	13.8
Michigan †	6.6	3.9	Mississippi	20.6	7.6
			Florida	29.7	11.9
Delaware	6.7	10.7			
Maryland	6.9	6.3			

Not Reported in 1919-1928

State	1956
New Mexico	1.7
Texas	10.5
South Dakota *	.5
Nevada	5.4

Sources: Bureau of Census Reports; *Uniform Crime Reports,* F.B.I., Washington, D.C.; *The Annals,* November 1952.

CRIME IN AMERICA

Appendix C

Table IV

HOMICIDE RATES OF STATES, 1954-1956, AND EXECUTIONS IN EACH STATE IN 1956

Key:
† Abolished Capital Punishment
* Abolished and Restored
‡ Abolished 1958

State	Hom. Rate 1956	Hom. Rate 1955	Hom. Rate 1954	Exec. 1956	State	Hom. Rate 1956	Hom. Rate 1955	Hom. Rate 1954	Exec. 1956
Vermont	0.0	0.0	0.0		Indiana	5.0	4.4	3.5	
New Hampshire	.4	.7	.4		Ohio	5.4	3.7	3.8	4
South Dakota *	.5	2.2	1.5		Nevada	5.4	20.2	18.0	
Iowa *	.9	1.2	1.0		Illinois	5.9	5.7	5.4	
Minnesota †	1.1	1.1	.5		Maryland	6.3	7.6	7.7	
Maine †	1.2	1.8	2.4						
North Dakota †	1.3	1.8	.0		Arizona *	7.3	6.7	8.4	
Wisconsin †	1.3	1.2	1.1		Mississippi	7.6	4.4	9.4	8
Massachusetts	1.4	1.2	1.1		Missouri *	7.8	7.2	6.8	
New Mexico	1.7	4.5	3.6	1					
					Kentucky	8.5	9.4	9.7	3
Rhode Island †	2.2	1.4	.9		Arkansas	8.7	7.4	6.4	1
Nebraska	2.3	2.0	2.6						
Connecticut	2.3	1.2	1.4		So. Carolina	9.0	10.	7.2	4
New Jersey	2.3	2.1	2.8	1	Virginia	9.1	8.4	10.	
Montana	2.3				Louisiana	9.9	8.6	10.7	1
Oregon *	2.4	3.1	2.3						
Washington *	2.5	2.1	3.1	1	Texas	10.5	9.9	9.7	7
Utah	2.8	2.4	2.7	2	Delaware ‡	10.7	3.9	5.7	
Pennsylvania	3.1	3.2	3.7	2	No. Carolina	11.5	9.9	11.0	1
New York	3.2	3.1	3.2	6	Florida	11.9	12.3	10.0	7
Colorado *	3.5	4.1	4.1	1					
Michigan †	3.9	4.6	4.3		Alabama	13.8	17.1	14.8	1
West Virginia	3.9	2.6	3.5	1					
					Tennessee *	14.8	10.8	17.0	
Idaho	4.0	3.0	1.8						
Oklahoma	4.2	5.2	5.4	1	Georgia	15.5	13.6	16.	6
California	4.4	3.7	3.8	5					
Kansas *	4.5	2.6	4.6						
Wyoming	4.5	3.8	2.7	1					

Sources: Uniform Crime Reports, F.B.I., Washington, D.C.; National Prison Statistics, "Executions," Federal Bureau of Prisons, Washington, D.C.

Appendix D

Table V

STATES WHICH ABOLISHED AND RESTORED CAPITAL PUNISHMENT

State	Date Abolished	Date Restored
Iowa	1872	1878
Colorado	1897	1901
Kansas	1907	1935
Washington	1913	1919
Tennessee	1915	1917
Oregon	1915	1920
South Dakota	1915	1933
Arizona	1916	1918
Missouri	1917	1919

Table VI

HOMICIDE RATES IN STATES WHICH ABOLISHED AND RESTORED CAPITAL PUNISHMENT

State	Average Rate 1919-1928	1954	1955	1956
Iowa	2.4	1.0	1.2	.9
Oregon	4.7	2.3	3.1	2.4
Washington	5.2	3.1	2.1	2.5
Kansas	5.4	4.6	2.6	4.5
Colorado	8.8	4.1	4.1	3.5
Missouri	11.1	6.8	7.2	7.8
Arizona	12.0	8.4	6.7	7.3
Tennessee	17.0	17.0	10.8	14.8
So. Dakota		1.5	2.2	.5

Table VII

HOMICIDE RATES IN "ABOLITION" STATES

State	Average Rate 1919-1928	1954	1955	1956
Maine	1.7	2.4	1.5	1.2
Wisconsin	2.0	1.1	1.2	1.3
North Dakota	2.0	.0	1.8	1.3
Rhode Island	2.6	.9	1.4	2.2
Minnesota	3.1	.5	1.1	1.1
Michigan	6.6	4.3	4.6	3.9

Appendix E

Table VIII

COMPARATIVE HOMICIDE RATES IN NEIGHBORING CAPITAL PUNISHMENT AND ABOLITION STATES, 1933-1951

Year	Massachu-setts *	Rhode Island †	Connecti-cut *
1933	2.5	1.7	1.2
1934	1.3	0.6	0.8
1935	1.2	1.7	1.7
1936	0.9	0.7	1.4
1937	1.3	1.6	1.2
1938	0.8	0.8	1.9
1939	0.8	0.6	1.6
1940	1.0	1.3	2.1
1941	1.5	0.9	1.9
1942	1.0	1.3	2.2
1943	0.6	0.9	1.2
1944	1.0	0.5	2.3
1945	1.2	0.8	1.4
1946	1.5	1.1	2.1
1947	1.3	0.5	2.2
1948	1.2	2.3	1.9
1949	1.1	0.5	1.8
1950	1.0	1.1	1.3
1951	1.1	0.9	1.7

* Until 1951 in both Massachusetts and Connecticut the death penalty was mandatory in verdicts of murder in the first degree.

† Death penalty abolished in Rhode Island except in prison murder committed by a lifer.

To most readers, Dr. Jack Kevorkian's proposals will undoubtedly appear brutal and shocking. However, the view presented in this chapter attempts to be both realistic and rational. Dr. Kevorkian makes no brief for or against capital punishment. On the contrary, upon the assumption that the taking of human life by the state at the present time in the form of capital punishment constitutes an egregious waste and an immoral practice, Dr. Kevorkian, as a research scientist, deplores the loss of opportunity for research which this senseless killing takes. Incidentally, he touches upon a great many subtle issues of the law and morality which are not ordinarily considered in a discussion of capital punishment.

If killing by the state does take place, he argues, shall it be devoid of all purpose and meaning, except for purposes of vengefulness and an archaic notion of utilitarian justice which has long been discarded? If the states persist in the practice of imposing the death penalty, should they permit the condemned person the matter of choice as to how he shall die? Isn't there a real problem, he suggests, concerning the possibility of providing some restitution for the victim in the form of permitting his killer to present himself to medical research?

Although such questions may be shocking and deeply offensive to those who regard capital punishment as particularly repellent, they probe deeply into the nature of public morality and the essential meaning of legal justice. Unwittingly, perhaps, Dr. Kevorkian raises issues which go far beyond the immediate aspects of his proposal to permit condemned persons to decide for themselves whether their deaths will be effected through medical research. In a profound sense, he raises the disturbing philosophical question as to whether the taking of life, through judicial process or not, can be made meaningful. This is a question, of course, at least as ancient as Socrates.

The utilitarian philosophers, in their well-measured theories of criminology, falsely reasoned that justice could be obtained on the basis of a simple calculus of pleasure and pain. To the men in the death-house, as indeed to all offenders, such theories have as much relevance as the fear of eternal damnation in curbing men's other predatory appetites. To the man in the death-cell, there is a fumbling and inarticulate concern with the reasons for his presence there and a dim questioning as to who might benefit from his death. Dr. Kevorkian visited the death-cell to seek an answer to the second question. The implementation of the proposal offered by Dr. Kevorkian, through state and international agencies, is of far less significance than the basic question of determining whether any social benefit may be derived by state executions.

Chapter 7

CAPITAL PUNISHMENT OR CAPITAL GAIN?

JACK KEVORKIAN, M.D.

As if the topic of capital punishment is not sufficiently controversial, I would like to introduce into the consideration of this subject still another variable, which, in itself, is controversial enough. Whether capital punishment is a good or a bad idea is an argument which, for the present, I choose to avoid. I would like to stress instead an idea which has probably flashed through the minds of many people today. The procedure I am about to recommend would affect every living person indirectly in a rather intimate way. Specifically, it is a proposed modification of the way capital punishment is administered, a modification which, upon careful scrutiny, appears so rational as to make elaboration in detail almost ridiculous. Yet it is surprising that no written works have actually dealt with the matter in recent times, in an age when everything conceivable appears in print. Therefore, at the risk of perpetrating absurdity through erudite elaboration of what is essentially a common-sense idea, I propose detailed discussion of a most serious matter, one which involves with equal importance the fields of medicine, law and criminology, other biological sciences, sociology, and philosophy, with only one end in view—the *maximum* benefit of mankind. I propose that prisoners condemned to death under capital punishment be allowed to submit, by their own choice, to medical experimentation under surgical anesthesia, to be induced at the set minute of execution, as a form of execution in lieu of the conventional methods prescribed by law. Ultimate death would be induced by an overdose of the anesthetic agent.

It is advisable to begin our discussion from the medical standpoint in order to visualize the several aspects of such a revolutionary proposal. Most of us are well aware that the ultimate "laboratory" for testing every medical fact, concept, or device is man himself. No matter how many animal and test tube experiments are done, validity is finally judged, as it should be, after clinical trials on sick or healthy human subjects. In this logical and proper sequence of trial, the human subject at the end, the "guinea pig," is, and always will be, the most difficult link to procure. The use of man for such purposes has always been a touchy problem. Whether or not it is a question of testing some radically new idea of therapy or normal physiology, or of merely verifying what gives assurance (from prior non-human experimentation) of becoming a useful drug or manipulation, the actual involvement of the human factor—either healthy volunteers for less dangerous undertakings or the critically, "hopelessly" ill in desperation efforts—has always aroused the most profound contemplation of the ethical, moral, and purely metaphysical considerations which are involved in such a decision. It is the complex of these abstract considerations, undergirded by the law, which has justifiably retarded, limited, and controlled the subjugation of men as test objects.

Acceptable human experimentation has, of necessity, been limited to a voluntary status during normal periods. Most cases have involved prisoners or other volunteers as well as scientists themselves. Experiments with anti-malarial drugs on prisoners during World War II are now common medical knowledge. Also, Simpson and Long first tested chloroform and ether on friends and themselves before making clinical use of the agents. The toxic effect of digitalis, a drug virtually indispensable to those suffering from many forms of heart disease, was studied by the great scientist, Purkinje, on himself. Pierre Curie used his own arm in investigating radium "burns." And most physicians are aware of the fact that cardiac catheterization was first carried out alone and on himself by an obscure and young surgical resident in Germany! In all these instances, the extent, and therefore the value, of experimentation was (and always will be) limited in that the danger to life must be minimized, especially in the case of non-condemned prisoners and other non-medical volunteers. Physicians in solitude can be more daring on themselves. However, as a rule, there is always a limit in every voluntary case which curtails the means to any medical end and thereby detracts from the full potential inherent in the undertaking.

Viewing the problem purely realistically, capital punishment, as it exists today, offers an unrivalled opportunity to break these limits. It can do this by introducing into the situation an involuntary factor without destroying the necessary safeguard of consent. I would like to present my proposal in detail; a proposal which, to say the least, would improve the present situation in every respect, and then briefly expand on its medical, legal, and moral implications. A hypothetical example will best clarify exactly what I have in mind.

An admitted and convicted murderer, male or female, age approximately 30, is condemned to die by hanging one year hence. He is informed at the time of sentencing that he may choose to die by hanging at the set hour or to undergo surgical anesthesia for the purpose of medical research in a conventional and well-equipped operating room at a research center to which he will be transported under guard. The condemned person may then deliberate at his leisure for a year with professional advice and consultation whenever he requests it. One week prior to the set date of execution, he is approached by authorized representatives of the medical and legal professions and asked for his decision. He is not transferred at this time regardless of which choice he makes. If he prefers to submit to experimentation but later balks, he has a week to make that reversal of decision known. Such a reversal would be final. I would be inclined to limit a condemned man to just one reversal to minimize wasteful and purposeless vacillation of a perhaps tortured or malicious mind. In any event, there could be no delay of execution or inconvenient, costly, and unnecessary transfers. The decision, if not reversed, would become irrevocable on the day of execution. The exact hour of execution would coincide with the time of induction of anesthesia and, for all practical purposes, an unconsciousness commensurate with irreversible death.

Since the whole decision is of such a grave nature, the legal authorization for such a move should be issued by highest courts of jurisdiction, either state or national. Once medical experimentation is involved, the entire case should be reviewed and final authorization granted solely by such courts in the remaining few days before execution. It would seem fitting that special legal representatives be present at all stages—when asking for final consent of the prisoner, when inducing anesthesia, during the entire experiment, and at the pronouncement of final, irreversible death, at which point conventional legal machinery would take over.

From the purely medical standpoint the situation calls for utmost concern in respect to the type of experiment to be carried out. To assure maximum gain, experimental plans specifically devised for such occasions should be funneled from all over the civilized world into a central agency, perhaps under the auspices of the United Nations. There, a medical panel composed of outstanding physicians of international reputation in medical research would consider the relative merits of the planned experiments in respect to the methods to be employed and the *gains* to be anticipated (not results *per se*). Of necessity, the experiments should be *extremely* imaginative, should deal with things completely *uninvestigable* in living men under usual circumstances. Once a plan is accepted, then the prisoner who consents would be transferred to the site of execution of that plan (if in the United States), or the research team or teams, if foreign, would travel to the nation in which the operation is to be performed. Multiple experiments may be done simultaneously or sequentially on different parts or systems of a single body and could conceivably last for days under uninterrupted anesthesia stringently controlled by at least two board anesthesiologists. If experimentation does not cause death, it would ultimately be induced by an overdose of the anesthetic agent.

Probably the most expeditious and concise way to consider the philosophical and professional values involved under these novel circumstances would be to evaluate the advantages and disadvantages from the point of view of the condemned, of law and medicine, and of society at large. Let us examine, first of all, the disadvantages.

(1) For the prisoner, there seems to be hardly any. The choice is his alone, with impartial consultation at his request. The only possible disadvantage would be that of injecting an added mental burden into an already chaotic and despondent train of thought in the mind of the condemned. But it would be hard to disprove that such a condition would, in fact, subjectively lighten a crushing burden instead of adding to it, regardless of the behavior manifested by the victim.

(2) For medical research, there is no seeming disadvantage, save perhaps the same inference mentioned above, *viz.*, that it may further burden an already overburdened human being.

(3) From the legal side, there are real and valid criticisms. An arrangement such as I propose would be tantamount to tampering with the *formality* of the law, which stipulates that executions occur at a prescribed time and in a prescribed manner as part of an impartial judicial process. Rather than shatter any legal foundations, what is advocated is a new form of execution, a new prescription of means, not for the sake of inhuman caprice, but rather because the innovation will endow the aged formula with an aura of benefaction hitherto lacking in the extinction of a criminal career. The time of induction of anesthesia would correspond to the appointed time of execution; only the process of execution, undertaken over a period of time and of which the subject will be unconscious, would be unusual. In this respect, it is instructive to consider those instances in which multiple shocks interspersed with medical examinations were necessary to carry out duly prescribed but inadvertently prolonged electrocution, of which the victim could have been partially or even fully aware. The method of execution is, in a sense, inconsequential, provided it is accomplished with an absence of brutality and a minimum of pain. An appraisal of the legal criticism of this form of execution can best be judged

only when weighed against the advantages to be elucidated.

(4) For society, there would be some added financial expense. Tax dollars would be required to support the new agencies and machinery to operate the plan. However, these costs need not be exorbitant. Further, many of our tax resources today, earmarked for costly research projects of long duration, and of doubtful value, might be saved if a few experiments on human subjects were to be substituted for them. The study of the structure and function of the human brain might be cited as one such example. Countless experiments on other anthropoids can only lead to inferences and assumptions. The uncontestable observations must be made on the human brain, to be found nowhere but in the human skull.

There is, I presume, the very remote possibility that transfer of prisoners might create added opportunities for escape. Such opportunities, however, could be effectively minimized to near impossibility through intelligently conceived and strictly enforced physical safeguards. Perhaps anesthetization before transfer to the research institute would be a better solution.

As compared to the more obvious disadvantages, a number of signal benefits might be cited. (1) For the condemned person, such benefits are manifold. In the first place, it imparts to him in his condemned and degraded status a perhaps unwarranted dignity in that he is granted the privilege of decision—the matter of *how* he should die. Although of no major concern to the problem under discussion, this psychological gain on his part nonetheless produces no commensurate loss in the instrumentalities of punitive justice and should, therefore, be granted him—if for no other reason than that of membership in the human species.

If it is argued that condemned men would choose the proposed method of execution only because they are masochists or out of feelings of guilt, then why do other *non*-condemned prisoners submit to experimentation? Who is to judge that their reasons are any different? Yet we allow them to do so. Furthermore, these latter prisoners usually have ulterior and, frequently, far from altruistic motives—special consideration at parole hearings. In the case of the condemned, there can be no hope for reward; his death is foreordained.

How does the plan fit in with the explicit purposes of capital punishment as presently conceived? The first and most obvious purpose of capital punishment, presumably, is that of punishment or retaliation; secondly, it is intended to serve as a deterrent by setting an example, to dramatize the harsh fate awaiting those who dare commit certain heinous crimes; thirdly, it presumably protects society from vicious lawbreakers by their irrevocable removal; and finally, it supposedly signifies atonement through sacrifice. Proponents of capital punishment insist that death is absolutely essential in fulfilling these purposes. The proposed plan of execution would allow the criminal to choose a mode of death at least as acceptable and calm as any now in vogue for capital punishment, and probably more so. It is difficult to subscribe to the notion that violence or purposeful harshness and horror are indispensable if capital punishment is to satisfactorily meet its objectives. The loss of life is punishment enough for the most repugnant crime, and making it more grotesque and tortured can do nothing other than to detract from the ultimate social significance of judicial execution as well as to tarnish our standard of values. It seems to me that to die under smoothly induced anesthesia (e.g., the administration of intravenous pentothal) is preferable to having bullets rip through the chest, to experience the momentary choking or snapping of the neck, to place one's head under a hovering guillotine blade, to experience the heat and the shock of an electrical charge, or perhaps to experience the suffocating effect or convulsions induced by cyanide gas.

In interrogating a number of individual concerning the method of death they would choose for themselves, the majority preferred anesthesia. A few dissenters chose the gas chamber, stating that they heard it was a comparatively painless death. None of the dissenters objected to anesthesia, which they classified as probably equally gradual, and professed to be indifferent as to which of the two, cyanide or anesthesia, they would choose to take involuntarily. If one doubted the subjective serenity of anesthetic deaths as compared to the listed alternatives, then he would, in effect, be saying that the thousands of patients undergoing surgery every day are risking a death as unpleasant as, or more unpleasant than, execution as it is currently practiced. Such a viewpoint is hardly tenable.

In every decision to submit to medical experimentation, it would be difficult or nearly impossible to assess the relative roles played by two factors operating on the mind of the victim. To what degree would he be motivated by a purely egotistical desire to avoid a harsh death and how much by a desire, either conscious or subconscious, to die a fruitful, productive, and meaningful death? By offering such a choice to the man, society would certainly not be pampering him but providing an opportunity for meaningful self-redemption through a process which is considered by many to be meaningless and senseless. For the first time since the period of the ancient civilizations, perhaps, a brutal and meaningless act would be endowed with some dignity, meaning, and purpose.

In the case of the execution of innocent persons (a remote possibility), it would give the victim perhaps a little solace in having an opportunity to transform an ugly act of human injustice into one of some gain for mankind, at least, and to thereby partially rectify the otherwise total injustice of it all. Furthermore, the procedure will ordinarily provide a type of "stay of execution," for as long as the condemned remains alive under anesthesia, he may be revived with minimal sequellae if evidence of innocence should by chance be uncovered after the experiment is under way. Rather than shorten the condemned's life and ruin his "eleventh hour" chances for commutation, the plan would actually lengthen his life in every case where experimentation is selected, and thereby create fuller scope for the operation of justifiable reprieves.

(2) For law, an obvious advantage would be the acquisition of another beneficial aspect, one of enormous potential good for the humanity it was created to serve. The proposed plan would detract somewhat from the decidedly negative nature of capital punishment *per se*, engendered by the law,

and would serve to make tolerable, no matter how little or effectively, a practice upon which there is bitter debate. In fact, it appears to me to be an acceptable compromise on this very controversial point, at least for the time being. Paradoxically, it might even create a new realm wherein law and medicine become an inseparable unity in fulfilling their avowed purposes in the purest sense—to better human life.

(3) The advantages to medicine are obvious enough to merit only brief mention. In a human body to be destroyed, what limits can be imposed upon the probing that one can do? Reasonably speaking, there can be no limits. Why study thousands of monkey brains to trace anatomic tracts when intact human brains could be made available? A single living human body would offer invaluable opportunities to study the effects of controversial drugs as well as the hazards and techniques involved in radically new diagnostic and surgical procedures on hitherto untouched structures which men dare not try on any human body under any clinical circumstances. Just as progress in the perfection of needle biopsy techniques for internal organs, progress in cardiac catheterization, and in liver, kidney, heart, and brain surgery would have been logarithmically compounded if condemned humans were used in experiments, so, too, will progress be affected in other realms of medicine which are now in their infancy or not yet even conceived. Examples are countless. The means are within reach.

(4) For society, the advantages are equally obvious and overpowering. When a criminal decides, for any reason whatsoever, to give his body for such altruistic purposes as we have outlined, he pays to the society which he wronged and which vengefully condemned him to extinction not only a bare, hardly gratifying "principal" of debt, but also an "interest," so to speak, a social gratuity which promises to far surpass any real gain through the "principal" envisioned by society. Through such a form of "judicial euthanasia," redemption on the part of the condemned will be as complete as it ever can be, transmuting the negative concepts of vengeance and punishment into that of recompensing. No known

form of punishment or imprisonment or retribution can recompense society as handsomely.

For a society intent upon killing certain of its offenders, nothing would be lost and the gains, on the contrary, might be substantial. Many aspects of medical science could almost instantaneously be advanced a decade or more to help assure us and our descendants of substantial improvements in health and the prolongation of life. Given the medical genius and imagination required to exploit such a situation, a convicted murderer, be he inveterate and calloused or dazed and remorseful, can help us get a glimpse at least into the medical science of the Twenty-First Century. Under anesthesia, all humans become identical in essence. Experimental surgeons could confidently perfect daring new techniques on healthy organisms, instead of desperate improvisations on aged or disease-ridden bodies of unfortunate, "hopelessly" ill patients, whose decrepit health almost assures failure.

The proposal which has been made will immediately invoke recollections of the perverted and brutal use of human experimentation by the third German Reich during the second World War and invite inevitable comparisons. Actually, there is nothing but the most superficial resemblance between the frankly immoral practices of the Nazis in this respect and the use of a modified form of capital punishment. The differences between the proposed plan and the Nazi crimes of World War II should be clearly emphasized. (1) The latter were *wartime atrocities*, which are difficult to prevent regardless of any safeguards, and which can in no way be justified. (2) They were done for the most part without anesthesia. (3) The victims were not asked for their consent. (4) The victims were condemned under fanatically inhuman Nazi "laws" on political or racial grounds; these "laws" were hardly compatible with international standards. (5) The "experiments" themselves were superficially thought out, and the results could have been fairly accurately guessed in most instances. (6) The objectives of the experiments were often frivolous and without profound scientific significance; any pretense toward serious objectives was primarily of a military nature only. (7) The scientists performing them were either outright sadists or fanatical party members. In virtually every case, they were medical mediocrities, or less. They by no means represented the medical genius, such as it was, of Nazi Germany, let alone of the entire world. (8) The entire program was under the jurisdiction of a morally perverted government based upon a nihilistic philosophy.

On the other hand, the proposed plan involves condemnations imposed through civil law during peacetime which is, in itself, the international standard. Experiments would be devised and carried out by exceptional and proven scientists whose merit and rationality would be determined by a distinguished panel of medical researchers under the auspices of responsible government authority. Experiments would be aimed at general objectives of great value, the results of which can never be predicted or even guessed at, to deal with unsolved riddles of *human* health and life for the good of *every* human being. Finally, and foremost, such experiments would not be done on any subject who withholds consent (or who even wavers when giving consent); every subject, freely giving such consent, would be thoroughly anesthetized— being executed after feeling no more discomfort than a needle prick in the arm.

A factor of prime importance in the set of circumstances triggered by tragedy, to be sure the most important factor, is the victim of the crime. If he is murdered, for what purpose will he have died? To merely snuff out the life of his killer merely increases the number of lives destroyed for no tangible reason of any worth. In this oft-repeated pattern of tragedy, there is no real glimmer of gain or profit to the victims, their families, or their culture. But by permitting the condemned, if he chooses, to give society something in return, to force nature to reveal to us a few of her most coveted secrets through the vitality of his body, he will have imparted some positive significance to the death of himself as well as his victim.

How will a condemned man react when faced with a choice as to whether he will accept the usual execution procedure of the state or whether he prefers exposing himself to voluntary medical experimentation? I posed this question to two men condemned to die.

The warden of a Midwestern penitentiary recently granted my request to be allowed to interview two condemned men with the above aim in mind. Two suitable candidates were selected, suitable in the sense that they had the intelligence and equanimity to endure a conversation which could be difficult and agonizing. The sentences of both of these men are now in the process of being appealed, but the men still languish under impending death by electrocution. I proceeded to the death house, accompanied by a custodial officer, who acted as witness to the oral interview.

Bill F. (not his real name), the first condemned person to be interviewed, is a young man in his twenties and the father of a three-year-old daughter. After introducing myself, I, a total stranger, peering through a screen and heavy bars into a troubled face, began to discuss with him the matter of his death. The conversation remained surprisingly calm. Avoiding an excessive display of compassion and sympathy, I outlined as objectively as possible my proposed alternative to execution and stressed the fact that the matter was a totally hypothetical one and that his decision, and my presence at this interview, could never at that time influence the subsequent course of his life. Having understood my plan, I asked for his choice. His first reaction appeared to be that of indifference. There can, very likely, be little real meaning to the concept of a fruitful or "profitable" death in the mind of one who is about to die, especially if the concept is new to that mind. Brief contemplation, however, and clarification of some misunderstood points led to an astonishing transformation. Bill F.'s previously troubled face brightened slightly and he seemed to breathe a feeble sigh of relief as he said, turning to the officer with me, "You know, Lieutenant, maybe the doctors can learn something from my body which could help my little daughter later in life—maybe twenty years from now. I would rather let them experiment on me." His voice was tranquil but firm and unflinching. His decision, at that instant, appeared unconditional.

Jack W. (also fictitious) 23, married, also facing electrocution, was next interviewed. He was more curious about details and cautious in his mental probing, which occasionally led him to forget that anesthesia would be involved in all such experimentation. Once reassured on this point and bluntly confronted with a choice between electrocution and submitting to my plan, he said he favored the latter but preferred to discuss the matter with his wife before finally committing himself.

So far as I know only two condemned men have been asked this question this year; in all likelihood during this century in peacetime; and probably for the first time in a period of many centuries. Both prisoners, still youths, answered in such a way as to condemn the mode of their deaths; to indict as criminal the methods and philosophy that we in organized society have prescribed as appropriate to end their lives or to extract retribution. They did not wish to avoid a harsh death, for neither even hinted to this effect during the interviews, despite my purposeful mention of that aspect. What seemed to be paramount in their decision was a desire to experience and ponder a sublime feeling of usefulness in death, especially to loved ones. If only one of every one hundred condemned men elects it, then such a plan is definitely worth perfecting. So long as capital punishment is in effect, and wherever it is in effect, there is a far more humane, profitable, and sensible way to implement it. Among the states comprising our nation, 40 endorse capital punishment—24 by electrocution, 10 by gas, 5 by hanging, and one by hanging or firing squad. Let us assume that, as an average, two to three persons are executed in each of the forty states per year. In the decade, 1938-1947, the average was 132 per year; in the decade, 1948-1957, the average was 86 per year; and the total average for the two decades, 1938-1957, was 109 per year. Surely, at least one of the 80 to 120 victims would prefer to undergo experimentation. Bill F. has proved that. In my possession, I have his eloquent written confirmation of his preference for the form of execution which I propose. Considering the number of condemnations each year in the many nations of all continents, the magnitude of the wanton and senseless waste comes into true perspective, especially when viewed through the span of a single decade.

Part II

Some Special Aspects of Crime
and Law Enforcement in America

A new phenomenon upon the American scene, since the period of the Second World War, has been the maintenance of a huge and continuing military establishment. The social structure of the Army, with its own system of mandates and prerogatives, heirarchical roles, and stratified system of incentives and rewards, is, in effect, a complicated organizational system within the larger social complex of American life. The legal obligations which the new recruit assumes upon his admission into military service places him under sanctions of a special type. During the period preceding the Second World War, the Army was strongly resistant to admitting into its organization known offenders with previous records and men on probation and parole.

Scientific research on the character of the social organization of the Army and the forms of adaptation and role-performances required by its members has been limited, with the exception of the voluminous work on The American Soldier *by Samuel Stauffer, and is just beginning to make some headway. There are few intensive pieces of research on the character of adjustment to the several segments of Army life of recruits from different backgrounds and especially those with records as offenders or other forms of maladjustment in civilian life. There is a gradual development of this type of research, however, as Army officials recognize the need to modify its former methods of selection and screening in order to maintain a permanent establishment of large proportions. Recent research evidence indicates that the forms of adaptation to the regimented patterns of military organization are frequently quite contrary to the patterns we might expect and to those obtaining in civilian life. Individuals with disabilities in encompassing the demands of normal civilian life may, for a variety of reasons, make effective adjustments to the more inflexible requirements of military controls while the seemingly well adjusted civilian personality may, upon occasion, become considerably maladjusted to the requirements of military routines. Recent research under the auspices of the Veterans' Administration, for example, has indicated that certain neurotically-oriented individuals may make relatively satisfactory adjustments to the requirements of Army life while such individuals, upon the expiration of their service, may relapse into behavioral disorders in the more permissive environment of civilian life.*

It is likely, upon the evidence available, that the social structure of the Army, in functioning selectively in the types of human adaptations and maladaptations it fosters, has a unique problem of criminal violators. In becoming cognizant of the nature of its special problems, the officials charged with the responsibility of custody and rehabilitation of its own offenders have been keeping abreast of some of the more recent and progressive developments in the entire field of penology. What is particularly instructive are the efforts to adapt many of these principles and procedures to the special requirements of Army life.

In one sense, the custodial and penal system of the Army provides an illuminating experimental laboratory of correctional procedures within a special social setting which might well serve as a point of contrast with procedures employed by civilian penal authorities. In many respects, the Army has proved extremely progressive in the development of its penal program, emphasizing as its major objective a realistic concern in restoring the offender to his military duties whenever possible while providing him, at the same time, with a sense of his dignity and obligation as a soldier. This is far more unusual than it may appear at first glance. Brigadier General Raymond R. Ramsey, Deputy to the Provost Marshal General of the United States Army, presents an historic development of this point of view, beginning with the first Articles of War adopted by the Continental Congress, and then provides a graphic description of the functioning of the Army's penal structure in its efforts to maintain these objectives.

Chapter 8

MILITARY OFFENDERS AND THE ARMY CORRECTIONAL PROGRAM

Brigadier General Raymond R. Ramsey

Deputy, Provost Marshal General, United States Army.

Law enforcement in the military has a two-pronged mission. The military policeman has a primary responsibility of assisting the young soldier to stay out of trouble. On the other hand, it is the responsibility of the Military Police Corps to provide for the custody and care of those unfortunate enough to find themselves in difficulty, and to assist those in confinement to rehabilitate themselves as soldiers or as successful citizens. It is the latter function, of which the public and even the specialist are frequently unaware, that is of considerable interest to us at the present time.

The soldier in the Army is in a position which has no counterpart in civilian occupations. A substantial change in environment faces recruits and inductees when they enter the Army. Offhand, it might seem that the adjustment to life in the military establishment would be quite easy—that it might not be too different from going away to summer camps or going to a private school away from home. But in truth, we find these young men being thrust suddenly into an entirely unfamiliar social structure.

Military society is quite different from the civilian, primarily because of regimentation. It is characterized by a chain of command that controls each member. Even customs and rules of army life are such that the average individual may feel that his new life is completely foreign to him. He is confronted with situations which he would never face in the civilian community. Regardless of the desires of the soldier, he may be assigned to any type of job that needs to be done in order to feed, house, and care for the group or to fulfill a predetermined mission. Prompt and systematic performance of duty is a requirement in military service. To insure it, the Army must establish and maintain high standards of conduct. Rigid discipline and acceptance of authority, particularly in the heat of battle, are essential and, in fact, the key to successful accomplishment of a mission. An army without discipline is a mob, worthless in battle.

The rules governing the administration of justice in the Army were formerly contained in the Articles of War. The first Articles of War were prepared by a committee headed by George Washington. They were adopted by the Continental Congress in 1775, three days before Washington took command of the Continental Army. They have been amended from time to time by Congress to meet changing conditions. These articles are now incorporated in the Uniform Code of Military Justice, a legal code established by civilian authority for the government of the Army. They specify the offenses for which soldiers may be tried. These are crimes of a civil nature, such as robbery, murder, and rape, and those military offenses which would not be crimes in civil life, such as absence without official leave, disobedience of orders, and being asleep on sentry duty.

The protection of society and the individual requires law enforcement of the first group of offenses. The protection and security of the nation requires punishment of those who commit military offenses. As you can readily understand, in the Army, as in any organization composed of a representative cross-section of the country, law violations of all types and degrees of severity must be anticipated. The springs of human action which cause soldiers to come into conflict with the military law are essentially the same as those inner drives which motivate civilians to transgress the law. The soldier, after all, is the civilian in uniform. Deviations from approved military conduct as well as offenses against military law reflect to a large extent an inability on the part of the individual to make the necessary adaptations to the activities, experiences, and demands of the military environment. The behavior of the individual offender reflects his weaknesses and potentialities. They represent either outlets through which he finds satisfaction for the fundamental human drives and needs which he is unable to satisfy in military life, or flights from experiences in the Army which he has found unpleasant or disagreeable, and with which he has neither the psychological equipment nor the endowment to cope.

Traditionally, the confinement, treatment and disposition of Army offenders has involved a three-phase operation. Those convicted of major crimes, such as murder, rape, armed robbery, etc., have been sent to Federal Penitentiaries. Others receiving sentences of six months or more and a punitive discharge for such offenses as desertion, AWOL, petty larceny, etc., have been confined in disciplinary barracks. The stockades have been used for the detention of personnel awaiting trial and the confinement of those not awarded a punitive discharge, as well as those serving sentences of less than six months. The system described above must be flexible. For example, during mobilization in wartime, it is necessary to expand both facilities and personnel. During the peak of World War II, 36,000 Army prisoners were in confinement. Conversely, during times when the strength of the military services is reduced and emphasis is being placed on developing a "hard core" cadre of stable, skilled personnel for rapid wartime expansion, the prisoner load drops radically. For instance, at this time the Army is enjoying a period of relatively low disciplinary problems with a corresponding low prisoner population.

In order to present a fairly comprehensive picture of the Army's correctional system, it should be helpful to discuss briefly each of the types of facilities and programs beginning with the stockade. All prisoners, without regard to offenses, first must be confined in the stockade at the local command level. There, while awaiting the processes of trial and initial sentence review or disposition, they are subjected to intensive screening as a part of the process to determine their fitness for further military duty or other disposition. The deserving serviceman who commits a relatively minor offense is salvaged for himself and for the service through trial in an inferior court, comprehensive screening and evaluation when first confined, and subsequent retraining in a comprehensive rehabilitation program. Even those tried by general court-martial are considered valuable to the service until proved otherwise. This was not always the case. Prior to 1957, the Army's stockade program can best be described as one of "all things to all people." It divided its charges into custody grades based primarily on their offenses. Common training programs were required of all prisoners and work assignments were almost entirely menial labor of a nonproductive type, such as cutting grass, garbage disposal and similar routine assignments. Custody within and outside the facility was generally the maximum that could be applied, rather than the minimum required. In general, the old guardhouses were operated primarily on the basis of custody and punishment, the program for prisoners being limited to work of a scavenger type and hard labor under armed guards. No provision was made for correcting attitudes and deficiencies, nor in helping the prisoner become a better soldier. In a sense, the stockades in the past were comparable to the status of "county jails" of the local command.

As far back as 1929, in view of the large number of prisoners to be confined in post guardhouses, the Secretary of War directed that a set of regulations be prepared to accomplish at post guardhouses the same rehabilitative results as were accomplished at disciplinary barracks. Further, orders were given that the regulations go into considerable detail as to how prisoners should be treated, worked, and cared for. The Secretary of War also directed that specially selected officers and noncommissioned officers should be detailed over prisoners in the post guardhouses. This program met with considerable resistance by the Army commanders since it was the consensus that adequate machinery for putting this provision into practical application was difficult if not, indeed, impossible to provide at various posts. However, since World War II, there have been two major improvements in the operation of stockades. The first has involved improvement of the physical plant to provide protection against loss of life and injury by fire or other disasters, improved living conditions, and minimum standards for the care and physical well-being of the prisoner, such as suitable clothing, health and comfort supplies, welfare and recreational facilities. The second involves the establishment of screening and training procedures specifically designed to permit the application of intensive rehabilitative measures to the individual on the basis of his probable disposition.

The current stockade program provides for the screening and evaluation of the individual prisoner. A prisoner in confinement can be disposed of by (1) return to duty; (2) administrative separation from the service following normal board action; and (3) transfer to a disciplinary barracks. In this process, the staff of the post is utilized: for example, the medical officer for health problems and physical evaluation; the chaplains for counseling, character guidance, and religious instruction; the mental hygiene units for determining mental and personality problems, and professional evaluation. In addition to determining the disposition indicated in each individual's case, this process is calculated to develop an understanding of the man and his capabilities which, when coupled with his performance and demonstrated motivation, will result in timely recommendations to the commander for shortening of the sentence and return to duty status if this is indicated. Manpower is saved in two ways by this new program. First, it allows the commander to effect the timely return to their units for duty of those potentially qualified prisoners prior to expiration of their full sentences; secondly, it is designed to effect manpower savings in reduced custodial guard requirements. If the Army has a valid analysis of the man, including what he is capable of doing, it can upgrade greater numbers of prisoners to the higher custody grades and employ the maximum number of prisoners under unarmed supervisors. As a result, what we expect to see when we go to a post nowadays are prisoners working in sizable groups on worthwhile service-support type of work operations, with a minimum of guards.

Provision is made for organizing prisoners capable of potential restoration into special training units for a period of at least twenty hours per week or they may be released to training units. If they are released to training units, they are expected to follow the training schedule of their own or similar units during normal training hours, returning to the stockade for custodial purposes during nonduty hours—the time when the majority of them got into trouble originally.

While this program is still young, some significant accomplishments have been achieved which would indicate its value. At individual posts visited in the recent past, it has been found that the screening and evaluation procedures are resulting in elimination of large numbers of substandard personnel by administrative discharge who would likely have found their way into more serious difficulty resulting in imprisonment and dishonorable discharges. There has also been a concurrent decrease in the number of prisoners reaching disciplinary barracks who have had numerous previous courts-martial. At the same time, there has been a great increase in the percentage of prisoners being allowed to function in parolee status or under unarmed supervisors, thereby eliminating the requirements for armed guards for each one or two prisoners. Posts which have adopted the policy of using unarmed work supervisors uniformly report greater work accomplishment with less prisoners and less guards.

The Army operates specialized confinement facilities, known as United States disciplinary barracks, for the confinement and treatment of offenders with sentences of more than six months but who are deemed amenable to rehabilitation and whose crimes are not so serious as to require their commitment to a Federal penitentiary. The disciplinary barracks were established by specific act of Congress, which has maintained close and continuing interest in their administration since before the turn of the century. The Army presently operates three United States disciplinary barracks located in the continental United States. The treatment of the prisoners in the disciplinary barracks, while firm, is humane and in no way calculated to humiliate or degrade. The attitude of properly trained custodial personnel is that of specially qualified leaders. The days are gone when Army men in confinement were made to break rocks, to dig ditches, and fill them up, or were kept in monotonous routine drills and exercises solely for the purpose of keeping them occupied without beneficial ends in view.

Routines at United States disciplinary barracks embody modern concepts of penology and are designed to further the rehabilitation of prisoners. One of the principles accepted as fundamental is that offenders possess marked individual differences and therefore cannot be effectively treated in mass. The attempt is made to learn everything possible about each prisoner and assemble this knowledge in usable form. The program makes extensive use of psychiatric and psychological services properly related to the problems of academic and vocational education, work assignment, self-discipline, and personal attitude changes; employment at tasks comparable in variety, type, and pace to the world outside; both formal schooling and vocational training planned in accordance with the individual's needs, capacity, and interests with major emphasis on job training; directed leisure time activities, both indoors and outdoors, so organized as to promote mental and physical health; a religious program so conducted as to instill a recognition of the value of spiritual faith on the part of the individual as well as on the part of the group; and discipline that aims at the development of self-control and preparation for life in free society.

Nowadays, a program is planned for each prisoner on the basis of his needs at the time of his confinement and for the future. Each individual is trained and treated in a manner designed to eliminate most effectively his handicaps and disabilities, and to instill in him adaptive knowledge, skills and incentives, together with positive attitudes toward his own conduct and future. It is the policy of the Army to encourage all physically, mentally, and morally qualified prisoners to earn restoration to duty with a view to eventual honorable discharge. If it is determined, after careful observation and consideration, that a prisoner is not qualified for restoration to duty, every effort is exerted toward effecting maximum rehabilitation possible with a view toward return to civil life.

Considered in the examination of the prisoner with a view towards his restoration are the offense of which he has been convicted, his civil record, his prior military record, his conduct in confinement, and determinations by the psychiatrist or psychologist at the institution as to his mental condition. In determining whether a prisoner may be returned to military duty in the peacetime Army, it is necessary that he not only meet the requirements of service for a "hard core" Army of men who will provide a highly trained nucleus for rapid wartime expansion, but consideration must also be given to his moral qualifications as well. The youthfulness of so many of our enlisted men makes it necessary that we protect them as much as possible from association with morally corrupt individuals. It is perfectly understandable how parents of young soldiers, who come into the service to do their duty for their country, feel about this. Consequently, even though a convicted murderer or sex offender, for example, may show evidences of reform and be well motivated for further military service, the restoration of such individuals to service must be viewed with extreme caution and they cannot normally expect to be returned to duty. Military service must be maintained on a high plane and the Army must be careful to protect the reputation as well as the character of those in its service. Before final restoration to duty, each restoree must successfully complete an eight-week training program in a military training company established at the United States Disciplinary Barracks, Fort Leavenworth, Kansas. Army prisoners in Federal institutions are transferred to Fort Leavenworth, Kansas, to undergo the preparatory training necessary.

In addition to restoration, the Army has made provision for clemency and parole. The Army strongly maintains that the length of a prisoner's confinement should depend primarily and within reasonable limits on the fitness of the individual for release. In fact, the prisoners come to the disciplinary barracks with what are, in effect, indeterminate sentences. The term, indeterminate sentences, is used advisedly because the terms of imprisonment imposed by court-martial serve in practice as maximum terms in which there are no minimums. Under the procedure established by law, the Secretary of the Army is authorized to grant clemency. The cases of all prisoners confined either in disciplinary barracks or Army prisoners confined in Federal prisons are reviewed for clemency consideration within the first six months of confinement and at least once annually thereafter. A prisoner in confinement at a disciplinary barracks becomes eligible for parole consideration when he has served one-third of the total of his term or aggregate terms of confinement, but in no case less than six months or ten years, if sentenced for life. All cases for clemency or parole consideration are presented to the Joint Army and Air Force Clemency and Parole Board for final action.

The discussion, thus far, has attempted to give some insight into the functioning of the disciplinary barracks concerning restoration, clemency, and parole. The Army, however, has been equally concerned with the other significant aspects of the correctional system—the actual confinement of prisoners, the administration of confinement facilities, and the programs of rehabilitation carried on in each installation. The correctional system of the Army is one of treatment rather than of punishment. Every possible step is taken to prepare each prisoner in the time available either for restoration to duty or for eventual return to a stable, decent, respectable, law-abiding life in the community which is to be his home.

The Army is concerned not only with encouraging work habits in its prisoners, it also provides opportunities designed to change their mental attitudes and guide them in their social thinking and outlook. To bolster morale, we encourage relatives and friends of prisoners to visit them; provide ample facilities for prisoners to send letters to authorized correspondents and issue them welfare and comfort items. A very important aspect of any effective rehabilitative program is the physical, spiritual, and moral guidance of the prisoners. Facilities are provided for physical relaxation and improvement of the individual. In each disciplinary barracks there are Army chaplains of the several faiths, who conduct religious services and spiritual guidance courses, and who are always ready to give individual counsel to those individuals desiring it.

The success of the Army in this field is believed to be the result of careful planning, including the advice of outstanding contemporary penologists. Carefully chosen, professionally qualified military personnel and civilian specialists are assigned to confinement activities to provide for stability and technical proficiency in day-to-day operations. The Army recognizes the importance and value of a progressive rehabilitation program in the management and care of its military personnel.

Probably in no area of corrections more than in probation and parole do we have evidence of clearcut contradictions between theory and practise. Both probation and parole, as phases of penal treatment, are based upon the assumption that rehabilitative techniques must be closely related to the entire process of correction. Since the time of the Boston cobbler, John Augustus, who undertook the responsibility of "friendly supervision" for the varied derelicts of the Boston courts as far back as 1841, the horizons opened up by these procedures have appeared vast and rewarding. The realities, however, are quite different. Legislators, and even the so-called informed public, frequently suffer from serious misapprehensions as to the functioning of these instrumentalities in modern penal life.

The great promise which informed and enlightened probation and parole procedures hold for penal development has never been adequately fulfilled. Instead, probation and parole in their organized forms have become rigidly institutionalized, emphasizing aspects which are congenial to existent bureaucratic patterns and policies. The sustained supervisory aspects of probation, for example, carried on in keeping with the conditions of an informed and progressive rehabilitative philosophy, have been neglected in favor of the need to maintain pre-sentence investigations, the mechanical routines of record-keeping, and the perfunctory limitations imposed by large caseloads. Within the professional context itself, serious disabilities occur in consequence of whether or not certain professional approaches are feasible or desirable. The great promise of these instruments of correction, however, still remains.

Dr. Vernon Fox, whose chapter on prison discipline appears earlier and who is well conversant with the several aspects of the entire correctional process, emphasizes some of these distinctions between theory and practice in the fields of probation and parole. Beginning with the assumption that sound theory, in any field, can never be fully prepared to encompass all the contingencies presented by emerging and novel situations, he suggests nevertheless that the modifications that have occurred in the application of principle to practice have erred on the side of bureaucratic expedience. Even more fundamental, perhaps, is his view that probation and parole, to be fully successful, must be integrated with the entire field of penology. This would mean that instead of such procedures being utilized only in the case of a selected few at a given time, the corrective process must be visualized as an ongoing and continuous process from the time of the offender's conviction until the time of his release. Release from custody or confinement would occur, under those conditions, at the time when the individual is considered most likely to benefit from such procedures without danger to society. Preparation for such treatment, to be realistic and fully effective, would begin from the period of the individual's institutionalization and, in many cases, even before.

What he suggests by implication is, perhaps, even more significant, viz., that the corrective process must be viewed as an integral and comprehensive system in which every agency and individual who plays a part must be informed with the same fundamental philosophy, from the functionaries of the courts and the custodial staff of penal institutions to the practicing probation and parole officer. It is ironic, perhaps, that the realities of such proposals have never been fully borne home in the minds of public officials in general, and a large segment of penal officials in particular—even in the face of the all-powerful tax argument indicating the significant savings of public moneys to be accomplished through such procedures as contrasted with sheer physical custody. In the face of an entrenched resistance to an adequately implemented and functioning probation and parole system, Dr.

Fox suggests a feasible starting point in order to develop an effective program through improved methods of selection of personnel for these important responsibilities, a greater awareness and sensitivity on the part of public administrations, and a reduction of caseloads.

Chapter 9

PROBATION AND PAROLE:
THEORY VERSUS PRACTICE

Vernon Fox

Florida State University

Theory develops from observations of practical situations and events. Similar and related observations from many different situations and events in various settings lead to generalizations. These generalizations, if well made, can be applied to similar situations and events at different times and in different locations. Consequently, good theory evolves from practice. Then, when a new service, situation, or event is inaugurated or observed, the generalizations which have been gleaned from the preceding situations or events can be used advantageously to pattern the implementation of the desired objectives. Consequently, good practice has good theory as its guide.

The difficulty of aligning practice with theory, however, is that theory must assume that all situations are relatively equal, as the physicist does when he demonstrates that objects of equal weight, whether lead pellet or feather, fall with equal acceleration in a vacuum where air resistance is eliminated. In the practical situation, all other things are not equal and disturbing factors are not eliminated. Consequently, corrective factors have to be introduced to determine how much the generalization must be modified to account for the variations of factors not controlled in a specific situation. The mathematicians and physicists make constant use of these "corrective factors" to modify the practical conclusions from the general principles. This means that the practitioner, no matter in what field he practices, has to evaluate the specific situation and the theory or principle involved and make his corrective modifications according to his professional discretion. The reconciliation of theory and practice assumes that the professional person so integrating theory and practice has a sufficiently broad knowledge of the principles involved in any given situation, a discriminating perception of all the factors involved, and the professional competence and flexibility to modify his approach to the problem accordingly. The congruency of theory and practice is dependent upon (1) the practitioner's knowledge of theory, his sensitivity to generalized and specific factors in the case, and his competence to focus the resulting effort toward the desired objective and (2) upon environmental factors which militate against the application of theory, such as overwhelming caseloads or unsympathetic administrations, colleagues, or related agencies. Theory and practice in any field, including probation and parole, become widely separated when the practitioner does not know the theory relating to what he is doing, cannot perceive accurately and objectively the extraneous factors that make his specific situation different from that for which the pure theory was generalized, or when the practitioner is not sufficiently flexible, perceptive, or professionally competent to make the necessary modifications.

There are few fields of human endeavor where theory and practice are farther apart, and for these reasons, than in the field of juvenile and adult corrections. The discrepancies between theory and practice in the field of corrections are shared by probation and parole. This opinion is reflected throughout the writings in the field, under such titles as Helen Pigeon's *Probation and Parole In Theory and Practice* [1] and the recent publication of the National Probation and Parole Association, *Parole In Principle and Practice.* [2] Because of the wide discrepancies sometimes seen between theory and practice in probation and parole, it is fitting that special attention be given to the area of "Probation and Parole: Theory Versus Practice" with the emphasis on the variations rather than the integrations. The variations between theory and practice are especially wide in probation and parole, particularly in the areas of treatment or quality of supervision. Quality of supervision is by far the most important aspect of either probation or parole and is the crux of the entire process. Yet, these treatment aspects are much more difficult to evaluate and supervise than are the more tangible results of the work, such as pre-sentence investigation reports and other needed paper work. This leaves possible the greatest variations between theory and practice in the most crucial phases of probation and parole which are most difficult to detect by the ordinary methods of supervision.

Probation

Theory and practice appear to be wide apart in the area of probation. It is estimated that the courts serving one-third of the American public are without any probation service of any sort.[3] The use of probation as a form of judicial disposition varies widely from ten percent in some courts to 70 percent in others, while wardens in most prisons estimate that 25 to 40 percent of their inmates could have been handled better on probation than in the institution.[4] Development of good probation and parole will make it possible for institutions to become rehabilitation centers, small in size, and specialized for the few offenders who really need institutionalization for a time.[5]

The two primary functions of probation are (1) the preparation of the pre-sentence investigation report and (2) the supervision of probationers. Pre-sentence investigation reports should be made on all persons convicted of crimes and should be made available to the judge prior to sentencing. The probation officer doing the report would, theoretically, be able to select out those individuals who could profit from supervision and casework in the community and would not have to be institutionalized. Such a screening process is a valuable service to society, economically and in the selective reduction of prison populations. The pre-sentence investigation reports provide the basis for complete and adequate casework services for the offenders who do not need to be incarcerated. Such a pre-sentence investigation report is mandatory in many States and merely "available" to different degrees in others.

The attitudes of the judges toward pre-sentence investigation reports vary quite widely. Many judges will not sentence a major offender without an adequate pre-sentence investigation report. At the other extreme, there are some judges, many in jurisdictions in which the pre-sentence investigation report is mandatory in felony cases, who want nothing to do with it, will not read it, and certainly will not ask for it. Between these two extremes are the large number of judges who accept the pre-sentence investigation report as a tool to be used with judicial discretion. The recommendations of the probation officers are followed in about 95 percent of the cases in which pre-sentence investigation reports are prepared.

In practice, the volume of work to be done by the probation officers and the attitudes of the judges toward the pre-sentence investigation may render the specific situation considerably at variance with the theory of probation. Overworked probation officers spend too high a proportion of their time preparing pre-sentence investigation reports because they constitute the tangible and routine paper work that may be seen and which can be evaluated. The pre-sentence investigation reports have to be physically available, while some equally or more necessary probationer supervision is less tangible and can be skimmed. Consequently, a probation officer may spend 50 to 85 percent of his time on pre-sentence investigation reports. This disproportionate amount of effort spent in the pre-sentence investigation detracts from the quality of supervision that can be given to probationers and, even more serious, perhaps, from the number of offenders who can be added to the caseload and have to be sent to an institution because the probation officer does not have time for supervision. This raises a question of overall economics in the American correctional system. When pre-sentence investigations and the preparation of the accompanying reports, conferences with the judge and other staff members, routine correspondence, court hearings, and other non-supervisory work is subtracted from a forty-hour week, the probation officer will experience considerable difficulty in adequately supervising and working with a caseload greater than twenty-five persons and families.

The problem of determining whether probation or parole supervision should be casework or surveillance has received more than its share of attention in the literature, where controverting theories have been evolved from limited experience on both sides. Practitioners from Social Work and related fields frequently practice in sympathetic environments and hold that probation and parole are casework. Practitioners with the same background in less sympathetic settings frequently grow cynical and antagonistic toward the "starry-eyed idealism" they were taught at school, and revert to surveillance techniques. On the other hand, other practitioners without casework training tend to view probation and parole supervision as surveillance in the first place and, if practicing in a setting sympathetic to professional growth, may pick up some casework techniques. The more generalized theory based on a wider sampling of experience appears to be that probation and parole can be a combination of modified surveillance and aggressive casework in an authoritative setting, which seems to furnish a common ground that provides a basis for communication for most viewpoints. Individual variations depend upon the professional competence of the practitioner, the setting in which, and the client with whom, he is working. Not all probationers and parolees need intensive treatment; some require only the stabilizing influence of an authoritative caseworker somewhere in the milieu.[6] These cases appear to be handled differentially in supervision, the variable being the needs of the individual client, rather than the method used, as indicated by studies of probationers with similar results whether the supervising methods were (1) routine reports, (2) a definite plan of treatment, or (3) casework techniques.[7] It is obvious that the individuals on probation and parole vary, and the methods have to vary to accomplish common results. This is the crux of professional competence.

While the average cost of keeping a person in an institution is now approaching $1,300 per year, supervision in the community in probation and parole programs is being accomplished at an average of a little over $100 per year.[8] The difference, however, is in maintenance and custody, not in professional services. It has been computed that if probation officers had a case load of 25 persons, probation services would cost approximately $150 to $200 per case per year.[9] Caseloads could be handled with greater speed and efficiency, and would not be loaded down with inactive and inadequately supervised cases. The total probation program would, in turn, be more effective. Good probation service would return $500 to $1,000 on every $100 invested in comparison with the present uneconomical practice.

Parole

Parole selection should be on the basis of optimum time for release, rather than on the expiration of predetermined dates. These optimum release times can be identified best by the treatment personnel working with the individual. Too frequently, however, selection for release is based on adjustment within the institution. Selection for parole should be based upon the optimum risk for favorable adjustment, rather than on institutional record alone. While institutional record may be used as a partial guide for selection for parole, good adjustment in the institution is no assurance of good adjustment when the institutional controls are removed.

Politics interfere frequently in the correctional field, but they interfere most frequently in designating certain individuals for parole. The intensity of political interference and how it can be handled or why it has to be tolerated varies quite widely and, fortunately for corrections, is apparently in the process of being reduced as a problem. An interesting observation from another study in progress by the writer is that a positive coefficient of rank correlation of +0.50 appears between a team judgment of political interference in corrections and the rate of illiteracy in the several States.[10] All the professional organizations of correctional persons are on record as opposing political interference, but it yet remains a persistent problem in many jurisdictions. It is difficult to study and report on, too, because the politicians involved constitute a sufficient threat to the personnel involved so that considerable apprehension is generated before resisting or talking openly. This writer has had the experience!

Institutional officials frequently recommend "inmate pets" for parole on the basis of excellent institutional records or what they consider to be exceptionally favorable attitudes, with no real recognition of past performance or realistic future risk. When they are paroled, they frequently fail to make an adequate adjustment when left to their own devices away from institutional controls. When, on the other hand, the parole board rejects the special recommendations, conflicts between wardens and parole boards occur, each wondering in what frame of reference the other is thinking. When the recommendations are made by classification and treatment personnel in the institution within the framework of objective and casework factors, however, including prison record, parole boards and institutional people are usually in agreement.

Parole prediction studies tend to emphasize factors which were present in the offenders' backgrounds and confronting situations outside the institution.[11] Although the use of factors relating to inmates' hunches as to probable success of fellow inmates on parole has shown some promise,[12] little has been done in this area of research. Judgment by discerning persons, taking into consideration intent and judgment of capability or adjustment, appears to be just as reliable and more desirable because of better accounting for emotional factors than are the parole prediction studies in release practice.

During the selection process, the inmate should participate in the proceedings because it gives him an unusual opportunity to learn how other people view behavior, particularly his reactions to social stimuli. The objectivity with which parole boards can review behavior and interpret it assists in developing some insight into his problems. Further, when he is aware of the thinking of the parole board, he is less confused, perplexed, and frustrated as a result of their decisions. Consequently, inmate participation in parole board hearings improves the morale of the inmate body as well as the communication between them and the parole board. At least, there is some assurance, assisted by the inmate "grapevine," that the parole board's frame of reference will be better understood by the inmates, thereby lending cohesiveness to the total process. Yet, in practice, there are many parole boards that never see the man nor interview him prior to decisions regarding parole. Some parole boards, such as that in Michigan, spend considerable time with each inmate, working out and interpreting their action in the presence of the inmate. Some other parole boards, such as the United States Board of Parole, provide for one-man interviews, with the decision coming from full board action several weeks, sometimes melting into months, after the interview. The insecurity, indecision, and apprehension experienced by the inmate, under any circumstances other than board interview with the decision made in his presence, renders any decision less effective and does not contribute to the corrective process. As a matter of fact, such procedure deprives the paroling process of much of its potentially therapeutic effectiveness.

A major discrepancy between theory and practice appears to be in the proportion of inmates paroled from prison and those discharged without supervision. Parole is an integral part of the total corrections program. The gradual and controlled release from long-term incarceration is an important phase in the de-institutionalizing process. Theoretical considerations demonstrated in all types of releases from mass treatment to community living show the necessity of gradual release, including releases from mental hospitals and even releases from the military services. The necessity for gradual and controlled releases from the prison situation is even more important for the safety of society and the adjustment of the individual.[13] Parole is not a reward for good behavior, nor is it a "parole privilege" as some parole people refer to it, any more than is penicillin a reward for good behavior or a privilege. Parole is an integral part of treatment. Therefore, all prisoners should be paroled if they are to be released at all. The timing of the parole is the important decision to make. It should be at the optimum time in the development of the casework process for the individual, and may be long past the expiration of the minimum sentence, but must be sufficiently prior to the expiration of the maximum term to permit controlled read-justment. Yet, during 1956, the practice in this regard in the United States was to parole only 55.6 percent of all prisoners released,[14] the percentages ranging from 100 percent in the State of Washington to 7.6 percent in Oklahoma and 8.2 per-cent in South Carolina. More than 41 percent (41.5) were released by outright discharge without any sort of supervi-sion. The proportion of first releases by parole was 57.1 per-cent as compared with paroled re-releases of 46.8 percent. To add to the confusion between theory and practice in this regard, it was the group of prisoners who needed the follow-up supervision the most and from whom society needed the most protection who were discharged without supervision. The releasing of more than two-fifths of all prisoners, the most disturbed and dangerous ones, at that, without benefit of or protection of follow-up parole supervision is a glaring discrepancy between theory and practice.

Pre-release programs should start when the prisoner ar-rives at the institution, the diagnosis and programming being aimed at eventual release. The intensity of pre-release pro-grams should increase gradually, with the release plan for employment and residence being tentatively consummated prior to the parole hearing. After the individual has been favorably received by the parole board, the pre-release unit should have full programming for the individual, including placement in a parole camp or, at least, a full-time pre-release program. Something must be introduced to counter the ill effects of institutionalization. Yet, there are very few pre-release programs in full operation in the United States. A few experiments with the "half-way house" and the parole camp and a few pre-release furloughs cover the serious attempts at pre-release programs of any magnitude. Many institutions and parole programs have some lectures and films as the pre-release program, but their inadequacy is obvious.

Supervision in parole is the most important aspect of the parole procedure, considerably more important than selection. A good parole supervisory staff can, through good casework, help some seriously disturbed inmates make a satisfactory or acceptable adjustment in the community. On the other hand, poor supervisory personnel can make a good parole board look bad by incompetent mishandling of the parolees. Quality of supervision is most difficult to evaluate and most difficult to supervise. Yet, quality of supervision is the phase that makes or breaks a parole program. The only way to assure good supervision is to reduce the risk by obtaining well-trained persons with a correctional orientation to do the job, then subject him to intensive in-service training and liberal exposure to professional literature and conferences; then reduce his caseload.

The most important factor militating against good supervision of parolees is the large caseloads prevalent in probation and parole. Caseloads for parole officers range from 313.6 in South Carolina to 50 in Delaware, Kentucky, and Wisconsin,[15] while the estimates of the "ideal" caseload range from 25 to 50. Probation caseloads are generally considerably higher than the parole caseloads. Time is needed to do anything well. When forty hours a week are divided to cover a caseload of a hundred people and numerous other necessary contacts and paper work, very little actual casework can be done with anybody. Further, the forty hours a week is theory, rather than practice.

Combined Probation and Parole

Theoretically, all correctional processes should be under the same general administration, including probation, institutionalization, pardon, and parole selection and supervision. This procedure is better geared for coherent correctional programs than are the more fragmentized programs. Some jurisdictions group probation and parole functions together, either in a bureau within a department or separate from the institutional services. Only a few jurisdictions have common administration for all correctional services. Some jurisdictions have parole boards appointed by the governor, completely separate from the rest of the correctional services. Such procedures fragmentize the services, are not conducive to coherent treatment programming and, sometimes, result in decisions made on individual cases on criteria other than treatment or response to treatment.

There is some disagreement that probation and parole functions can or cannot be handled by the same person, since both involve supervision of offenders in the community. When it is attempted, the size of the caseloads force the emphasis to be placed on the preparation of pre-sentence investigation reports and on supervision of parolees, thereby ignoring the most important contribution of probation, the supervision of probationers. Consequently, the effectiveness of both functions is impaired by failure to concentrate on one phase or to relate fully to one group of persons. Poorly trained officers who perform both functions have reported that probationers are more difficult to supervise because they engage in more nuisance activity, while parolees do not require so much attention from the supervising officer. Well-trained officers have reported the reverse, that probationers are easier to supervise because their defenses are less well systematized and they can be easier reached in the casework process; while the parolees have been previously screened out as being sufficiently disturbed that prison was indicated, had been conditioned by it, and that their defenses had been so well systematized that it became difficult to break through them and establish a therapeutic working relationship. In good practice, it becomes obvious that different approaches need to be used in supervising probationers and parolees, although in the more prevalent poor practice, the methods are undifferentiated.

Conclusions

Probation is available in some form in all States, and parole is available in all States. Though the theory in probation and parole is similar everywhere, the forms and practices vary quite widely. These variations are particularly wide in the area of quality of supervision because of the difficulty in evaluating it. Large caseloads cannot be handled adequately by even the most competent professional practitioner and, perhaps, less anxiety would be generated by a less competent practitioner who knows no better. Group therapy techniques offer the best approach to handling large caseloads, but they cannot replace individual supervision. It is certain that if caseloads remain as high as they are now in the United States, there will never be a measure of the effectiveness of casework in probation and parole, for it cannot work until it is given a chance to work. Effective casework and group therapy is impossible with caseloads greater than fifty, and only difficult with caseloads greater than twenty-five. Legislatures have to be convinced that probation and parole are economical ways, not cheap ways, to do the corrections job. More money is needed not only to improve the professional level significantly, and not only to increase the staffs so that caseloads for each officer can be reduced to manipulable proportions, but also to increase the staffs enough so that all persons leaving prisons will be released to adequate supervision.

Many persons going into probation and parole have law-enforcement philosophy, rather than casework and corrections philosophy. With inadequate knowledge of theory, of which philosophy is a part, an officer's perception of the situation does not differentiate for him the theoretical considerations from the extraneous factors, so theory can not adequately be applied and integrated for him. Further, the surveillance or law-enforcement philosophy renders the person less sensitive to the diagnostic and treatment aspects of the probationer and the parolee. Better personnel selection would have to aim at determining the prospective officer's basic philosophy. It takes much training to change philosophy, though it can be done. It is much easier to select for philosophy and train for content in in-service training, if no perfectly trained candidates are available.

Much of the variation between theory and practice comes in the changing philosophy and improvement programs that bring in new ideas and personnel and threaten old ideas and personnel. The major organizational problems in bringing practice into closer agreement with improved theory are either (1) entrenched leadership resisting new methods rising around them or (2) line resistance from untrained staff protecting themselves from the newer and unfamiliar methods and approaches being promoted by an enlightened administration.

In order to integrate theory and practice in probation and parole, then, it will be necessary to (1) improve selection and training of personnel, (2) develop administrations sensitive to their overall purpose, and (3) reduce caseloads so that casework and group therapy can have some effectiveness. The achievement of these objectives will require considerable movement from the present status of corrections in the United States, but are necessary if ever probation and parole are to avoid references to theory *versus* practice.

REFERENCES

1. Pigeon, Helen D., *Probation and Parole in Theory and Practice* (National Probation Association, New York, 1942).

2. NPPA National Conference on Parole, *Parole in Principle and Practice: A Manual and Report* (New York, 1957).

3. Turnbladh, Will C., "II. Current Status of Probation," in Paul Tappan, *Contemporary Correction* (New York, 1951), p. 394.

4. Turnbladh, Will C., "Substitutes for Imprisonment," *The Annals of the American Academy of Political and Social Science: Prisons in Transformation* (May, 1954), p. 114.

5. Turnbladh, Will C., "Foreword" of the *Standard Probation and Parole Act, 1955* (National Probation and Parole Association, New York, 1955).

6. Prigmore, Charles S., "Surveillance or Treatment—the Supervisor's Decision," *Focus* (January, 1955), pp. 8-10.

7. Diana, Lewis, "Is Casework in Probation Necessary?", *Focus* (January, 1955), pp. 1-8.

8. For amplification, see Edgar S. Vaught, "Probation and Parole from Viewpoint of the Trial Judge," *Federal Probation* (December, 1954).

9. MacCormick, Austin H., "The Potential Value of Probation" *(Federal Probation)*, March, 1955.

10. Fox, Vernon, "An Evaluation of American Prison Systems," presented to the Florida Academy of Sciences, Jacksonville University, December 5, 1958. Partial report of a study still in progress.

11. Ohlin, Lloyd E., *Selection for Parole* (New York, 1951) and Vold, George E., *Prediction Methods and Parole* (Hanover, New Hampshire, 1931).

12. Laune, Ferris, *Predicting Criminality* (Evanston, 1936).

13. Giardini, G. I.; "Parole," in Vernon C. Branham and Samuel B. Kutash, *Encyclopedia of Criminology* (New York, 1949), p. 289. Also, see United Nations, *Parole and After-Care* (New York, 1954), p. 79, which mentions obligatory parole in Sweden after expiration of five-sixths of the prison term.

14. Federal Bureau of Prisons, *National Prisoner Statistics; Prisoners in State and Federal Institutions, 1956* (Washington, 1957), No. 17.

15. Jacks, William L., "A Comparison of Parole Agents' Salaries, Caseloads, and Supervision Duties," 1957, in Charles L. Newman; *Sourcebook on Probation, Parole and Pardons* (Springfield, Ill., 1958), p. 215.

To the layman, one of the most intriguing aspects of the vast field of criminology is that which deals with the efforts to establish through scientific means the authenticity of legal evidence and the identity of criminals—the branch commonly referred to by criminologists as "criminalistics." The individual commonly identified with the establishment of this branch of criminology is the Austrian jurist, Hans Gross (1847-1915), who, in the course of an active career as examining magistrate, became convinced of the unreliability of much of the evidence presented before him. It was the great Alphonse Bertillon (1853-1914), however, who, as head of the famous Service d'Identité Judiciare *in France, laid down the first basic methods, now associated with his name, and which prompted a wide variety of applied procedures for criminal detection, derived from the physical and natural sciences.*

During the present period, an age of unparalleled technical and scientific achievement and promise, there is increasing recognition of the type of assistance which science may provide in the apprehension and detection of criminal behavior. Most of this interest, however, is centered upon problems of conventional crime where the work of the modern police laboratory, an indispensable present day adjunct to any modern police system, has become highly standardized. Mr. Paul B. Weston however, the author of this chapter, states an urgent case for the help of science in dealing with a problem not ordinarily associated in the minds of the public with criminal activity. Becoming increasingly dependent upon machines in our daily lives, especially the automobile, Mr. Weston turns our attention to a completely different type of problem. Like the weather, the automobile is always with us. Unlike the weather, except upon infrequent occasions, the automobile has daily become a growing menace to the safety and property of thousands of citizens. The highway and traffic law enforcement official is asked to control a problem which, upon occasion, seems almost beyond control. The growth of traffic laws, and with them, the high volume of traffic violators, creates a problem of lawlessness and, commonly, serious danger and destruction which is frequently neglected.

The extension of criminalistics into this area—for this is what Mr. Weston actually suggests—places demands not only upon the physical scientist, but even more so, perhaps, upon the behavioral scientist. Unless the overwhelming congestion on our highways and the almost limitless expansion of our car ownership and travel continue to overwhelm our already over-burdened technical age with serious further dislocations, it is imperative, Paul Weston argues, for us to gain more effective control methods on our highways through the active intervention of scientific aids.

Chapter 10

HOMICIDE ON THE HIGHWAY

Paul B. Weston

Deputy Chief Inspector, New York City Police Department (retired); formerly Commander of New York's Accident Investigation Squad and Special Traffic Enforcement Squad.

Figures and statistics are hardly required to make us aware of the importance of homicide on the highway. The figures dealing with these casualties, as tragic as they are, can be dry and boring. It is sufficient to recognize, as we all do, that there are too many needless deaths resulting from the operation of motor vehicles on our streets and highways. The startling feature of these deaths is that we now know that the biggest single factor in this type of accident causation is the drunken driver.

Over the years, we have come to realize, tragically, that the principal cause of violent deaths in the United States is automobile accidents, followed by homicide and suicide. Despite periodic, and more recently, sustained efforts by regional and national traffic safety councils, governmental agencies and outstanding public figures, including the President of the United States himself, the annual mounting toll of these deaths becomes a matter of profound concern. In a country such as ours, with an extent of car ownership and a total annual volume of traffic mileage exceeding any country in the world by far, the prospects become truly alarming. When we recognize that almost 70 percent of American families own one or more cars, and that this index of ownership will tend to increase rather than diminish, the possibility of significant further increases in the annual death by violence on our highways is a cause of growing national concern. Aside from the human factors of carelessness and inadequacies brought about by mechanical defect and dangerous highway conditions, the principal factor responsible for this annual record of roadside catastrophes is the alcoholic driver.

Actually, however, from the standpoint of the law enforcement official charged with the difficult responsibility of developing adequate protection safeguards on our highways, there are two distinctive phases of the problem of securing highway control—particularly in the effort to curb the inexcusably high death rate and violations of the law. Both of these phases are of particular concern to us. The first involves the problem of preventing drivers under the excessive influence of alcohol from operating vehicles, and the second is to develop scientific safeguards which will provide indisputable authenticity to the testimony presented in the courts in cases of serious traffic violation and highway accidents. In both cases, law enforcement officials require and earnestly solicit the assistance of workers in the scientific field.

For the first problem, an extremely difficult one involving educational procedures, mass communication, and an elaborate procedure of conditioning processes, the active assistance of the behavioral scientist is sought. In the case of the second, a far more simple problem to resolve, the aid of engineering technicians is required to provide conclusive safeguards for the testimony produced in the courts. It is to the first of these problems, the educational, cultural, and psychological one, that we will turn.

In early 1958, New York's research-minded Police Commissioner, Stephen P. Kennedy, reported the results of a joint one year study, conducted in collaboration with the office of the Chief Medical Examiner of the City. Over half of the "killed operators"—i.e., drivers who, in effect, were responsible for their own deaths while at the wheel of a car—were found upon post-mortem examination to yield significantly high percentages of blood alcohol in their bodily systems.

Thirty-eight of the total of sixty-nine drivers in this study were found, upon examination, to have a blood alcohol level of from .10 to .40 percent, dangerously high levels of alcoholic content.

Recently, at a symposium on "Alcohol and Road Traffic" at Indiana University, a reporting physician, Dr. William Haddon, Jr., revealed that in a study of alcohol in "single vehicle" fatal accidents in Westchester County, New York, almost half of eighty-three drivers who were killed while at the wheel of a car met their deaths without the involvement of another car. The impact that brought death occurred solely through the agency of a fixed obstacle, either a tree, bridge abutment, or other stationary object, while these drivers were intoxicated in a legally-defined sense. An additional twenty percent, according to this survey, had a blood alcohol level of between .05 and .15 percent—drunk enough apparently at the time of the accident to have their critical judgments fatally impaired. Up to now, however, scientific research has done little to help us resolve this problem of the drunken driver.

What motivates a man or woman, seriously under the influence of liquor, to get behind the wheel of a car and drive a lethal projectile of two or more tons at high velocity speeds through crowded thoroughfares and roads? What type of peculiar sense of mastery does this type of driving impart? What can be done to stop such individuals from this reckless and irresponsible behavior? Aside from a more complete understanding of alcoholism itself and methods of its control, what can be done about the association between the mania for speed and movement, and the tendency to drink to excess? In what ways does the penchant for speed and movement find expression through alcohol, and at what point does the loss of inhibition create a threshold for physical disaster and destruction? Even if we find the answers to these and related problems, how can we scientifically induce methods of control so that these excesses are less likely to occur? Shall we, as has been suggested elsewhere and in a form which has been approached in the Scandinavian countries, assume the responsibility for licensing drinkers, similar to the process in which we license drivers, particularly those whose activity—professional and personal—indicates frequent or constant operation of a motor vehicle?

Improved devices for giving chemical tests to suspected drivers are apparently not the answer. Although such devices can be relatively effective, they are primarily procedures which can be satisfactorily employed only after the dangerous driver is already successfully apprehended, frequently a matter of chance and good fortune. Such devices in themselves simply confirm a condition which has already been prevented. The crucial problem is one of preventing the possibility of the occurrence itself. The essential problem is to prevent the accident before it occurs by keeping the alcoholic driver from behind the wheel of a car. Neither the law nor the police, in themselves, are sufficient to prevent this. Up to now, both have signally failed. Help is required from the social scientists, the psychologists, and the behavioral technicians studying human behavior so that instruments of detection and techniques of prevention may be improved.

It is even possible that some form of subliminal communication on television, as distasteful as such procedures may appear to the American public, may have a legitimate use here in serving the public good. Mass communication specialists and scientists who are conversant with this novel subconscious form of communication might legitimately work with our television networks as a public service measure. The ramifications of mass educational procedures, designed not only to reach the potentially dangerous driver but those in a position to prevent his taking the wheel, might extend to a variety of salutary safety measures. Scientifically devised educational procedures during an era of unparalleled mass communication have not even been conceived as yet. Principally, however, such measures might initially be aimed at preventing the intoxicated driver from getting behind the wheel of a car.

A less difficult problem to cope with involves the development of physical instruments which can be of use in the courts in determining the actual conditions of an accident and thereby help to establish legal responsibility. A key problem in the field of accident reconstruction, for example, involves the establishment of impact speeds at the time of collision. It should not be too difficult for technicians working with servo-mechanisms and data recorders to give us a small device to record impact speed. Such a device could be welded to a car's frame by the manufacturer and provision made by federal law that only a police investigator could remove it—and only after a serious accident. The self-recording and correction feature of this device could be such that it would return to a zero-setting in twenty-four hours if not removed, thus making it good for the life of the car—until wrecked.

Civil rights adherents may, very likely, protest bitterly that an individual should not be placed in a position where he is compelled to testify against himself. To slow down a certain segment of our driver population, however, it is necessary that such malefactors know beforehand that the police can prove their impact speed after an accident. The fact that such violators could no longer hide behind the common plea, "I was only doing twenty miles an hour," might in itself serve as a strong deterrent.

Such a device may take time to develop and adopt legally, but until we get it, why can't the workers in the physical sciences give us greater assistance in determining the impact speed of cars in collision from a study of the physical damage to each car involved? In accident reconstruction, the paths of the cars involved are plotted and we have as physical evidence the result of the energy expended in the accident—the damaged cars themselves. It would seem that a constant might be developed for bumpers bent upon impact in an accident. It appears perfectly feasible that a motor of known weight and method of mooring must require a readily measurable amount of energy to push it into a driver's lap!

Captain Charles Lehman of New York City's Accident Investigation Squad and myself have repeatedly been able to estimate speeds within twenty miles of actual impact speed from damage done to the front of a vehicle. Although we were forced to resort to rule of thumb, constant checking and rechecking time and again confirmed the accuracy of our estimates. One of my former graduate students, now the head of our police laboratory in New York City, in a research project under my direction was also able to confirm the accuracy of such judgments when conducted under objective and carefully stipulated conditions.

Many people are under the impression that speed can be readily reconstructed from skid marks at accident scenes. It must be remembered, however, that highways are not laboratories and police at accident scenes are not laboratory technicians. This method is generally dependent upon such variable factors as road conditions, the state of the weather, and the training level and experience of the police at the scene of the accident.

The need for these new devices and scientific techniques is not urged solely as a means of pinning guilt on the person causing an accident, as important as it is to serve accurately and impartially the cause of justice. The need for such technical aids is based upon the firm belief that public knowledge that the police were armed with devices of greater scientific accuracy and evidential value would be a far better deterrent to death on the highway than police action *after* an accident.

In addition to instruments for determining with greater accuracy impact speeds, there is likewise a need for a simple instrument for recording the speeds of automobiles on the highway. The determination of such speeds should be registered in such a fashion that identity of the vehicle will be positive and a written record of high integrity provided. Such a record should be so easily understood by motorists that prompt acceptance by the general public will be assured, as well as acceptance by the courts. The accuracy of radar speed management has unfortunately, in many instances, been clouded by court cases. Many attorneys, defending their clients in speed cases in which police paced the suspected vehicle, have questioned both the integrity of the method and the policeman. All of us, I am certain, know of someone who received a ticket for speeding who claimed, with complete equanimity, that he never drives over the legal speed limit— well, hardly ever!

There is, it appears to me, a grave need for science in its several branches to come to the aid of highway law enforcement agencies to curb a condition which, if not actually homicide in the legal sense, constitutes through indifference and irresponsibility a problem equally as grave perhaps. There is available a vast reservoir of knowledge and technical skill which can help in this respect, just as the fruitful development of criminalistics and forensic medicine in this century has been so signally aided by the natural sciences. The areas of such assistance are being well-defined; there is need for technical assistance in speed management, in the determination of impact speeds, and finally, help in the tragic problem of curbing the alcoholic driver. In an age of vast scientific progress, this important segment of our lives in the motor age can no longer be neglected.

It was the dictum of the late nineteenth century social philosopher and sociologist, Herbert Spencer, that a highly developed and advanced society in the evolutionary scheme of things was characterized by its penchant for specialization of function and complexity. Although Spencer confused the notions of evolution and progress, there can be little doubt as to the validity of his basic observation. In an era marked by enormous specialization of function and resultant complexity, many of our basic social organizations, while not lagging behind through intent, have found themselves seriously handicapped in the ability to mobilize their resources effectively because of excessive demands and competitive pressure. Modern police organizations find themselves in this peculiar dilemma. While freely acknowledging the new demands which an epoch of specialization has placed upon them, and the intricacies of law enforcement which a plethora of modern statutes impose, the police are asked to do far too much with too little.

There are very few people today who comprehend the difficulties which the modern police department daily confronts. In the course of social change, many of our former agencies of social control have appeared to abrogate their functions and former responsibilities. The police, consequently, are constantly being asked to assume ever new responsibilities in what comes perilously close, upon occasion, to constituting a social vacuum. The work of the modern police officer, so frequently misunderstood by the public, is not only an arduous task but one which increasingly calls for special skills and training. Whether police work may be dignified by being referred to as a profession, as is commonly done in certain quarters, remains, however, a highly debatable issue. That it makes difficult and technical demands upon its practitioners, however, there can be little doubt.

During the present period, when manpower planning and management have come to constitute a significant facet of our public thinking, the problem of police recruitment and training raises some difficult problems. This is especially true in an era where the monetary rewards for service are not always commensurate with its wide-ranging social importance. How to recruit able and qualified personnel for the police today, and how to train them when they are inducted into police service, is a far more formidable problem than the public is apt to appreciate.

Mr. John Duffy, a veteran police official of many years of service, views this problem realistically and from the police standpoint. The police are not unmindful of modern methods of manpower selection, recruitment, and training. The police, however, have been seriously handicapped by lack of an enlivened public interest which may be implemented in terms of active fiscal support for modernized methods and facilities. It is useful to examine this problem from a police perspective and with the realistic understanding which an experienced police official can bring to the subject. This, John Duffy attempts to give us.

Chapter 11

A PROPOSED EXPERIMENT IN POLICE SELECTION

JOHN DUFFY

New Jersey State Police

During a lengthy and active career in police work, a career largely devoted to scientific crime detection and the instruments of such detection—cameras, microscopes, spectographs, fingerprint equipment and the rest—I have become constantly aware of a problem even more basic than the use of such aids, as invaluable as they are. During the present period, when police work has become far more complex and difficult, I have become acutely aware of the need to improve personnel, if we are to raise the levels of professional performance, and the need for improved methods of recruitment. In probing this problem, however, a more basic question comes to the fore. What characteristics should we look for in the modern police officer?

In investigating various police departments in the United States and in discussions with their administrators, in training men from many parts of the United States and of the world, one question invariably came to the forefront of our discussions. "In your opinion," I would ask, "what qualities should a good policeman possess?" Initially, the answers were so diverse that it appeared rather hopeless to establish a pattern. Eventually, however, a composite conception began to take form and substance, based upon the varied experiences of my subjects. The good policeman these men had been describing was not an objective evaluation, but a highly subjective impression. It was a former instructor in some cases; in others, it was someone in the field who had left a deep impression. A large group, interestingly enough, gave a word portrait of themselves. Although this last group may appear at first to be somewhat egocentric, it is probably a good thing for a policeman to have a sense of pride. Eventually, however, one conclusion appeared to emerge: what makes a good police officer differed widely from man to man.

Some might point out that the problem of identifying the competent police officer has already been resolved, offering as examples Cincinnati's excellent record under Chief Schrotel, or J. Edgar Hoover, with his efficient handling of the Federal Bureau of Investigation. Although such outstanding administrators may provide excellent examples for all of us, it becomes extremely difficult to reach into a diffuse mass of police applicants and come up with a man to fit that pattern. Let us go back to our basic question: "What qualities should a good policeman possess?" If we were to stop at this point and make a list of all the desirable qualities such an individual should have, the length of the list of such traits would be overwhelming and staggering. It is somewhat ironic that even those of us in the police profession expect a policeman to be a demigod on the salary of an upstairs maid. It is important to limit such a list to the very basic qualities without which no man could be an efficient law enforcement officer. It should also be recalled that eventually the superior officers in any department will be appointed from the pool of our initial selections.

A primary factor agreed upon by all experienced administrators questioned on this subject is the need of the candidate to possess a certain level of intelligence. By implication, this would also mean intelligence of a certain defined character. It is not only the *level* of intelligence which concerns us here, but the *kind* of intelligence best suited for police work.

What do we actually mean by the designation of intelligence for our police recruit? We must ask ourselves whether the definitions we have in mind are functional in character— that is, do they state how intelligence operates (learning, adaptation, abstract thinking, etc.)—or do our definitions describe the nature and structure of intelligence, its under-lying factors?

It is assumed in some departments that it is not necessary for us to know exactly what intelligence is as long as there is some tried and true method of measuring it. There are, of course, academic specialists and able personnel administrators in the industrial and business world who have devoted many years of study to this particular problem. These specialists have developed instruments that can be fairly well relied upon to measure certain phases of intelligence. The instruments thus far developed to measure intelligence have a positive and negative margin of error. While this does not preclude their use, it does suggest a note of caution in interpreting the results of any one test. Just as we know that no one test can measure intelligence perfectly, we are likewise aware that all pur-ported tests of intelligence are not equally valid. As a matter of fact, we could expend our entire discussion in the matter of adequate selection on this point alone. We will limit this phase of our discussion, briefly, to two main types of intelli-gence tests: the so-called Group Scale and the Individual Test.

The preponderant weight of expert opinion appears to be in favor of individual testing, as opposed to group testing, to get a truer measure of intellectual level. And yet, as we have pointed out before, there are so many factors that can affect the results of even a carefully administered individual test, that any numerical evaluation must be determined with a note of caution. For reasons largely beyond our control, we never-theless persist in testing people in groups. For one thing, such tests are less time consuming, and certainly they are con-siderably less expensive. What is more important, however, is that individual testing, for the most part, requires a person highly trained in the technique of psychological testing, whereas group tests can be mass administered by individuals without highly specialized clinical training. We must learn to accept the fact, therefore, that while the group type of test is not all that is to be desired, we will have to try to under-stand its limitations and do the best we can with it. For the time being, at least, we must depend upon some form of group testing as one element in our selective process.

Let us assume a group scale with perfect reliability and validity and even go so far as to imagine that every man taking that test is in peak form when he takes it. We might even go so far as to imagine that men at all levels of intellectual ability are interested in taking the test. Let us picture such an examination process. The day of the examination rolls around, and large numbers of applicants appear to compete for forty or fifty positions. The papers are returned for scoring, and the men with the top one hundred scores are selected for subsequent personal interview and investigation. These men are, by selection, presumably far above the mean intellectual level of the general population as determined by the testing scores. Those who pass the physical standards, the personal interview, and the private investigation are notified to report to the training school or police academy. In due course, further selection and the rigors of training reduce the group to the desired forty or fifty. This is what we set out to do, but it may be questioned as to whether this is at all desirable.

There is no doubt that the pre-training group contained a number of men with superior intelligence, by our very method of selection, and there can be little question but that they in turn would represent an increasing proportion in any academic elimination schedule. Our graduates, then, are presumably intellectually keen and physically able. They are eventually given a badge and a gun and the authority to enforce the law. Their postgraduate days are usually exciting as they eagerly set foot into their chosen field.

We must recognize, however, that these men have twenty to thirty years of hard, dangerous, often distasteful work ahead. For some of these men, the daily toil of obedience to seemingly unintelligent orders, the long hours, the frustrations encountered in the aspirations they initially held for themselves, slowly irritate their above average intelligence. For many, there comes the painful realization that years of service and acquiescence are better credentials for a sergeant's stripes than all the arguments won, however harmlessly, and all the initiative displayed, which may have been resented by some superior officer. The results, ten years later, are fre-

quently seen in a group of bitter and perfunctory police officers, disliking their jobs intensely, and afraid or unwilling
to leave the service because of the investment of time already
put into their careers. Every department has a sizable quota
of such men.

There is another phase to this problem. Let us, for example, consider the policeman with so-called superior intelligence chasing a gun-toting criminal up a darkened alley. He
would, very likely, do just what you and I would do—stop
and think: "There must be some other way of capturing this
madman without getting myself killed." Yet that stopping
and thinking may cost the life of some citizen he is paid to
protect. I do not mean to infer that intelligent men lack
courage, but you will very likely find more men in the
average range of intelligence who will fly into the face of
danger than you'll find in a group of superior intellects.

How intelligent, then, do we want our competent officers
to be? Shall he be like Officer Brown who is approached on
the street by ten-year old Bobby Green, an avid reader of
Dick Tracy, and asked, "What is a spectrograph?" "Why I
think," hazards Officer Brown, "I think it is something the
Russians use to launch satellites," and he smiles benignly.
Bobby turns away and mutters, "Dumb cop." Or shall he
be the type who cannot win the respect of the inhabitants of
a tough neighborhood because he is so far above them?

It may be pointed out, of course, that a modern police
department can use men at all levels of intellectual ability
above average. The term, average, is a peculiarly deceptive
description, however. A variety of physical and psychological
factors must be considered. Maintenance of continuity in
service must certainly be considered. There is evidence to
support the contention, for example, that those departments
with a large percentage of men with superior intelligence
quotients among their personnel have a much greater turnover rate than departments which select men somewhere
below the top. Turnover rates represent serious monetary
losses, and that is important. More important still, however,
is the fact that a policeman's value to his department is represented in length of service. While the high I.Q. man may be

excellent as a specialist or as an administrator, he doesn't always thrive on the daily monotony, the arduous routines that constitute "grass-roots" police work. Such a man, therefore, may never acquire enough years of the right kind of service to make him a police officer of high calibre.

An experienced training officer recently derided this idea completely, offering himself and his department as good examples. The claim was made by this officer that selections were made, in part, on competitive scoring of intelligence levels, and that the resignation rate was very low and morale maintained on a high level. It is difficult to believe that the situation represented depicted the facts in their true light. An analysis of his department's selection system, plus a look at its high pay scale, excellent side benefits, and early retirement age did not support his basic premise. It is easy to whet the appetite, and keep it sharp, with a big fat goose in the oven, not too far distant.

What I have said thus far should not be construed as implying opposition to any form of intelligence in police work. Far from it. It seems, however, that we may have over-emphasized intelligence as a selective factor to the neglect of another aspect of the candidate's mental makeup, *viz.*, his "social balance." In considering such a complex of traits, it is not to be implied that the significant psychological characteristics contained within such a complex are to be avoided. Actually, the term is being employed in its broadest sense. Why do we have policemen in the first place? Is it to protect us from invading aircraft? From wild animals? From the scourge of disease? Of course not! Policemen are employed to protect man from man. Therefore it is not surprising that we propose "social balance" as a strong attribute for any police officer. Probably no other profession places greater demands for such qualities upon its practitioners.

Ironically, it is frequently pointed out by police personnel administrators that there is no need for determining "social balance" so long as an adequate intelligence test is given. The assumption upon which this assertion rests is that a high score on an intelligence test presupposes an individual's social adjustment. The fatuity of this reasoning is self-evident. The classical arguments and definitions do not help us here. We all know men of unquestioned superior intelligence with whom, nevertheless, we would not want to associate ourselves in police operations. All that may be said is that we expect intelligent people to behave according to some acceptable social pattern, which, incidentally, will not apply equally to all parts of the world, nor even to all parts of the United States.

A consideration of the problem of "social balance," as a necessary requisite for sound police performance, opens up an area of wide scope for discussion. In the highly diversified American cultural scene, it is almost impossible that a policeman will deal exclusively with his "own kind." He must associate with and protect people characterized by language barriers, people of different races, people with different religious and political views. His work-a-day world covers all the social strata, all economic levels, all degrees of education. He will represent something to all men, and yet, theoretically, will impart special favor to none. Hence it should prove helpful to know what he thinks of his fellow man, and how he might react in certain situations. If he has a deep-seated feeling toward some group, it is fair to assume his judgment will be warped when members of that group are involved in his work.

The judgment of the staff at the usual Police Training School is hardly adequate in making effective selections in these terms. Further, the training school experience is a peculiarly isolating experience for the recruit. Personal evaluations may have some value, but unless the person or persons doing the rating have been thoroughly trained in the technique, value, and failures of different types of standardized rating scales, we might be doing ourselves a grave injustice by relying so heavily on them. Further, since ratings are frequently performed during the training period, it represents a waste of manpower, money, and time to do it then, if there is a reasonable chance of doing it beforehand.

Are there ways of reaching into the undifferentiated mass that represents the preselection group and coming up with the type of man we want, without leaning so heavily on intelligence tests alone? The first method that comes to mind is the use of structured interview procedures. There is, of course, a wide margin of error possible if such procedures are used uncritically. Much more research is needed before they may be considered sufficiently valid to be used by other than professional personnel who are versed in their use, interpretation, and limitations. Nevertheless, a discriminating and cautious use of such procedures may be helpful.

Much more sensitive in assessing perceptual and adjustment possibilities are the psychological projective techniques. The flexibility of such instruments, especially when conducted by trained technicians, constitutes in itself a singular advantage for their use. Situational tests offer another fertile field. The situational tests I conceive are not the haphazardly applied and often clumsy methods used during the training period, which frequently amount to little more than superficial hazing. I am referring here to carefully planned tests that can be conducted and evaluated objectively; tests from which we can learn something about the man and advance our own thinking thereby. The Office of Strategic Services has employed situational tests and has found them basically sound in assessing the traits of recruits, in that a qualified observer can make detailed observations, not in an unrealistic situation, but in actual life situations.

Most police administrators will admit the merit of more extensive testing, but they point out the paucity of personnel trained in the administration of such techniques and the length of time required to give the tests. These are not insurmountable barriers. Once we decide to move ahead, the problem is one of selecting the most feasible and logical approach. Experimental and tentative programs may be established by personnel chiefs, provided initial incentive and encouragement is offered by department heads. Such programs should include as a first step an objective study to determine the profile of a good police officer. This is a most important first step. It must be done carefully by an intelligent person with an unjaundiced eye. He should start, not in his files, but in the field, culling both subjective and objective characteristics. He must have the sensitive ear of a musician, the wary eye of a frontiersman, the impassivity of a poker player. Such devices as the Moreno Technique may be employed, as well as other situational or inter-personal studies. He should have a working knowledge of psychological testing and be fully capable of synthesizing and reporting. He should himself be a man of broad interests and stable personality.

After the primary study reveals the type of man who will make a good policeman, we must make some radical changes in our method of attracting applicants and selecting them. There are a number of common ways used by most police departments in obtaining candidates for competitive examinations. In some instances, persons interested in the prospects of police work have written to the police department. When the test comes up, they are notified to report to the testing center. Other departments advertise forthcoming tests in the classified section of the press or in public places. These advertisements are for the most part sterile; notices are frequently tucked among the obituaries of the local newspaper, posted in some dark corner of a subway station, or attached to a telephone pole. Economy frequently takes precedence over common sense, for the printing is so small as to discourage inquiry. The more modern departments pursue a publicity program of greater scope, mailing attractive brochures to interested men, and sending speakers to high schools and colleges. These departments also make good use of human interest stories in the press and on the radio. A few permit interesting cases from their police files to be dramatized on television.

There is a common objection to all of these methods—they simply do not reach enough men of the calibre required. The police personnel director in one of the world's largest cities recently reported that whereas, formerly, five applicants would inquire for each position available, the current ratio is less than two to one. Further, he insists, the quality of those applying has seriously degenerated. Are conditions really this bad, or is the position of policeman today of such low order that very few want it anymore? Neither of these views is correct, it appears to me. There is a myriad of men in every jurisdiction who would respond to a well conceived recruitment plan. Police work is just one of the packages in the labor supermarket, and if we want to catch the shopper's eye, we must redesign our package.

How do we go about this? First, we must set up an educational recruitment program using the techniques of modern mass communication methods in order to reach our selective audience. Techniques similar to that used by the military services, using attractive posters, or placing well designed advertisements in the news sections of the public press, in addition to other sales ideas, will reach a larger segment of the population than the methods now in use. These, in turn, will eventually provide us with a wider base from which to make our original selection. Next, the traditional procedure of a one-hour or one-day testing program must be discarded. Being a policeman is not a transitory phase. It is, or should be, a lifetime job. Why do we persist in selecting our police candidates in the course of a single day, or at the most two, and then naively expect them to be effectively adapted to their arduous emplyoment for the next thirty years? The saving of time during this preliminary stage should not be that important. It seems to me that one week of testing should constitute an absolute minimum.

It may be pointed out that under the existent procedure in most departments, it is necessary for the man who wants to be a policeman to lose one or two days' work in order to take the preliminary tests. If he is accepted, he must resign or leave his job to enter a training school or academy. During the training period the pay is low and the mortality high, which means the recruit who fails to make the grade suffers a multiple loss: money, prestige, tenure in his former position, and possibly the job itself. Under the more extended period of selection we have suggested, the loss would be greater, or so it seems. But it need not be. To this observer it appears obvious that the type of man we are seeking is a steady, forward-looking individual, who, between the ages of twenty-one to thirty, has already assumed some small measure of responsibility in his field of employment. He is not particularly the impetuous type who will jeopardize his established position in order to venture into an unknown field. The man we seek is not an irresponsible itinerant. He will have social responsibilities which he accepts, and rightly so. By asking him to give up the security and responsibility he presently has with such low odds facing him may appear to be anomalous. Actually, this need not be so.

Along with the tests given during the day, a parallel series should be given during the evening hours. This will give us a sizable increase in our selection base without penalizing the applicants. Further, on the basis of previous experience, it is also quite likely that the average grades scored will be higher in the evening group. Having a larger number of applicants to choose from and knowing the type of man we are seeking, we can apply our predetermined selective methods more carefully and extend their scope. It should again be emphasized that police candidates should be screened and selected only by someone fully acquainted with police work. In the last resort, it hardly seems feasible or sensible to expect an examiner who has never done a day's police work or who has only a passing acquaintance with it to select men or women for such a highly specialized task. It may be argued that the cost of such a selective procedure may be prohibitive. In reply, the cost will never be higher than the security the people demand.

Lastly, since at least the early weeks of training are a form of selection, and since the greatest percentage of recruits are dropped or leave during this period, why can't we follow the lead of the colleges and universities and have night classes for at least a part of the program, making residence a requisite for the remainder? It would not be necessary to do this in all departments, only where conditions justified it. Besides the benefits gained in better personnel, these methods could result in considerable savings to a large department which clothes, houses, and feeds its men in training. But more important is the man himself; he does not lose his place in the world about him if he decides, after a week or two, that police work is not for him, or the instructors decide it for him.

As elementary as some of these procedures may appear, few of them have been attempted. With the growing complexity of modern police operations, and the intensive competition from other employment fields, we must proceed to reorganize some of our time-honored concepts of training and recruitment. Is not today the right time to make a fresh start? Our present concept of police selection is a museum piece, largely contrived through accident and consisting of a patchwork that has been thrown together through many decades. We must gaze ahead twenty or thirty years and revitalize from the ground up to meet the growing challenge of specialization and planned use of manpower. This will take courage and long clinical study, but at least a pilot experiment should be started now so that our rapidly evolving law enforcement needs will find us equal to the task.

One of the great paradoxes existing in our democratic culture is the belief that all men are equal before the law and the failure to implement this basic principle in our courts of justice. Litigation, today, is a prolonged, complicated, and technical process—and, above all, a costly process. Theoretically, each accused individual is tried on the basis of the offense he has presumably committed. The legal safeguards embodied in the procedural law and the rules of evidence are supposed to function impartially and solely as a means of establishing innocence or guilt. The actual operations of a court of law, however, are a far cry from this ideal conception. In many cases, the true picture makes the ideal version appear almost a naive notion.

Although counsel is assigned to defendants who are charged with a crime, if they cannot afford to retain their own, the differentials in legal talent, the loss of employment during trial, and the social and psychological disabilities which result, may produce a highly distorted version of the common impression of "equality before the law." For the middle class individual, the problem may become especially acute in many instances. Investigation procedures, required in many criminal actions, are costly and the use of technical experts and facilities contribute to the heavy financial burden which the defendant must bear for himself. For the defendant, such costs must be borne alone—or by his friends or relatives—as compared to the vast resources which the state can amass in prosecuting its case. The scales of justice, thus, are not weighed in favor of a preponderance of evidence pointing to guilt or innocence, but rather in terms of the differing capa-

bilities of prosecution and accused to collect and present suitable evidence. The net result is a disproportionate sense of equity, largely controlled by economic factors, instead of the pure justice envisioned by the philosophers of jurisprudence. A greater evil is the operation of selective factors of class and economic status, inducing a discriminatory and differential process of adjudication.

Dean Roscoe Pound, some years ago, indicated that a sharp distinction must be drawn between the rules of equity practiced in law and the behavioral operations of the courts of justice themselves. The vast distinction between them which frequently exists suggests some of the value-patterns which exist in the social structure itself. Students of jurisprudence and state bar associations are keenly aware of some of the discrepancies which these conditions presuppose and there is increasing concern on the part of the legal profession generally to remove some of the inequities produced by a dual system of justice. The use of the public defender, the opposing counterpart of the prosecuting attorney, has been urged by many of our leading judicial figures as a means of bringing about the system of equity to which a democratic system aspires.

Mr. Martin K. Tytell, as an experienced investigator and a consulting expert used by the courts in a number of prominent recent cases, has had the opportuntiy of seeing at first hand some of the inequities he describes in the following chapter. His skill as a document examiner is well known and highly considered, and as a technical expert in one of the most celebrated trials of our day, the Alger Hiss case, he is fully aware of the significance of competitive costs in resolving so many of our contests in law.

Chapter 12

THE HIGH COST OF JUSTICE

Martin K. Tytell

Lecturer on Criminal Investigation,
New York Institute of Criminology

I. *Introduction*

Many observers on the American legal scene are becoming
increasingly convinced that the high financial cost of justice
is rapidly reducing the constitutional concept of "equality
under law" to a mere abstraction for most citizens.

For centuries, crusading reformers have charged that the
poor were disadvantaged in the legal process, but this recent
development does not apply to the destitute at all. Quite on
the contrary, it is the relatively secure, solid citizen who now
enjoys what Alistair Cooke, in his book *Generation on Trial*,
calls "the right to go bankrupt to pay for interminable
litigation." [1]

According to one authority, Allen Murray Myers of the
New York Bar Association, "If you are accused of a crime
in the United States today, you probably could not afford
adequately to defend yourself." [2] Mr. Myers takes a fairly
commonplace situation—a motorist is accused of having left
the scene of an accident after having struck a pedestrian.
A defense in a trial of this nature, he estimates, would cost
between $2,000 and $5,000, depending on the circumstances.
A charge of murder would involve a defense costing as much
as $10,000. [3]

A recent case is cited involving a man who was indicted

for the murder of his wife. His trial cost him $10,000; he was found guilty. An appeal from the verdict cost $5,000. A new trial was granted, and cost another $10,000. Again he was found guilty, and again he appealed. This time, he was set free on appeal. But the total cost of proving himself innocent cost the man $30,000.[4] For a man of modest means, such an ordeal would not only wipe him out financially, but probably take the savings of members of his family and loyal friends. The case of Alger Hiss, with which this writer has some familiarity, cost the defense over a quarter of a million dollars. This does not include the services that were rendered as a contribution in the search for justice by some outstanding attorneys at no cost to the defense, but at heavy cost to themselves both in time and actual money spent for expenses. Were we to add this to the cost of the Hiss defense, the probable total would be well in excess of three hundred thousand dollars.

Aside from the fact that litigation, like almost everything these days, costs more than ever, there are several recent developments which have served to make the price of justice hit a new high. First of all, in American jurisprudence there seems to be a distinct tendency for litigation to take increasingly longer periods of time. A murder trial which in Great Britain might take a few days, such as the recent trial of Dr. John Bodkin Adams, would involve weeks and even months of litigation in American law courts. Secondly, with the development of the science of criminology, the technological aspects of crime detection and solution have become most important. When a defendant must match the virtually unlimited resources of the government in obtaining evidence scientifically and retaining highly trained experts to work in his behalf, he is certain to "go broke" financially. These two aspects of the problem will be further developed in the course of this discussion.

II. *The Lawyer*

When people think of the law, they think of a lawyer. Individuals accused of a crime retain a lawyer usually as their first move. Legal retainers, like all professional fees, have risen considerably in recent years.

A lawyer's fee will vary widely. It depends upon the complexity of the case, the duration of the litigation, and the ability of the client to pay. The skill and reputation of the lawyer are, in addition, important determinants. But, as will be explained, the lawyer's fee is frequently a minor expense in litigation, important as his services are.

Again, contrary to the opinion held by most laymen, it is not the poor who feel the pressure of increased lawyers' fees. Nor, of course, is it the rich. It is the middle class individual who finds attorney's fees difficult to manage.

The destitute usually obtain counsel, in many areas, through the Legal Aid Society. Each year about seven hundred defense assignments are made in the Southern District of New York Federal Courts alone.[5] In other jurisdictions, members of the bar generally volunteer their services when called upon by the court, and assume a defense without charge. It has been estimated that about one defendant out of eight is indigent, and must depend upon assigned counsel.[6] Only in murder cases is the defense compensated.

This system, though it affords the poor the elemental right to counsel, is hardly a satisfactory one. Lawyers working without compensation may not always put forward their best efforts. Frequently, inexperienced attorneys seek court assignments merely to gain trial experience. And those lawyers who are conscientious in fulfilling their assignments often suffer severe financial loss. One lawyer became involved in a case which lasted eight months. He received no pay for his work, and as a result, he had to mortgage his home to meet his own expenses while engaged in this extended litigation.[7]

As far as the poor are concerned, some communities have remedied the situation by appointment of a Public Defender. Three states and thirty-one cities already have adopted a public defender system. Several authorities have advocated extension of this system, perhaps under Federal auspices.[8]

A bill now before Congress has won considerable support. It has the endorsement of the Department of Justice, the

Judicial Conference of the United States, and Legal Aid Societies.[9] If enacted, it would authorize the Federal district courts in large metropolitan areas to appoint public defenders either as full-time or part-time officers of the courts, as the volume of work requires. In less populated districts, where the court concludes that a public defender is not required, the court would be authorized to appoint counsel in particular cases and to pay reasonable compensation.

This measure, however, applies only to the indigent. A person with resources has no recourse to the public defender under the proposed bill. An individual with a modest income who has managed, over the years, to save a small amount of money, must still face the prospect of being left penniless and in debt as a result of litigation.

III. *Expert Assistance*

Even though a person might be in a position to retain a lawyer without undue financial strain, "this may be a minor financial item in a trial." [10]

Expert assistance may well turn out to be the most expensive item in the judicial process. Incidentally, it should be noted that even under the proposed public defender legislation, only legal fees are paid for. Expert assistance is not furnished, even to the accused poor. How a person who is unable to afford even a lawyer is expected to retain specialized experts in cases which require them is unexplained.

Experts such as psychiatrists, document examiners, private detectives, and the like come high. A document examiner, for example, may charge $150.00 per day for his services. This writer, for constructing a specially built typewriter for the Alger Hiss defense which was not even admitted into evidence, was paid $7,500.

Our law enforcement agencies have established elaborate facilities to obtain convictions. They maintain large staffs of trained operatives in every area of crime detection. They have crime laboratories with modern scientific equipment set up at great expense. They may even summon outside experts, when the situation warrants, out of their budgets.

It is estimated that the United States government spent a million dollars in getting the Hiss conviction. The Manhattan District Attorney's office spent nearly a million and a half dollars last year for law enforcement. Although this is as it should be, how is the accused to be enabled to meet the resources of government in defending himself adequately?

Theoretically, governmental law enforcement agencies are as much concerned with the establishment of innocence as of guilt, and some observers might maintain that their resources are applied for the good of all. But, as one writer has noted, "although the police supposedly undertake an impartial investigation of the facts in each case, they actually only look for that evidence which will convict. We are now duty bound to create machinery that will help those who are accused." [11]

Many cases may be adduced to prove that the cost of expert assistance is an impediment to justice. In one instance, a young man discovered the strangled body of his girl friend when he went to her apartment on a Sunday night. In a panic, he fled the apartment and the body was not discovered until Monday noon. His whereabouts for all of Friday and Saturday were well accounted for, but the medical examiner in error estimated the time of death as Sunday night instead of Friday, when the murder actually occurred. The young man's presence in the girl's apartment on Sunday was established, and he was convicted of murder. After he had spent four years in prison, it was discovered that the girl had been murdered days earlier.

If the young man had been able to afford medical experts —if he had at his disposal the laboratories and expensive equipment of the state—the innocent might not have suffered unjust punishment. The real criminal might have been apprehended and tried.

Another case involved a woman accused of murdering her husband. Actually, she had been on a bus going to another city at the time of the crime. But her bus ticket had been surrendered and she had no evidence at hand to prove her alibi.

If she could have retained private detectives to go out of

the state and locate the bus driver, other passengers, taxi drivers, ticket sellers, redcaps, or anyone else who might remember her, her innocence might have been established. But then it would have been necessary to transport these witnesses, pay their expenses and compensate them for time taken from their work. The lawyer in the case estimated that at least $1,640 was needed for this phase of the defense alone. The woman could not afford this expense so the search was never made.[12]

Obviously, if the prosecution needed out-of-town witnesses to gain a conviction, it would have been a relatively simple matter to obtain them. Police agencies in other jurisdictions would cooperate. Operatives could be sent anywhere —even to foreign countries—for evidence. It is clear that the contest between the accused and the prosecution is an unequal one. In cases where innocence or guilt is not clear-cut, in instances where circumstantial evidence is all-important, the accused must stand more than an even chance of losing.

Until the accused can meet the prosecution on even ground, it is plain that justice will not be done in many cases. Several proposals have been made so that this goal may be attained. One suggestion is that the public defender bill be expanded to include the costs of expert assistance as well as that of counsel. Another proposal is that even an individual who can afford counsel should be entitled to use, for his defense, investigators, crime lab technicians, and other skilled personnel on the government payroll.[13]

In other words, the facilities which are now dedicated to establishing guilt should be equally devoted to proclaiming innocence.

IV. *Other Expenses*

There are other considerable expenses which an accused person must assume in his defense. One is the price a defendant must pay in order to get a transcript of his trial. Such a transcript usually costs between $750 and $1,000.[14]

In the Hiss case the cost of printing the appeal ran between $15,000 and $16,000, and this figure was low because it was done in a small print shop in Pennsylvania at great inconvenience to the Hiss attorneys. The New York City printing estimates for the same job were between $25,000 and $30,000.

Every convicted criminal has the constitutional right to appeal the verdict against him to a higher court. But a higher court cannot consider his appeal unless it is furnished an official transcript of all the testimony at his original trial. Unless the accused has the money to pay for this transcript, his constitutional right is a mythological one; he cannot have a higher court review his case in actuality. There are many prisoners serving time in penitentiaries all over the country who have never been able to appeal the verdicts against them because of this financial factor.

It would seem only fair that the government assume the expense of supplying the transcript to individuals who wish a judicial review of verdicts against them.

Another constitutional right is the one to reasonable bail. Even a fairly well-to-do individual seldom has the resources to "put up" the bail required in many criminal actions. Family and friends must be called upon for assistance. In cases where the accused cannot raise the bail, commercial bondsmen will, for a fee, bail out the prisoner. The abuses which have arisen in connection with bail bonding are well known. The "bail-bonding racket" has been widely publicized. Police officers and bail bondsmen have been known to work in collusion. And obtaining bail for the accused has developed into just another expense added to all the others.

V. *Some Case Studies*

Many individuals feel that the problem of defense against accusation will never confront them. They have the instinctive feeling that "justice will be done," and even if an accused person cannot adequately defend himself, it is no great loss, for he is probably guilty anyway.

Needless to say, the guilty deserve the full protection of

the laws just as the innocent do. If guilt is to be determined, it is to be determined fairly in an even contest for the minds of the judge and jury.

But the very premise of this kind of argument is wrong. Innocent individuals are accused of crimes almost daily, and frequently convicted. Accusation may be the result of mistake or malice, but it is a threat over all of us. And financial ruination faces all of us as a result.

Several well-publicized cases may be cited to prove the point. In his film, *The Wrong Man*, Alfred Hitchcock dramatized the actual case of a night club musician, Christopher Balestrero. Balestrero was picked up by the police one night as a suspect in a series of armed robberies.

He was identified by several individuals as the man who had perpetrated a number of hold-ups. In the dramatization, Balestrero is held incommunicado for hours; his family is not notified of his whereabouts; he is questioned, fingerprinted, jailed, and degraded.

He is finally arraigned, indicted, and freed on bail. His first trial is terminated in a mistrial because of a technicality. Throughout the film, Balestrero is engaged in a frustrating search to establish his innocence, but witnesses he might have used have disappeared or died. He has an understandable difficulty accounting for his whereabouts on specified nights months ago.

Finally, Balestrero is cleared when the real criminal is caught in the act of robbery. The same witnesses who identified him now identify the real culprit.

However, the film—dealing as it does with the human elements in the case—overlooks the financial debacle suffered by the accused. Balestrero loses time from his job. He must retain an attorney. He tries to conduct investigations which will establish his innocence.

As a result of the arrest, his wife suffers a nervous breakdown and must be placed in a sanitarium. Only two years after his vindication is she ready for release. In the meanwhile, the burden of caring for two small children falls upon his shoulders.

In the film version, the police are only too helpful and

sympathetic to Balestrero, almost regretting the fact that he seems to be guilty. In reality, however, if this accused man had had the resources of agencies of law enforcement at his disposal, it would have been relatively simple for him to have established his innocence.

In a more recent case, a man named Russell Ericksen was suspected of murder.[15] The mother of his fiancee, Mrs. Dorothy Campbell, was found bludgeoned to death in a parked car. Ericksen was accused, his motive traced to the woman's double-indemnity insurance policy, and his fiancee suspected of complicity in the crime. After protracted questioning, the police actually obtained a confession from the girl. However, Ericksen was not brought to trial on what was apparently a flimsy case. But for weeks he was summoned for questioning at odd hours, for long periods of time, and kept under surveillance.

Then a Mrs. Mary Rasmussen was attacked in the same neighborhood. Ericksen was picked up by the police and identified by Mrs. Rasmussen as her assailant. He was indicted on this charge, and was awaiting trial.

But another murder—that of young Patricia Ruland—led to the arrest of Thomas Higgins, who reportedly confessed both the Campbell killing and the Rasmussen attack. Mrs. Rasmussen changed her "positive identification" to Higgins. Although Higgins was later said to have repudiated his confession, Ericksen and his fiancee at present writing seem to have been cleared of the suspicion of murder and criminal assault.

But in any case, innocent or guilty, here was the financial loss suffered by Ericksen *before* he had even come to trial:

1. He was suspended from his job as a recreational leader at a Park Department playground.
2. The constant questioning and suspicion, added to the shock of her mother's violent death, led to Barbara's loss of her job as a dictaphone operator with a medical instrument supply firm.
3. Ericksen had to give up his night school courses in physical education at Hunter College. The police had

held him for questioning the night he was to register
for the current semester.

4. Ericksen was held in $50,000 bail. It was reduced to
$5,000 after he had spent nearly a week in jail.

5. An attorney, John Norton, was retained to defend
him.

6. His parents suffered physical as well as financial set-
backs in the course of his defense.

Another case involved a college professor who was
charged by a disgruntled woman student with attempted
rape. The professor was later cleared of the charge, but not
until after he had been suspended from his post, been indicted, and had undergone severe mental strain. Although he
was acquitted of the charge, the man, an outstanding scholar,
gradually deteriorated. He took to drink, and was subsequently dismissed from the college. His death several years
ago on Bowery's Skid Row as a broken alcoholic derelict revived newspaper stories of the old charges against him.

Many other "wrong man" cases have been publicized, but
it is the unpublished ones which should really give us pause.
There are men behind bars in every state who were unjustly
convicted, and frequently simply because they did not have
the financial resources to pay the high cost of justice.

VI. *Conclusion*

There are other factors which make justice not only
expensive but hard to come by. Witnesses, for example, are
seldom as eager to testify for an individual accused of crime
as they are to testify for the government. The prosecution
may, more often, gain cooperation in presenting its case than
can an accused person, particularly if the crime is heinous
or revolting. And there are frequently rewards, tangible and
intangible, for the witness who assists the government in
obtaining a conviction in a widely publicized trial.

Another factor to consider is that the law courts are not
the only places, these days, in which an individual may be
called upon to defend himself. With the increased tendency

of Congress to devote itself to committee investigation—a relatively minor function assigned to it by the Constitution as an aid to legislation—an individual may find himself confronted with a subpoena to appear before one of the many Congressional investigation committees. A lawyer with Washington connections is usually retained, and even though the line of questioning may be associated with a perfectly innocent activity, the person summoned suffers a certain amount of anxiety and expense in this quasi-judicial process.

The cost of justice is rising all the time in our society. It has now become imperative to enable any accused individual to defend himself without suffering bankruptcy, whether innocent or guilty.

REFERENCES

1. Cooke, Alistair, *Generation on Trial* (Knopf, 1950), p. vii.
2. Myers, Allen Murray, "Could You Afford a Fair Trial?", *This Week*, November 28, 1954, p. 7.
3. *Loc. cit.*
4. *Loc. cit.*
5. Rogers, William P., "Plea for the Public Defender," *New York Times Magazine*, April 21, 1957, p. 26.
6. *Ibid.*, p. 56.
7. *Ibid.*, p. 26.
8. Rogers, *op. cit.*, p. 26, and Myers, *op. cit.*, p. 22.
9. Rogers, *op. cit.*, p. 58.
10. Myers, *op. cit.*, p. 7.
11. Myers, *op. cit.*, p. 22.
12. *Loc. cit.*
13. *Loc. cit.*
14. *Loc. cit.*
15. Seely, Nancy, "Racking Our Brains," *New York Post*, April 24, 1957, p. 3.

There is considerably more agreement among criminologists and correction officials as to the essential goals of penology than is generally recognized. A primary difficulty in atttaining such agreed-upon objectives is lack of procedural insight, i.e., the development of appropriate techniques for the ends we have in view. Closely associated with this problem is the great dearth of professionally trained workers and specialists who can accomplish the objectives which have been set forth. Further, there is the complicated problem of the enormous institutional and bureaucratic structures which we have created which, because of their deeply patterned and routinized procedures, have engendered processes which frequently appear directly inimical to the corrective process itself. This is a problem which is strongly implied by Dr. Vernon Fox in his earlier chapters on prison organization, and probation and parole.

Professor John P. Kenney, recognizing the improbability of gaining adequately trained staff and sufficient facilities within the immediate future, suggests that, irrespective of such augmentation, a realistic approach to our goals can be made. The application of modern management principles to the operating law enforcement and correctional agency, whether police department, prison, or division of probation and parole, may bring our goals closer to effective practise. This involves, as he would suggest, a realistic acceptance of the limitations and capacities of the functioning human relationships of the staff of each institution and the actual framework within which each staff operates. Even if only to bring about a fundamental reexamination of the rigidity of bureaucratic structure in most large-scale penal and law enforcement agencies, the use of such a perspective may be beneficial.

Chapter 13

A MANAGEMENT FOCUS FOR CRIMINOLOGY

JOHN P. KENNEY

Former President, American Society of Criminology;
Associate Professor, School of Public Administration,
University of Southern California

Criminology as defined in the constitution of the American Society of Criminology is "a study of the causes, treatment and prevention of crime; law enforcement, criminal
justice; and allied fields." This pluralistic approach is necessary, perhaps, if criminologists are to meet the essential obligations of a professional organization for the improvement
of society as a whole.

There exist many approaches in dealing with the substantive concepts of criminology. The traditional concern
has been with the protection of society and recognition of
the inherent worth of the individual. The police and prisons
have traditionally emphasized the protection of the society,
whereas probation and parole operations appear to focus
more on the individual. If one reviews the literature on delinquency, crime prevention, and treatment, there seem to be
as many answers set forth for the problems as there are
schools of thought on the subject.

The agencies, both public and private, responsible for
implementation of programs of criminology provide, in the
final analysis, the test for all of the concepts and theories
which have been developed. It appears that there has been
too little concern and study of the means by which the

agencies meet their responsibilities. An evaluation of the "machine," its structure, command lines, internal relationships, and utilization of personnel, essential for getting the job done, can give us insight heretofore unknown.

There is, however, a more basic concern in which criminology as a science is involved, and that is the determination, through accredited scientific methodologies, of causes and conditions which tend to create varying problems of crime in differing types of environments. Although the process is slow, there is an encouraging and heartening attempt today of agencies of correction to begin to implement and to put into operation such findings as part of an organized program of objectives. It is possible, I believe, to develop a more effective means by which agencies concerned with problems inherent in the field of criminology can approach their obligations of protecting society and in dealing with the individual. The subject is "management," which may be regarded as the effective utilization of human resources and material to reach the known goal.[1] The assumption is made that agency goals have been defined and that the task at hand is implementation.

Since management and organization are interrelated, let us define organization for the purpose of more precise orientation. It may be regarded as the division and unification of effort toward some goal or policy.[2] Thus, there is established the agency institutional setting, from which a management focus for criminology may be developed and an expanded, more meaningful understanding of administration of criminological programs created.

The scientific management movement began in the last quarter of the nineteenth century, emphasizing productivity and efficiency through human engineering. Such names as Frederick Taylor, Gantt, and Gilbreth are immediately associated with the movement. Coordinate with this development, principles of organization and administration were being identified and clarified in the writings of such men as Luther Gulick, Urwick and Mooney, providing the basis for what is now recognized as the orthodox theories for management and organization.

The past three decades have seen development of a whole new body of management and organization theory. Central to these theories is a recognition of men as social animals, even in a work situation.[3] Beginning with the writing of Mary Parker Follett and the Western Electric Studies of Elton Mayo, a whole new body of literature with this theme has developed, with such outstanding scholars as John M. Pfiffner, Rensis Likert and Herbert Simon leading the way. A cross-disciplinary approach to organization and management has evolved, with theory reflecting beliefs and trends currently prevailing in psychology, sociology, anthropology, and social welfare.

Man in his work situation is no longer perceived along with machines and material as merely one of the elements of production. The worker is much happier and productive if motivated by a democratic leadership which recognizes human dignity, fosters a satisfying social environment, cultivates a feeling of belonging, and develops two-way communication.[4]

Application of the several theories, principles and concepts of dealing with groups and individuals advocated in criminology, provide the very core for effective internal management of the different types of agencies concerned with the corrective process. By such judicious application, we should be able to improve performance within agencies concerned with criminological problems. Seen within the context of management principles, our understanding of individuals and agency groups provides many essential elements of current theory in management and organization. It remains for us to review the orthodox principles and concepts, now more often than not referred to as the "proverbs of administration," and to gain an understanding of the proposition that management institutions are organized on the basis of hierarchy.

Much too long, it seems, we have focused on achievement of the goals, protection of society and helping individuals, commendable and laudatory as they are, but in an almost abstract sense. Effective utilization of available manpower, mobilized towards realizable and operational goals, would appear to be a more realistic approach. Production is primarily service in nature; therefore materials and machines are of considerably less significant concern. It is now time for us to take a critical look at the means by which we are expected to meet the goals.

I submit the proposition that across-the-board improvement in the management of criminological agencies can be made. However, to be more specific, a few areas of current concern will suffice to point up the scope of the problem. The following problems highlight situations for which the agency itself can do something, if it is willing to accept the "management approach" in dealing with its problems.

1. There is serious doubt as to the effectiveness of some institutional treatment programs. A recent preliminary study revealed that varying periods of institutionalization of convicted young adults seemed to show little correlation with rehabilitation.

2. A preliminary study of institutional treatment reveals that perhaps the greatest therapeutic-impact on inmates is made by artisans and custodial personnel, not professional therapists. Perhaps our institutional organizations should change in focus to give more importance to the non-professional employees.

3. Probation and parole care is considerably cheaper than institutional care, and for most delinquents and criminals, probably more effective. Have we not a responsibility to contrive more boldly conceived programs of non-institutional care?

4. A critical look at the duties of probation and parole officers raises the issue of control versus treatment. It is suspected that probationers and parolees are on the average seen less than half an hour monthly by an officer, suggesting a complete new approach to utilization of probation and parole officers.

5. Recent studies of police departments reveal that less than twelve percent of departmental personnel time is spent on criminal cases, and a considerably less amount of time in dealing with delinquents and criminals. These studies suggest a new focus for utilization of personnel which may create

an "environment" less conducive to crime and delinquency.

In summary what appears to be needed is considerable internal realignment in all of our agencies dealing with crime and delinquency. Too long have we concentrated on the goals and let the "machine" fall apart. Reappraisal of jobs, introduction of good office techniques, clarification of relationship between staff and line, better program planning, and improved internal coordination and communication can do much to improve effectiveness. Such an internal audit, the taking of stock of what we have to do the job with, will give us a more solid base for the future.

REFERENCES

1. Seckler-Hudson, Catheryn, *Organization and Management: Theory and Practice* (The American University Press, Washington, D. C., 1955), p. 12.

2. *Ibid.*

3. Pfiffner, John M., and Presthus, R. Vance, *Public Administration* (The Ronald Press Co., N. Y., 1953), pp. 148-149.

4. *Ibid.*

In the development of modern institutional trends towards crime, one of the most difficult problems is that brought about by the growth of enormous secondary and impersonal institutional patterns with which most citizens are identified in one way or another. Indeed, it is virtually impossible to function in contemporary society without some sort of identification with these significant agencies of modern life. Crime, in earlier epochs, was able to assume an immediacy of character and personal effect which is lacking in these large institutional agencies. The average individual is compelled to identify his own interests with vast professional and occupational associations whose complex and intricate organizational structures appear far removed from the immediate personal reference of his daily concerns. Such reference groups, as the sociologist frequently refers to them, provide a particular point of departure for the highly specialized interests which each citizen pursues.

Probably nowhere are these highly specialized and depersonalized forms of identification best exemplified than in the growth of managerial and labor organizations. With the growth of these organizations, the burden of responsibility for administrative control and decision-making falls upon delegated and elected leadership, whose permissive scope for action and decision-making becomes increasingly difficult to control and to define. Even when attempts are made towards careful and precise definition, procedures of control are difficult to articulate and enforce through operating sanctions. The result is a vast penumbra of social action in which abuse *of institutional prerogatives and leadership responsibilities are not only possible, but almost inevitable.*

This is not a problem alone of the labor movement; it is a problem common to all of our vast supervening social institutions, governmental and non-governmental. Government, business and labor have equally become concerned with the problem of abuses both within and without their own special spheres of operation. It would not be entirely human perhaps if this feeling of concern were not focused more commonly upon some agency other than one's own. Since illegal behavior and dishonesty frequently become difficult to define adequately in this relatively uncharted area, except in certain clearcut cases already established by the criminal statutes such as actual peculation or embezzlement, other devices are sought. There has been a marked tendency to resort to internal policing actions by large organizations themselves, primarily in the form of illy-defined prescriptions laid down by Ethical Practises Committees.

Because of the growing strength of the labor movement in this country, and the peculiar position which labor has occupied in an institutionally patterned business economy, the abuses occurring in labor organizations have been particularly subject to serious scrutiny during the past decade. The exploration of the problem of abuses by labor officials of the responsibilities vested in their leadership, a highly controversial and disputed issue, has become the special target of recent legislative investigating bodies.

The increasing use of these legislative committees, however, opens up a problem equally as significant as the problem of possible abuses. This is the serious question of the extralegal prerogatives employed by such bodies, and the far-ranging implications for law enforcement and quasi-judicial process which the extended operations of such bodies assume. What is actually occurring in American life at the present time is the intrusion of a novel form of administrative justice and a new conception concerning the imposition of legal sanctions upon newly defined forms of criminal behavior.

Senator Patrick McNamara, Democratic Senator from the State of Michigan, while writing from an unquestioned par-

tisan view, nevertheless indicates the character of the problems which are emerging as a result of this new trend in legislative investigation of large-scale social institutions. As a former member of the Senate Committee on Investigation of Improper Activities in the Labor or Management Field, popularly known as the McClellan Committee, he reveals the conflicting forms of social pressure which function in the operation of such investigative bodies. There is likewise evidence that where legal processes are not clearly defined in the responsibilities of newly emergent leadership, the dangers of criminal abuses and racketeering are not only possible, but very likely inevitable.

In a sense, this may be viewed as the reverse side of the coin of "white collar crime," performed with less finesse and subtlety, and without the protection of the civil statutes afforded to other agencies where legal evasion can take place.

Chapter 14

CRIME AND THE LABOR MOVEMENT

PATRICK MCNAMARA

United States Senator, Michigan; former Member, United States Senate Committee on Investigation of Improper Activities in the Labor and Management Field.

It is quite likely that the factors that produce crime and criminality are pretty much the same whether the criminal is connected in some way with the labor movement or any other form of activity or business. If I may be permitted to generalize, which is very unscientific, I know, these factors probably are greed for wealth and the desire to get something for nothing, a desire for power, and so forth. I think these will hold true for the bank embezzler, the second-story man, the welfare chiseler and the man who pads his expense account, as well as for a crook in a labor union. Assuming that there are certain common elements in all forms of crime, it should then be possible to go into the fine points of whether he came from a broken home, whether his mother hated him, or whether he once fell out of his swing onto his head. Once we accept the fact that crime is crime, no matter where it arises, I think we can better discuss crime as it may occur in the labor movement in particular.

While the law must look equally on crime no matter where it occurs, I would like to note here a very personal feeling I have on the subject insofar as it relates to the labor movement. Over the years, from inside it and out, I have viewed the American labor movement in action. It has been an inspiring experience watching men and women forming unions, watching the unions grow, and watching the resulting increase in the standard of living, in the national prosperity, and the growing dignity of the individual. The labor unions have been effective spokesmen for their members, both at the local bargaining table and at the governmental levels where the laws are made.

The responsibility of the union official to his member is a great one. A tremendous amount of trust is placed in him. Therefore, any union official, at any level, who uses his position for unethical or illegal personal gain, I feel, is practically guilty of treason to his members and to the labor movement as a whole.

Crime and the labor movement is a subject that has been much in the headlines over the past two years, primarily as a result of the activities of a Senate committee. This, of course, is the Senate Committee on Investigation of Improper Activities in the Labor or Management Field, more popularly known as the McClellan Committee. Unfortunately, because of the sensational manner in which the press frequently has treated these hearings, a number of serious misconceptions have arisen. I would like to try to clear up some of the misconceptions and to indicate what, if anything, might be done about the real problems that do, unfortunately, exist. Some of these observations are based upon my service as a member of the McClellan Committee from the time it was established in January 1957 until April 1958.

In March of 1958, the Committee issued a 462-page book which it called its interim report on the first year's activities. It contained, in part, several recommendations for legislation in the labor-management field. The report also contained nine pages of my individual views on the committee's work and its recommendations. Primarily, I was critical of the Committee's report, for I felt it unfairly served to stigmatize all of labor for the sins of a few.

It groped for new headlines through the use of such unsupported and ill-defined statements that ten million dollars in union funds had been found to be "stolen, embezzled or misused." And it further made charges, allegations and recommendations which I honestly felt were not always supported by the hearings which I had faithfully attended.

While I did note that I thought the Committee's report had strained its reputation for objectivity, I also said this: "As is true in any other field of activity, the labor movement unfortunately is not immune to corrupt influences. The Committee, in a number of areas, has already demonstrated this, and it is to be commended for it. The bulk of the labor unions, through the AFL-CIO, have publicly praised the Committee for this service. I believe the labor movement will join the rest of the public in endorsing constructive legislation at the Federal level."

Not long after the report was issued, I left the Committee because I felt it had accomplished its purpose in developing recommendations for legislation. The next step, it seemed to me, was not more investigation, but for the proper standing committees of the Senate to study the recommendations and draft any necessary legislation. This is, of course, what subsequently was done by the Senate Labor and Public Welfare Committee, of which I am a member. However, while we in the Labor Committee were doing that, the McClellan Committee was continuing its hearings. On the basis of its record, a publicized committee such as this will come before the Senate and ask that its life be extended for an additional period. In keeping with common precedent, such extensions are frequently granted with the result that another half-million dollars or so may be added to the one and a quarter million dollars which this committee, for example, has already spent.

Personally, I haven't changed my opinion that the Committee has long since served its useful purpose of conducting a legislative search. I don't think the Committee's 1958 hearings added anything substantially new to what had already been revealed in 1957. And I doubt very much whether hearings in 1959 have proven any more productive. They will, of course, have produced an occasional new headline, but we can hardly base sound legislation on those.

Such investigative committees have become, in fact, a sort of sacred cow, which people hesitate to criticize for its excess

for fear they will be charged with giving aid and comfort
to crooks. An example of this came not long ago when a
prominent clergyman offered the suggestion that the Committee might well end its hearings in the near future. The
Committee greeted the suggestion with the comment that
"every hoodlum, gangster and racketeer . . . will heartily
applaud it." If the people genuinely want the Committee to
continue, it is all right with me. But I think they should
recognize exactly what they are buying.

They are buying a sort of extralegal police force, complete
with all the dangers to due process of law and individual
rights inherent in the Congressional investigating committee
system. They will *not* be getting a committee whose primary
function is to help in the development of sound legislation.
No matter what the future of the McClellan Committee,
however, our Labor and Public Welfare Committee will continue its legislation functions in this field. As is well known, we
got a good start on this last year.

As far back as April of last year, we had drafted and
passed in the Senate the pension and welfare fund reporting
and disclosure act. Work on this legislation preceded the
McClellan Committee by several years, and adoption of the
legislation was held up by management opposition. Then,
after extensive Labor Committee hearings, the Senate passed,
by a vote of 88 to 1, the Labor-Management Reporting and
Disclosure Act. This was popularly known as the Kennedy-
Ives Bill. This bill, unfortunately, was rejected by the House,
thanks to a rather unprecedented lobbying and pressure job
by some business interests.

Despite this, I expect that proposed legislation very similar
to the Kennedy-Ives Bill will again receive the most serious
consideration for some time. This bill had provisions in it with
which I disagreed, but I nevertheless believe it was a conscientious effort to meet problems and recommendations in
this important field. It did, in fact, cover all the areas contained in the recommendations of the McClellan Committee
report, with the exception of the pension and welfare legislation. Had this bill been enacted, I am sure it would have

been effective in curbing a number of abuses not now adequately covered by law.

The Kennedy-Ives Bill covered several specific areas which I will briefly run through. First, it required unions to file detailed financial statements which would become public and available to the members. Second, employers would be required to publicly disclose direct expenditures of $5,000 or more to influence or affect employees in the exercise of their rights under national labor laws, and any indirect expenditures for this purpose. Third, the so-called labor relations experts or "middlemen" would be required to file financial reports on their activities.

This, incidentally, would help curtail one of the greatest abuses exposed by the McClellan Committee—the work of these experts in union busting. In addition to the reporting requirements, certain protections were given local unions placed under trusteeship and union members in electing their officers. It was the reporting requirements for employers and their middlemen friends that raised the roof in certain business quarters, and became the major reason for opposition to the bill in the House. It was perfectly all right, it seemed, to adopt legislation that might put severe restrictions on labor unions. Applying the same standards to employers, however, suddenly became abhorrent. Apparently what employers were doing wasn't looked on as unethical or criminal, but as good business practise. Perhaps this goes to prove the saying that "successful and fortunate crime is called virtue."

This leads to one of the most serious misconceptions that has come about, one which, unfortunately, the McClellan Committee seems to have nurtured rather than discouraged. This is the idea that the labor movement generally is shot through with criminal elements. And that improper and criminal conduct is typical of the behavior to be expected from union leaders. These leaders, the story goes, rule their unions with an iron hand for their own profit and advantage, rather than for the welfare and benefit of the union members. They gorge themselves through use of the members' dues and freely use these dues to support political candidates favorable to their own interests. This is the line actively peddled by a number of organizations such as the National Association of Manufacturers and the United States Chamber of Commerce.

It would be idle to suggest that none of this conduct exists in the labor movement. The McClellan Committee, and before it, the Douglas Subcommittee, investigating pension and welfare fund abuses, have shown instances where some officials of some unions have abused the trust placed in them, conducted themselves unethically if not illegally. Now, it is no more fair to use these persons as representative of the labor movement than it is to use the bank embezzler as representative of the business world. Yet, there are those whose remedies for corruption in the labor movement would subject all unions to severe restrictions that are totally unwarranted.

These restrictions in the guise of cleaning up corruption would interfere with such legitimate practises as negotiating for the union shop, organizing workers, or even collective bargaining. In short, these restrictions would reduce the labor movement to a completely ineffective institution. It had been necessary to fight off more than a dozen of these restrictions which were proposed as amendments to the Kennedy-Ives Bill, and before that to the pension and welfare bill.

Another widely-held misconception concerns the alleged power of union officials. This view holds that union officials can dictate the terms and conditions under which the nation's economy is allowed to operate. It also pictures the unionists making and breaking politicians and political parties at will, squandering vast sums of dues money for this purpose, completely oblivious to the desires of the members.

There can, of course, be little doubt that the labor movement has had a significant impact on the economy. Far from being adverse, however, this influence has largely been beneficial. The increases in wages won through collective bargaining have in turn paid for more goods, resulting in a higher gross national product, and more jobs in an expanding economy. The extent to which higher wages have resulted in higher prices is vague, at best. But it has become a handy excuse for some profit-hungry industrialists. Pension plans and other social welfare programs pioneered and fought for by organized labor pay off daily in a higher standard of living and in economic security.

It is truly remarkable that so much has been accomplished by a labor movement which, even today, represents only about 37 percent of the American wage earners. This means union representation for only eighteen and a half million of the more than sixty-eight and a half million workers in the total civilian labor force. Whole industries and trades, such as the retail and service trades and office employees, have little or no broadly effective union organization.

Labor unions have every right to support political candidates, but the argument that they exercise massive or sinister control over elections is false on either of two counts. Such an argument either ignores the very existence of millions of voters who actually make the decisions or it implies that these voters are simply sheep, and not very bright ones at that. The N.A.M. and like interests already are devoting considerable time and spending vast sums to advance their own programs. It is inconceivable that the labor movement should be denied the same right.

Now, are these matters crimes in the usual sense of the word? Is it, or should it be, a crime for labor unions to bargain collectively with employers for higher wages and better working conditions? Or for unions to take an active part in the political affairs that affect them and their members? Or should it be a crime for union members to spend their money for things which some outsider might not approve of?

When we were debating the Kennedy-Ives Bill in the Senate during the summer of 1958, one amendment offered actually would have permitted court action if union funds were spent for anything besides collective bargaining. This could have effectively prevented a union from contributing to local charities or even buying a new typewriter for the office.

It seems to me what we really are talking about in this area are two basic kinds of crime or would-be crime. One is the plain old garden variety type, where someone puts his hand in the till and shouldn't. Or where he beats up someone else or practises extortion. I don't think these are the kind of crimes that we can seriously consider on the Federal level. After all, theft, violence and extortion already are crimes in every State of the Union. Should Congress single them out for special Federal penalties just because the culprit may be found to have a connection with a labor union? The answer to that is obvious. Crimes of this nature must be dealt with on the local level where they occur. It is up to the States and their local prosecutors to enforce these laws just as they enforce any other.

The other kind of crime, or alleged crime, is a matter of ethical conduct, and determining what that is, puts us into the greatest area of controversy. Here it is especially necessary to recognize what the labor movement itself has done. I noted in my individual views on the McClellan Committee report that the lack of democratic procedures and corruption among a small minority of unions have been matters of great concern in the labor movement for many years. Until the American Federation of Labor and the Congress of Industrial Organizations merged in 1955, however, principles and traditions of local trade union autonomy prevented effective action in many instances. Even so, the labor movement must be credited with being among the first to recognize the dangers of communist infiltration and for acting forthrightly against it. The A.F.L., for years, had strong anti-communist policies and the C.I.O. moved courageously in the late 1940s to expel several communist-dominated unions. The A.F.L., several years ago, expelled the racket-ridden longshoremen's union. At the very meeting at which the AFL-CIO merger took place in 1955, the new federation acted promptly. A resolution adopted by that convention stated the following:

> "The American labor movement has ever been quick in its denunciation of public officials who betray their trust.
>
> We have been equally critical of businessmen who have used corrupt methods and bribery to gain their selfish, acquisitive ends.
>
> We must be equally quick to recognize and condemn

those instances of racketeering, corruption and disregard for ethical standards when they occur inside our labor movement."

That was what the new AFL-CIO said in 1955, and they were not merely idle words. First, a powerful Ethical Practises Committee was created. This committee, in turn, ultimately developed a series of ethical practises codes which were adopted by the merged federation. These codes laid down rigid standards of conduct dealing with local union charters, health and welfare funds, racketeers, crooks, communists and fascists, conflicts of interest among union officials, union financial practises, and democratic processes within unions. Subsequently, the AFL-CIO moved to clean up or expel several affiliated unions where these codes were violated. Thus, the leaders of the American labor movement, who are sometimes alleged to be so dues-hungry, unceremoniously expelled unions with more than a million dues-paying members.

This was hardly a move taken lightly, not because of the loss of dues money involved, but because the vast majority of the members of these unions were completely innocent of any wrongdoing. If they were guilty of anything it was for neglect in not taking enough interest in the internal affairs of their unions. It is sometimes argued that such action by the AFL-CIO is very well on the surface, but that the corrupt leaders who are booted out are free to pursue their evil ways outside the federation.

The facts are, however, that expulsion from the AFL-CIO is a far more serious penalty than is generally recognized. Expulsion from the federation can pave the way for the chartering of a new, clean union to take the place of the one that was expelled. Members of the old union, if fed up with corrupt leadership, can find a new home in the labor movement. This has been done, as a matter of fact, in the cases of two unions expelled by the AFL-CIO.

In other instances, the members have taken care of matters within their unions by doing their own housecleaning. Another expelled union, the Teamsters, operates today under a unique Federal Court order which provides for supervision of its affairs by a court-appointed board of monitors. I have recited this record of labor's own efforts to deal with corrupt and unethical practises because it is often ignored in discussions of what ought to be done to cope with the problem. It is hardly feasible or sound to pass a law whenever some improper activity is uncovered by Congress. We must not legislate by whim, hysteria or headlines, but only when the need for Federal legislation is clearly shown.

The strong steps taken by the AFL-CIO to keep labor clean are unique in the annals of organizational development. They reflect a sensitivity to ethical concepts and a sense of responsibility for the welfare of union members that few, if any, private groups have ever manifested. Certainly, the business world hardly leaped to curb malpractises or unethical conduct exposed in its ranks. Last summer, the NAM did announce publication of a so-called code of ethical employer practises. But this was so vague, inadequate and devoid of provisions for enforcement as to be meaningless. Is there any wonder that there is skepticism in many quarters as to the genuineness of management's pious concern about crime in the labor movement?

From what has been said, it seems evident that any new Federal legislation should be minimum legislation. I would lay out a four-point course of action that I think should be followed in meeting the problems. First, I would favor prompt adoption by Congress of legislation similar to the Kennedy-Ives Bill. Particularly important are the provisions for financial reporting by unions, management, and these so-called middlemen or union busters. Second, the AFL-CIO should be encouraged in its efforts to root out corrupt influences within the labor movement and be strongly commended for its past action. It is far better for corrupt or unethical practices to be dealt with by the members themselves, whenever possible, rather than by new punitive laws. While we are encouraging labor unions to continue their self-policing activities, we should encourage management at the same time to make a start at least in the same area. Third, State laws against misappropriaton of funds, stealing, violence, extortion, and other crimes should be vigorously enforced by States and local prosecutors. If there are occasions when these laws are not enforced, the people should demand to know why. Fourth, members of labor unions themselves must recognize and live up to their responsibilities. Rank-and-file apathy, I am sure, has been an important factor in the infiltration of any criminal elements into the labor movement. This four-point program, which certainly is not a difficult one, can accomplish far more than restrictive or punitive legislation.

Nothing is more repellent to the community than the act of murder, and certainly nothing more deeply disturbing than when a child commits a murder. This is even more heinous in the public mind when the victim of the murder is a parent of the child, and in slightly lesser degree, when the victim happens to be some other family member. The inviolateness of the parent at the hand of the child, so deeply entrenched in Western culture through the Judaeo-Christian ethic and profoundly reinforced by traditional custom and sentiment, makes the very thought of killing a parent extremely abhorrent and frightening.

Dr. Melitta Schmideberg, one of the handful of psychiatrists devoting themselves exclusively to problems of crime, deals with the problem of the child murderer as a phenomenon and symptom of our times. In two respects, Dr. Schmideberg's approach is distinctive. In the first place, unlike many of her practising professional colleagues, she is extremely sensitive in her approach to sociological and cultural factors which tend to induce patterns of crime, although she has illustrious predecessors in Karen Horney, Erich Fromm, and Harry Stack Sullivan. Secondly, and this is quite distinctive from the usual psychiatric pattern, she is sharply critical of some of the tenets of orthodox therapeutic practise and, of greater pertinence perhaps, the socio-ethical practises they may tend to foster.

While many of the positions she assumes in her discussion are open to serious reservation and question, she touches nevertheless upon some of the widely sensed, rather than proven, tension-areas of contemporary society which bear upon the relaxation of traditional social standards generally.

She is one of the few lone voices, in a profession which ardently espouses greater compassion for the offender through deeper understanding, who urgently appeals for a renewed sense of the sanctions of punishment. She alludes to what the writer has referred to upon a number of occasions as the growing "psychopathic dimension" in modern life, with the accompanying erosion of the traditional sense of moral guilt and its replacement by a purely personal sense of shame, or even worse, indifference.

There is considerable research evidence which must be compiled to support such assertions. The limitation of the fields of research to restricted and researchable areas where such problems may be effectively studied constitutes a genuine need. We cannot even be too certain that, despite Dr. Schmideberg's special pleading, there is actually greater child violence occurring today than in previous periods and in other cultures. It is true, nevertheless, that the concern about what appears to be a growth in the manifestation of violent crimes among children is widespread and a matter of considerable agitated popular speculation.

Accompanying this expressed concern on the part of an adult generation which frequently displays its alarm in fatuous and meaningless ways, there are basic modifications of our family patterns and the exercise of parental authority over children. There is, further, mass exposure to accounts of violence through the press and other popular media of communication which is unprecedented, although the degree to which individuals are motivated to violence by such exposure is highly debatable. As one of the expressions of our contemporary culture mentality, however, this mass interest in violence is, probably, deeply suggestive.

In an age which is gradually extending the conception of therapeutic reform from its application to child offenders to ever advancing age levels, Dr. Schmideberg's comments, by implication, would tend to raise serious questions concerning the entire issue of legal sanity, as defined by the famous M'Naghten rules. The problem of the child murderer, as she sees it, is less a problem perhaps of the individual child offender than it represents a deeply disturbing symptom of our age.

Chapter 15

THE CHILD MURDERER

Melitta Schmideberg, M.D.

Director of Clinical Services, Association for the
Psychiatric Treatment of Offenders, New York

Crimes are conditioned by individual factors inherent in
the personality of the offender, in family attitudes, and by
socio-cultural conditions and trends. Each society has the
crimes it creates, condones or fails to nip in the bud. Punishing the relatively few who commit an offense is only one
method, perhaps a relatively unimportant one, in the community's fight against crime. More important are the innumerable ways in which a society continuously disapproves
and suppresses the steps that mentally or in actuality lead
towards crime, the methods by which it establishes values and
controls, and teaches its members to respond to them. More
important than its deterrent value, punishment reflects the
community's intense disapproval, and this disapproval, if
wholehearted and unanimous enough, is the most powerful
inhibiting factor.

Psychoanalysts tell us that the jungle still survives in our
unconscious and that the small child has cannibalistic impulses. Yet, though there is no law against cannibalism, the
thought of it is so repellent to every member of the community, even to the worst criminals and murderers, that it
hardly ever occurs in civilized countries and then only is
perpetrated by full blown psychotics.

The same does not hold true for murder. Although it is

punished, it is not altogether abhorred. It is much more frequent in this country than in some others. Homicide committed by children under sixteen, relatively frequent here, is practically unheard of in other civilizations.

The fact that we all probably have unconscious wishes and sometimes even a conscious impulse to kill does not in itself explain the phenomenon of murder. Homicide is the combined outcome of the murderous impulse and the weakness of controls, individual and social. Though murder is punished and regarded as the gravest of crimes, we are not revolted by it in the same way as cannibalism revolts us; it is condoned to some degree and sometimes even glorified. Homicide of family members, and in particular of parents, is generally regarded as the worst; yet in recent years, there have been a number of such cases committed by children under sixteen that have rightly perturbed the nation.

Another feature of our society is the degree to which violence is permitted and even encouraged, and the fact that children are not taught sufficient discipline and self-control. As compared to many other cultures, our children appear to be excessively self-centered, and oversensitive to frustration and reprimand. The steps that mentally lead to murder are not sufficiently discouraged. These steps include violence, disregard for others, little family sense, lack of social or religious consciousness, absence of fear of social consequences and punishment, and regarding murder as an everyday event.

Most of the homicides committed by children under sixteen are the outcome of gang warfare, often not premeditated. Less frequent but more puzzling and disturbing is another type: that of children killing, on impulse or premeditation, near members of their own family. The following features, sometimes in combination, have made these crimes particularly disturbing. (1) They are committed by children under sixteen, sometimes as young as eight or ten. (2) The victims are members of the close family, often the parents. (3) They show little emotion and virtually no remorse about it. (4) The provocations have been trifling and the reasons given inadequate, such as a quarrel over television, jealousy of a sibling, and resentment against the father for ordinary punishment or reprimand. Sometimes, in fact, almost bizarre reasons are offered such as the decision of three young children to kill their parents in order to rule the household themselves. (5) Occasionally, murder has been carefully prepared, as in one case when the child practised rifleshooting for weeks, sent the parents to the movies, and pulled the blinds in order to kill his younger brother. (6) In the case of impulsive homicide, it is strange that the child can sometimes just take a knife from the kitchen and use it with such uncanny certainty as to kill the victim by one stab. (Soldiers, during the war, had to be taught for long periods to practise killing by use of the bayonet.) (7) A generation ago in this country, and even today abroad, criminals usually came from the lowest strata of society or from grossly inadequate homes. Frequently, they appeared abnormal to a degree that was obvious even to the untrained observer, or else acted under excessive strain or provocation. In this country, in recent years, there have been a number of child murderers from good middle-class homes, where, if the murder had not occurred, nothing overt might have been found wrong with the home, the family life or with even the offender. (8) This applies even to Jewish families who, abroad and here in the past, have been identified with the most law-abiding, respectable, nonviolent section of the community, and marked by strong family structures.

It has been reasoned that children do not have a proper concept of death during the early years. While this argument probably holds true to some degree for the very few instances of small children killing infants, this can hardly apply to children over ten, and probably not even to those over eight or even six years of age. In this respect, there is very little difference between them and adults. Nobody may be said to have a proper concept of death or murder unless he has actually witnessed it. If a boy of eight jumps into the pond to save his little brother from drowning, he has as clear a concept of death as another boy of the same age who pushes his brother into the water. Again, if failure to realize the implication of the deed might be considered as providing a full explanation of child murder, there would not be cultural differences as to the incidence of such offenses.

Our evaluation of child murder is often faulty because we take for granted the attitudes and standards of the past with which we ourselves grew up and perceive the act in relation to such standards. Yet, in many sections of the community and in certain age-groups, these standards have often been weakened to such a degree that the act of murder must be appraised in terms of a different type of value background.[1]

The average citizen assumes as a matter of course that to take a life is such a heinous occurrence, that the murderer must be deeply abnormal or carried away by an irresistible impulse. Yet this is not necessarily so; sometimes to the murderer, the other person's life is just cheap and murder does not seem a matter of great consequence. Hence, he needs little provocation before and has little reaction after the act has taken place. Also, he is so highly self-centered that he regards an injury as experienced by himself as an act of "lèse majesté" that justifies every and any type of retaliation.

The concept of the "irresistible impulse" usually presupposes the notion that the barriers against killing are so powerful that an impulse of well-nigh overwhelming strength is necessary to overcome them. We should, nevertheless, keep in mind the fact that sometimes the barriers are weak, and hence an impulse of ordinary temper may be sufficient. Thus, the issue, frequently, is one of an uncontrolled impulse rather than of an uncontrollable impulse. Past generations grew up with the concept of the sanctity of life, even irreligious members of such generations. Thus, we automatically assume today that whoever commits a murder must have gone through agonies of struggle or is necessarily deeply abnormal. Many of us, thus, are a little too prone to sympathize with the "sick" child murderer.

The more humane treatment of young offenders and the propaganda for psychiatric therapy may sometimes have an undesirable effect on the offender himself, by helping him take his offense too lightly. One such patient, who knew that his murder of a member of his family was merely adjudged "juvenile delinquency" and which, legally, he did not have to acknowledge when filling out applications, argued with me that he had merely been sent to an "institution for emotionally disturbed children." In the legal sense this, of course, was true. Another one, who failed to a striking degree to show any remorse over his killing, nevertheless criticized the court psychiatrist and social worker for their lack of disapproval, claiming, "I, at least, have a sense of morals," adding, "though I fail to live up to it." The boy was correct in criticizing a tendency to lean over backwards in sympathizing with the so-called agony of the murderer and forgetting the victim, particularly since many murderers undergo no such contrition. In discussing the case of a certain child murderer with a social worker, I was informed that, upon discharge from the institution to which he had been committed, he might be sent to college since "his case would have sentimental appeal" for certain persons ready to offer the necessary funds.

The M'Naghten criterion—"Does the offender know right from wrong?"—is based on a society with rigid beliefs in the distinction between right and wrong. Large sections of present day American society have no strong convictions of right and wrong, not necessarily because they are in sympathy with lawbreaking, but because it is considered reactionary to be moral.[2] Ignoring the parents who set a bad example for their children, there are those who hesitantly impose their own moral and cultural standards and with too great restraint: this is an important factor in middle class delinquency. In other countries and here in the past, the middle classes constituted the bulwark of respectability, overconcerned with their children's education and future. Nothing was more greatly feared than that the child might become a lawbreaker and for a member of the family to become a murderer was an unthinkable threat to the family's existence.

It is a peculiar situation in which liberalism, progressive education, attempts at judicial reform, the plea for psychiatric therapy and humane treatment of offenders—in their struggle on behalf of offenders and children—have helped to undermine moral standards and the respect for the law and the family structure. Ironically, these forces, in abetting the standards of the underworld, lawlessness and crime, are the more effective since they emanate from superior, intelligent, well-meaning, respectable and responsible persons, and coincide with the waning of strong religious and moral beliefs. The present day ideology in this country insists more on the freedom of the individual than on his responsibilities to the community, somewhat in contradistinction to the European democracies.

We are still so accustomed to the standards of past generations that it is too easily assumed that parental overseverity may help to cause murder. When newspaper reports are published in which it is implied that a boy killed his father because of some punishment, it is forgotten that in civilizations where parental punishments were infinitely harsher, there were no murders of parents. If a boy kills his father for a relatively trivial punishment, this is not necessarily an indication of the father's severity, but rather an indication that the child has not learned to accept the concept of punishment and is oversensitive to any hurt inflicted on him. Such a child may regard any form of punishment as something so terrible that it justifies any type of retaliation, including murder. Also, he places himself and his father on the same plane, ignoring his father's support, his bringing him up, and his general status as parent. In previous periods, children were not only punished but had impressed upon them the moral and religious justification of punishment in a myriad of ways. The idea of killing one's parents was regarded as the most abhorrent of all crimes; even for a small child to raise his hand or voice against his parent was most sharply condemned and punished. In patriarchal societies, children had no right to answer back, had to accept even ill-treatment and unjust punishment, and owed their parents unquestioning obedience.

Our society is child-dominated. There has been a relative breakdown of family structure and ideals, and of parental authority. Although this is highlighted by child murderers, it may be observed in other areas as well to quite a degree. Recently, I encountered some difficulty in explaining to a twenty-year old patient why he should not assault his parents, since he argued that the physical inequality between them now was no worse than when his father beat him as a child. A ten-year old who was a misfit in the home, and flagrantly disrespectful and offensive in school but who had committed no serious offenses, told his mother, "The world is ruled today by children and you better get used to it." Both patients were from the middle-class and came from respectable families. The indifference and lack of guilt after the act can be called psychopathic or schizophrenic, but it is conditioned to quite a degree by the fact that in certain states no severe punishment is meted out to child murderers and that children are frequently well aware of it. It was recently reported that a boy who sat through his murder trial of three days with indifference and was sentenced to life imprisonment, a punishment that had not been meted out to children of his age for many years, went into hysterics when sentence was pronounced and he had to be carried out of the courtroom. Obviously, he had not expected such a sentence. Many delinquents state that they have no sense of guilt unless or until they are caught and have developed an expectancy of punishment; this probably holds true for many murderers as well.[3]

With many persons there is no sharp delineation between guilt and fear. In delinquents, in particular, guilt and remorse are usually evoked only by fear, either of immediate or of eternal punishment.

In the past one of the strongest barriers against murder was the religious concept of the sanctity of life with ensuing eternal punishment. If, in such a society, murder occurred because of a genuinely irresistible impulse, at least there was an overwhelming reaction of remorse and guilt.

Delinquency breeds delinquency, murder breeds murder. An important reason for the lack of cannibalism is that for many centuries there have been no cases and hence none have been reported. The practise of detailed reporting, often without any serious show of disapproval, not only appeals to sensationalists but familiarizes the community with the act.

Murder is nothing unheard of anymore. Our crime resistance is broken down and we cease to be shocked.

Not only comics, but television, movies, and lurid news accounts have helped to break down the nation's crime resistance. If we believe in the power of advertising there can be little doubt that the frequent and detailed reporting of murder helps to break down normal inhibitions and social controls for certain individuals. If we smoke cigarettes because others do, murder becomes more acceptable as it tends to become a commonplace event. While millions are spent on advertising soap and cigarettes, only one form of advertisement is free—the advertisement for crime.

Moreover, it is sometimes implied or even stated that the act of murder is a great thrill to the murderer. In one case, a sixteen-year old murderer, after committing homicide, said in a disillusioned vein, "I did not get the thrill I expected." Obviously, what he had heard or read made him expect the thrill. If eating human flesh were described as a rare delicacy, and such cases were reported frequently, probably some individuals might be tempted to try it.

The individual factor is highlighted by the fact that, fortunately, it is as yet only a small number of children who kill. Most psychiatrists who have studied such child murderers do not feel able to explain their mentality adequately. While they are obviously not normal, it is too glib merely to call them "sick," "psychopathic," or "schizophrenic." In any event, they do not fit the typical picture of schizophrenia. In all these areas, much more research is needed.

It has become a scientific commonplace that disturbed family life and wrong parental attitudes are essential factors in delinquency. One emotional abnormality should be stressed in particular: the failure of parents and other members to react with adequate normal feelings. In several cases of child murderers it is striking that not only did the offender himself fail to appear unduly upset but that other members of the family also showed little concern. Although the parents sometimes vocalized their shock and grief, their behavior did not indicate it.

More research and detailed follow-up studies of how the child murderer develops in later life is needed. In New York State, many are discharged from mental institutions or training schools after a few years and returned to the community. In the majority of cases, we do not know with certainty what happens. It is widely believed that they do not commit a second murder, but there is no reliable evidence to this effect. Both from a practical and from a theoretical point of view, it is of paramount importance to study the problem intensively and scientifically.

REFERENCES

1. ". . . children soon learn that . . . being a minor puts them in control of an incredible power, that of excuse and toleration of juvenile delinquency. Delinquency provides excitement, and even in the event he is caught, the delinquent knows that punishment will not be harsh, and often he considers punishment just another excitement. Children consider childhood their 'first life,' distinctly separate from their 'second life,' adulthood, and they find it hard to believe that juvenile delinquency will affect their future life." (This was written by a youth who, at the age of thirteen, after careful preparation, killed his sister in cold blood.)

2. Schmideberg: "Out of the Mouths of Children," *APTO Journal*, 1959, Vol. 3, No. 3.

3. The current trend to regard "punitive" as wholly bad is unjustified. Punishment, if fair, has a socializing, educative effect, and provided it is certain, it acts as a deterrent in most cases. See Schmideberg: "The Offender's Attitude toward Punishment," *Journal of Criminal Law and Criminology*, 1960. Schmideberg: "Making the Patient Aware," *Crime and Delinquency*, 1960.

Part III

Sex, Sanity, and Society

The criminal statutes are based upon the conception that, in the commission of an offense, the individual possesses the rational capacity to exercise freedom of judgment and, consequently, must be held responsible for a crime. There is a further presupposition in this traditional legal point of view, viz., that the individual, in exercising freedom of choice, is aware of and capable of distinguishing between right and wrong. Within the present century, and especially within the last two decades, this legal assumption of free volition in the commission of an offense has been subject to serious, and occasional, bitter discussion and debate.

Since the mid-nineteenth century, both English and American courts of law have tended to follow the famous M'Naghten Rule, first laid down by the British courts in 1843, as a result of the attempted assassination of Sir Robert Peel and the formulated response to the House of Lords as to the basis of Daniel M'Naghten's acquittal. On legal grounds, the well-known criteria of the M'Naghten Rule appear simple and unequivocal. These criteria simply stipulate that the offender, at the time of the commission of his offense, must have been aware of the "nature and quality" of his act and, if he did not know it, to have been able to distinguish right from wrong. The growth of the sciences of psychiatry and psychology, since this period, has not only caused the courts to reexamine the capacity to which such criteria may be employed effectively by juries and judges, but the very assumptions upon which such criteria rest.

There have, consequently, been a great many efforts towards basic revision of these fundamental criteria, extending *as far back, in fact, as 1843, the very year in which the M'Naghten Rule itself was laid down. In that year, Judge Shaw of Massachusetts and Judge Edmonds of New York State both advanced points of view which stipulated that the "right from wrong" distinction was an inadequate test of mental capacity and that overriding emotional factors, such as irresistible impulse, must likewise be considered.*

More recently, the famous Durham decision of 1954 in the District of Columbia has provided a new basis for the determination of legal responsibility on the part of the accused. This much debated recent decision, restricted in its application to the federal district, holds that criminal responsibility may not be imputed if it can be shown that the offender was suffering from a mental disease or defect at the time the act was committed, and that the unlawful act was the product of such mental aberration. The discussion in the next chapter is based upon a somewhat similar proposal brought before the Assembly of the State of California.

Dr. Frederick Hacker and Dr. Marcel Frym are well equipped, by virtue of legal and psychiatric training and experience, to examine this issue. The point of view they present is in refutation to the psychiatric opinion of an experienced psychiatrist and administrator of a mental hospital who, for reasons not always of a psychiatric nature, sees some merit in the retention of the M'Naghten Rule.

This is a critical period in the efforts towards eventual resolution of the bitter conflict between the M'Naghten protagonists and their legal and psychiatric opponents. Equally significant, it would appear, are the eventual social and legal implications of this resolution. A drastic liberalizing of the traditional M'Naghten Rule may eventually have a profound effect upon the entire conception of legal responsibility before the courts for a variety of criminal acts not ordinarily considered within this context and for different age groups.

Chapter 16

THE M'NAGHTEN RULE AND LEGAL INSANITY

Frederick J. Hacker, M.D.,

Chief of Staff, Hacker Psychiatric Clinic,
Beverly Hills, California

Marcel Frym, J.D.

President of the American Society of Criminology;
Senior Staff Member, Hacker Psychiatric Clinic,
Beverly Hills, California; Schools of Law and Public
Administration, University of Southern California.

(*Editorial Note:*

Recently, a bill was introduced into the California Legislature, California Assembly Bill 437, which would supersede the traditional M'Naghten Rule, ordinarily followed by the courts, to determine the presence of legal sanity in the commission of an offense. This interest by the California Legislature, in reconsidering one of the most controversial of all areas in the field of criminal jurisprudence, is paralleled by an extensive interest by legislative bodies throughout the United States and Great Britain. We are, very likely, standing on the threshold of important modifications in determining the legal bases upon which innocence or guilt may be established in relation to the offender's mental state. The California bill would attempt to replace the essential legalistic conception inherent in the M'Naghten Rule by a definition which would limit legal insanity only to clinically proven cases of psychosis and severe mental deficiency.

Dr. Reginald S. Rood, Superintendent and Medical Director of the Atascadero State Hospital in Atascadero, California, has had the occasion to comment critically on the proposed substitution. Unlike what appears to be the preponderant opinion by most psychiatrists, he defends the continuing use of the M'Naghten Rule and expresses skepticism as to whether the proposed changes have any special merit. Among the several arguments he advances in favor of the retention of the M'Naghten Rule are: (1) the use of the expert witness, in the new law, would produce a situation in which "the expert witness becomes the judge, and we (should) have a shift from government by law toward government by men"; (2) in trials without jury, the psychiatrist might, in effect, become the judge, since many judges are on "the point of seeming oversold on psychiatry"; (3) departure from the M'Naghten Rule would permit the courts to "go loose-reined," permitting their decisions to wander from the uniformity required by justice; and (4) the M'Naghten Rule is not affected by the changing concepts of modern psychiatry and psychology.

Since many of the arguments employed by Dr. Rood have been used before and have, frequently, become part of the conventional defense of the M'Naghten position, the criticism by Dr. Frederick Hacker and Dr. Marcel Frym of this point of view has a reference extending far beyond the reply to the standpoint entertained by Dr. Rood. It is, in effect, the position frequently maintained by the critics of the M'Naghten Rule who are interested in having the law recognize modern psychiatric findings in determining the mental states of offenders.)

The controversy about the M'Naghten Rule has been joined by one of the few remaining psychiatric voices defending the retaining of this "simple and definite test." The rule is simple and definite indeed, as well as the reasons for its retention; the understanding of the world by the primitive or uneducated, the primitives' knowledge of physics, chemistry, sociology, and psychiatry, is also simple and definite. Yet it is believed to be the accomplishment of higher learning and of human progress to tolerate the burden of greater complexity because of the gain in understanding, knowledge and effective ability to help. Truth cannot be traded for simplicity even though it be admitted in all humility that human truth is and always will be subject to human errors and subsequent correction.

Dr. Rood asks, "Has anyone, so severely deranged as to come within the proposed bill's defense of legal insanity, ever, in our time been sentenced to a California prison? Or has any contemporary District Attorney ever invoked the M'Naghten Rule to prove an admitted lunatic to be legally sane and responsible?" The answer to Dr. Rood's questions is an unequivocal "Yes." Not only have a large number of people been executed who most likely would have been diagnosed as psychotic and/or mentally deficient on the strength of a scientifically meaningful psychiatric examination without the limitations and restrictions of the M'Naghten Rule, but an even larger number of people who qualify as psychotics in the meaning of the introduced Bill AB-437 are still held in facilities of the Department of Corrections of California. This can be proven by inquiry addressed to the Department of Corrections, especially to the Medical Facility of this Department in Vacaville, California.

All the arguments against the M'Naghten Rule cannot be reviewed in detail in this context. Suffice it to say that these arguments were strong enough to determine leading psychiatric authorities to suggest a radical departure from the M'Naghten Rule and to induce a growing number of prominent American jurists to propose a complete change in the Rule and the reformulation of our concept of criminal responsibility. To mention just one convincing argument that all psychiatrists know from observation, or ought to know and would if they took sufficient time to examine the individual patient-offender—that the so-called knowledge of right and wrong is often purely verbal and entirely divorced from all emotion or real understanding. From this observational fact, which is characteristic of mental illness, it frequently follows that the offender has no capacity to act according to a knowledge for which he has to give no other proof than to indicate on insistent questioning that he possesses it. Psychotic patients suffering from severe degrees of mental illness, totally unconnected with any criminal act, also know right from wrong, as can be observed on the wards of any state hospital.

It has been claimed that many judges are conditioned to the point of seeming oversold on psychiatry. Now psychiatry is a legitimate medical specialty. It has developed rapidly in the last few decades—in that respect similar to modern physics. The concern with ill people and the search for the means for their understanding and cure is hardly comparable to a commodity that is sold to or presumably bought by gullible judges, the price being restoration of mental health and the enjoyment of a good life. But even granting this strange lack of confidence in the diagnostic and therapeutic equipment of modern psychiatry, it is hard to see how any psychiatrist can seriously accept a pseudo-legal formulation that is clinically non-existent, psychiatrically nonsensical, and even of questionable moral and legal value, instead of using the results of careful clinical studies according to the best available medical knowledge of the time. This, incidentally, was recognized as early as 1843, at the time of the M'Naghten trial, by the great American psychiatrist, Isaac Ray, who attended the trial in England. Dr. Rood's position is the more surprising since even authorities in the field of criminal law and the administration of criminal justice, who can hardly be expected to overlook the interests of society and to "mollycoddle" criminals, are utterly dissatisfied with the Rule.

The American Law Institute, as well as the British Royal Commission on Capital Punishment, came out in favor of abolishing the Rule and of reformulating our concept of criminal responsibility. *The M'Naghten Rule represents the unique case, in which an expert in a professional field is instructed by the law as to what professional criteria he must apply in reaching his expert opinion.* Why a psychia-

CRIME IN AMERICA

trist should defend his own frustration that prevents him from acting as a psychiatrist is hard to understand. In analyzing Dr. Rood's position, one cannot help observing Dr. Rood's overwhelming preoccupation with the idea that defendants might be able to "beat the rap" (his words) and escape conviction on an insanity plea. This emotionally charged concern leads Dr. Rood so far astray that he equates the major premises underlying the Ten Commandments with the M'Naghten Rule. While the Ten Commandments represent moral concepts enunciated by divine revelation thousands of years ago, any concept of criminal responsibility purports to *clarify*, in our time, a state of mind which would exclude the type of volitional control which the law requires as a criterion of criminal responsibility. In regard to identifying such a state of mind, modern psychiatry and psychology have made tremendous strides. There is no excuse for eliminating scientific progress in one field of science from consideration and application in court, while in all other respects the newest scientific developments are admitted in evidence for fact-finding purposes.

Dr. Rood has stated that, "A lay jury or judge is better prepared to decide under the M'Naghten Rule, since its test relates to what they know, namely themselves. They are less qualified and must depend on experts, when the test involves an entity which is strange to them." Dr. Rood entirely overlooks the fact that courts, juries as well as judges, continuously have to decide issues where "entities which are strange to them" are involved. Can it really be seriously defended to reduce a matter of life and death to scientifically undefendable over-simplification, because of the limited qualifications of average jurors?

What the Rule produces is a kind of "escapist" movement on the part of judges and courts of appeal, to evade the limitations imposed by the legal concept of "insanity" and to permit the introduction of adequate psychiatric evidence on a "not guilty" plea in regard to the defendant's ability to entertain a criminal *intent* as required by law. This is an openly admitted subterfuge, being necessitated by the backwardness of the law. See, for instance, the recent decision of the California Supreme Court in *People* vs. *Nicholas Gorshen*, Crm. No. 6310, IN BANK, March 11, 1959.

There are only a few countries left in the civilized world in which the concept of criminal responsibility has not been developed far beyond the outdated M'Naghten Rule. And since Dr. Rood refers to the Ten Commandments, it might be especially interesting to note that the law of the Catholic Church (which can hardly be suspected of being morally too permissive), the Codex, in Canon 2229, requires for "dolus" or a "delictum colosum," the will to violate the law and deliberation in the act of violating it. It speaks of a "dolus" in which knowledge and complete deliberation are necessary.

The required criminal intent is precluded by any diminution of that fulness and completeness of activity on the part of either the intellect or of the will. The enlightened requirements for imputability (criminal responsibility) of the law of the Catholic Church are still not accepted by our obsolete penal law.

In conclusion, reference may be made to the Sexual Psychopath Act of California. The very fact that in the same state, in which the M'Naghten Rule still prevails, a new law could be enacted that, for a specific type of serious crime, i.e., sex crimes, introduces the most extensively formulated criteria for mental disturbances and actually substitutes treatment for punishment, is the strongest indication of the trend in protecting society from crime.[1] The interests of society and the interests of the individual offender clearly coincide in the social enactment of those answers that science helped formulate. The ultimate beneficial effect will, however, depend as much on new scientific findings as on the human courage in their application, in order to reconcile the demands of the changing world with the highest moral goals of mankind.

REFERENCES

1. Cal. Welf. & Inst. Code, Section 5500: "Sexual psychopath" means any person who is affected, in a form pre-

disposing to the commission of sexual offenses, and in a degree constituting him a menace to the health or safety of others, with any of the following conditions: (a) Mental disease or disorder; (b) Psychopathic personality; (c) Marked departures from normal mentality.

The problem posed in the effort to establish the mental and moral responsibility of the individual in committing a criminal act is hardly novel. As far back as the thirteenth century, Bracton, in commenting on the canon and Roman law, raised the issue as to whether certain individuals, adjudged insane, could be held accountable for their acts. In stipulating that the insane person is one who lacks mind and reason, and is not far removed from the brute, he posed a classic dilemma which has extended beyond the field of jurisprudence. Since Bracton, there has been a lengthy history of opinions and judgments by jurists and juridical philosophers concerning the determination of legal and moral responsibility. Conspicuous in the landmarks of this historic discussion have been some of the most prominent legal minds of the Old World, including the seventeenth century Coke and Lord Hale, and the brilliant and eloquent Lord Erskine of the early nineteenth century. It was the famous M'Naghten case of 1843, however, which established a pattern that has molded the thinking of the courts in the United States and Great Britain until the present day. Within the present decade, the Durham decision in the district of Columbia has begun to undermine the foundations of a legal pattern which has tended to become inflexible and rigid.

Dr. Philip Q. Roche, as a psychiatrist conversant with the thorny problems of expert psychiatric testimony, traces the development of legal thinking in the attempt to fix moral and legal responsibility. He is primarily concerned, however, with a realistic attempt to establish the role of the psychiatrist in the courts. In assessing this problem, he formulates certain *fundamental questions concerning the differences in the basic assumptions of jurisprudence and psychiatry. The character of the questions placed before the expert psychiatric witness, he asserts, are of an ethical and moral nature, and as such, unrelated to the diagnostic findings of the scientifically trained psychiatrist. The issues here are clearly drawn and Dr. Roche indicates that it is hardly feasible to expect expertness on such matters which are, fundamentally, issues to be determined by the "triers" of the case, as he puts it.*

This is a clarion call on the part of Dr. Roche for psychiatrists to adhere to the scientific responsibilities of their profession and to eschew evidence which departs from their professional competence. The rest, he asserts, is a matter for the courts. In establishing his position, he appears to endorse strongly the procedure of the recent Durham decision which enables the psychiatrist to give evidence only in relation to medical and psychological matters. (A view which appears closely analogous to the position taken by Dr. Roche has appeared in one of the editor's recent publications, "Psychiatric and Sociological Variations in the Interpretation of the Criminal Act," in Crime and Sanity, *edited by R. W. Nice [New York, 1958]. The viewpoint expressed in this analysis would tend to support, in part, Dr. Roche's position).*

Chapter 17

PSYCHIATRY AND THE M'NAGHTEN RULE

Philip Q. Roche, M.D.

"A practical man is a man who practises the errors of
his forefathers."   Benjamin Disraeli

The advance of science since the nineteenth century and
the progress of psychiatry, although based upon common
scientific precepts, present a pattern of divergent growth.
In 1843 the Judges of England formulated a legal rule for
determining the criminal responsibility of mentally ill persons accused of crime. A year later, 1844, the American
Psychiatric Association was founded. In this span of over a
century, the advancement of science has effected a miracle
of change in our physical environment; in the same span we
have not achieved a comparable advancement effecting our
social relationships, particularly in the area of the applications
of psychological science to moral problems. In this span is a
long chronicle of conflict between two systems of thought
and reality evaluation, represented respectively by traditional
criminal law and by medical psychology, in which the latter
has had its concepts and forms of discourse aligned with what
we have come to accept as the realm of science. In recent
decades, this conflict has sharpened with the advances of
psychiatry as a scientific discipline. It will be helpful to
examine briefly the essential alignments of this conflict and
some proposals for future study and change.

Let us first consider the unique Anglo-American legal
position regarding criminal responsibility of the insane. In

the 13th Century, Bracton, an ecclesiastic and Roman law writer, set forth that an insane person is one who does not *know* what he is doing, is lacking in mind and reason, and is not far removed from the brute.[1] In this dictum are the lineal ancestors of what have molded the common law into its present form, the familiar notion that an insane person does not *know* what he is doing, and that he does not *know* what he is doing because he has lost mind and reason. This is in common with our folkway view of the insane person as one who has "lost his mind." We note these attributes again with a later writer, Fitzherbert, who proposed minimum requirements to determine responsibility—whether a person could count to twenty or tell his age, or tell who his mother or father was. In the 17th Century, Coke laid down no formal test but suggested that no crime could exist without a felonious intent and purpose, and that since a madman does not know what he is doing and is lacking in mind and reason, he could not have a felonious intent. In the latter half of the 17th Century, Lord Hale likewise made criminal intent the pivotal integer of culpability. From him we have the earliest test based again upon the partition of the mind whereby the accused, afflicted only with a "partial" insanity, could not be excused; only "total" insanity dissipated felonious intent. Lord Hale set the measure of this test in these terms, ". . . such a person as labouring under melancholy distempers hath yet ordinarily an understanding, as ordinarily a child of 14 years hath, is such a person as may be guilty of treason or felony."[2] This was the "child of fourteen test." Hawkins, the succeeding law writer, reiterated the older attempts and set forth an omnibus of his own. He wrote: "Those who are under a natural disability of distinguishing between good and evil, as infants under the age of discretion, idiots and lunatics, are not punishable by any criminal prosecution whatsoever."[3] Embedded within this language is a religious view of mental illness as a punishment in itself—*furiosus solum furore punitur*. We would do well to respect this humane sentiment as it is expressed in the formal statement of the law. However, let us examine how it has been translated into secular applications.

Passing note may be made of further embellished variants

of the means whereby English courts met the issue of insanity and crime. In the Arnold case in 1724,[4] the presiding judge attempted to define for the jury the demarcation which determines penalty. In his instructions, a series of conditions were set forth; namely, total deprivation of understanding and memory, lack of knowledge in the accused of what he was doing, ". . . no more than an infant, than a brute or a wild beast . . . the incapacity to distinguish good from evil, and . . (to) understand what he did." Arnold was found guilty but reprieved. In 1760 the Earl of Ferrer was tried in the House of Lords. The accused had a long history of mental illness, but since, in following Hale's dictum of partial insanity, Ferrer had sufficient capacity to "form a design and to know its consequences," [5] he was found guilty and executed.

An interesting development occurred in the case of James Hadfield, who made an attempt on the life of George III in 1800. Hadfield, a depressed paranoiac, who hankered for the death penalty for himself, was acquitted on the ground set forth by his counsel, Lord Erskine, that "delusions, therefore, where there is no frenzy or raving madness, is the true character of insanity." [6] Erskine declared, "If a total deprivation of memory was intended by those great lawyers to be taken in the literal sense of the words, then no such madness ever existed in the world." [7]

Erskine's eloquence failed to bring judicial adoption of delusion as a test in place of the knowledge test of right and wrong, as came to notice in the subsequent trial of John Bellingham in 1812.[8] This case has been called the "most notorious in the medico-legal annals of England, because of the indecent haste" with which Bellingham was dispatched to his doom. "Eight days after the crime he was dead." [9]

In a still later case in 1840, one Oxford [10] was tried for shooting at Queen Victoria. Again the court's language centered on the intellectual capacity of the defendant in the familiar phrases which satisfied the jury of "that species of insanity" which would determine culpability.

Three years later, Daniel M'Naghten, a paranoiac, was tried for the shooting of Edward Drummond, probably mistaking him for Sir Robert Peel. The defense raised the question whether M'Naghten was affected by morbid delusions so as to be bereft of control and incapable of perceiving right from wrong. M'Naghten's acquittal evoked a public clamor and no small concern to the Queen, whose recent memory of Oxford moved her to press the issue of proper rules governing judges in their charges to juries. Quite sensibly, the Queen protested that the judges did "allow and advise the jury to pronounce the verdict of not guilty on account of insanity—whilst everybody is morally convinced that both malefactors (Oxford and M'Naghten) were *perfectly conscious and aware of what they did*." [11] (*Italics ours*.) The matter reached debate in the House of Lords. In due course the Lords submitted five questions of law to the Judges of England. Out of their deliberations came what is known as the M'Naghten Rule, the final crystallization of a long series of formulations beginning in the 13th Century. The rule follows:

> ". . . *to establish a defense on the ground of insanity, it must be clearly proved that at the time of committing the act the accused was laboring under such a defect of reason, from disease of the mind, as not to know the nature and the quality of the act he was doing, or if he did know it, that he did not know he was doing what was wrong*."

It does not appear that medical psychologists of the time had a hand in shaping this Rule in the sense of the exchange between Justice Charles Doe and Dr. Isaac Ray in framing the New Hampshire Rule in this country in 1866.[12] From the reading of the Judges' discussions, there is little to indicate that to them the observations of actual behavior of psychotics, as amply reported by the medical witnesses at M'Naghten's trial, had any relevance to a rule of law.[13] In the Judges' comments there is no mention of medical authority, although in M'Naghten's trial, his counsel, Alexander Cockburn, made great flourish of the authority of Dr. Isaac Ray's evaluations of the medical and legal merits of the preceding notable trials of Arnold, the Earl of Ferrer, Hadfield, and Bellingham.[14] Cockburn gave convincing demonstrations of the compelling force of delusional motivations of the madman, his awareness of his design and execution of his intentions, and of the moral and legal consequences of his acts. The Judges passed over these realities, and merely gave reiteration to an ancient maxim, of which the most that can be said is that it is an amiable figment of the "ought to be."

The Judges put no medical content in the Rule beyond that imposed in the assumption that, if medical men can describe and name mental illness, they can also determine from the same descriptions and designations when mental illness affects reason so as to impair knowledge of the nature, quality and wrongfulness of an act. This Rule prevails in England and in the United States in all jurisdictions except New Hampshire and the District of Columbia. In its lineage the M'Naghten Rule has had an application tied almost exclusively to the retributive death penalty. The Rule is applicable as a defense to any crime, but its use in cases other than homicide is rare.

On examination we perceive that the M'Naghten Rule of today is essentially a literal restatement of the 13th Century medieval dictum of Bracton. Both have the same bones and sinews. A common vocabulary accommodates and perpetuates the early idea that the madman's mind is emptied of reason, will, and felonious intent, the remaining void imparting to him the aspect of the wild man, the brute, the idiot, or the child.

We need not look far to discover in the language of our present criminal law of insanity reminders of the lag which marks the distance between mid-20th Century reality and the conceptions of Bracton and Hale. In a recent American murder trial, the jury was instructed on the law of insanity interpreted by the Supreme Court of Pennsylvania, thirty-six years after M'Naghten, in the following: (1) *general insanity*, which "must be so great in extent and degree as to blind him to the material consequence of his moral duty, that it must have utterly destroyed his perception of right and wrong"; (2) *partial insanity, hallucination and delusion*, a defense upon which the law of Pennsylvania frowns; and (3) *homicidal mania.* In respect to the latter, the Court stated: "We are obliged by force of authority to say to you that there is such a disease known to the law as homicidal insanity; what it is, or in what it consists, no lawyer or judge has ever yet been able to explain with precision." The Court then added this comment: "Physicians, especially those having charge of the insane, gradually, it would seem, have come to the conclusion that all wicked men are mad, and many of the Judges have so far fallen into the same error as to render it possible for any man to escape the penalty the law affixes to crime." [15]

In these classes of mental operations of insanity, as known to law by the force of authority, we can discern in "general insanity" and "homicidal mania" Bracton's raving man (*furiosus*) and brute. In the partitioned segment of the mind set off from an otherwise sane person, we likewise find the "child of fourteen years" and the "partial insanity" of Lord Hale. These descriptions are souvenirs of the forms of thought and practical life in the Middle Ages, when, as Huizinga writes, "once an idea received a name and form, its truth is preserved; it glides, so to say, into a system of spiritual figures and shares in their credibility." [16]

In this metamorphosis of the right and wrong rule is a reiteration of classical phrases and we observe among some legal scholars today the same tendency that moves us to garnish ancient generalizations with new words. In this respect we may take notice of the most recent proposals of the American Law Institute which, at its 32nd Annual Meeting, submitted a substitute for M'Naghten as follows:

"Mental Disease or Defect Excluding Responsibility. (1) A person is not responsible for criminal conduct if at the time of such conduct as a result of mental disease or defect he lacks substantial capacity either to appreciate the criminality of his conduct or to conform his conduct to the requirements of the law. (2) The terms 'mental disease or defect' do not include an abnormality manifested only by repeated criminal or otherwise antisocial conduct." [17]

The second paragraph is designed to exclude the so-called psychopathic personality as a category of mental illness or defect, notwithstanding the fact that this category constitutes the larger problem of present day jurisprudence. It may be that in denying the psychopath a status of mental illness, we are making a confession of our inability to move with our times, to break away from habits of thinking and acting enunciated by Bracton and Hale.

The American Law Institute proposal adheres essentially to M'Naghten. It makes changes in wording and adds a second element which recognizes impairment of volitional capacity as a defense. It abandons the words, "know," "nature," "quality," and "wrong," and adopts the word, "substantial," which removes from the formula the *all* or *none* alternative of cognition imposed by M'Naghten. The Code framers suggest that ambiguity will be minimized with the substitution of the word "criminality" for the word "wrong." The accused must lack "substantial capacity either to appreciate the criminality of his conduct or to conform his conduct to the requirements of the law." If this criterion imposes upon the accused that he must "appreciate the criminality of his conduct," it ignores the observations of everyday life that mentally disturbed persons who commit criminal acts are, as remarked by Queen Victoria regarding Oxford and M'Naghten, perfectly conscious and aware of what they do. They are indeed "substantially" appreciative of the criminality of their conduct. To some it may seem that in abandoning some words and replacing them with others, this proposal will achieve a revelation beyond a verbal circularity. Professor Weihofen comments that "The Model Code formula is a recognition that definiteness in this field is a mere *ignis fatuus.*" He adds, "The most significant and most hopeful thing about the Institute's formula is that a group of eminent lawyers have at long last recognized this fact, and are ready to stop chasing will-o-the-wisps." [18]

From the foregoing, may we echo Lord Erskine's declaration that if the words of the great lawyers are taken literally, "no such madness ever existed in the world." But such madness does exist within a metaphysical system of self-contained legal abstractions which have yet to be established as demonstrations of the mental operations of madmen as they live out their madness in the real world.

The futility of redesigning tests of criminal responsibility of mentally disabled persons is assured as long as we continue to erect test questions which do not reveal the properties of nature but only the properties of language; as long as lawyers put to psychiatrists questions which are unanswerable by psychiatrists; as long as psychiatry has not developed a means of quantifying moral qualities. This futility will persist in the absence of a device whereby one can take the measure of "knowledge" of the nature, quality and wrongfulness, as impaired by "a defect of reason, from disease of the mind"; as long as law insists that the psychiatrist deal with what the eminent jurist, John Biggs, calls "mental states and conditions which do not exist save as legal conceptions." [19]

These arguments are familiar to those who have followed the long controversy over the M'Naghten Rule. It is well trod by the critics of the Rule and can be reduced to the statement that it has never been reconciled with any past or currently accepted medical theory of mental illness. These arguments have come largely from the side of medical men. We are left with the conclusion that M'Naghten, as a matter of law, is an independent, supernatural, and self-contained folk theorem of mental illness, which may or may not have more than an accidental association with the descriptions of a few uncommon mental conditions as understood by psychiatry.

Yet, a further consideration demands our attention. That M'Naghten is alien to accepted medical theories of mental illness is not comprehensive of its essential utility and purpose as a public-centered, arbitrary moral testing device which, as a matter of law, need not have necessarily the verification of science. In fact, M'Naghten was never intended as a test to determine the existence of mental illness in an accused, but on another level of abstraction to determine the public moral issue of penalty. It has been a ritual employed as a moral exercise, not intended for the adjustment of the individual offender, but as a folkway therapeutic adjustment of the community. Considered strictly as a matter of arbitrary law and within its own logic, the M'Naghten Rule has a validity as a moral testing device. The legal view that "a defect of reason, from disease of the mind," impairs one's "knowledge" of right and wrong, or its American Law Institute substitution, is logical as long as it in action remains within an epistemological system of its own. Its validity is independent of what detached observers report of the actual behavior of mentally disturbed persons. The earlier determinations of guilt by fire or water ordeal had a logic of the same order. In time, it may transpire that in following the precedent set by the jurisdiction of the District of Columbia, judges will assign M'Naghten to the same antiquarian company.

The alignments of this century-old conflict in the issue of responsibility of the insane are now better outlined. It is clear that much of the criticism of M'Naghten and kindred tests, on the score of unscientific content, has been misdirected. Considered as a matter of law, M'Naghten has validity as a moral testing device. How well it meets the needs of mid-20th Century society is another matter. A more cogent defect of any test as a matter of law, and subsequently determining penalty, exists in the fact that when set in action in the trial, it does not remain in the realm of law but reaches into the realm of science. This was Justice Doe's reason for setting up the New Hampshire Rule. He concluded that the "great masters of our law" never made the distinction between law and fact in cases of mental illness of the doer. He said, "By setting up various theoretical criteria of legal responsibility, they not only invaded the realm of science, but also betrayed the spirit of the common law." [20]

Restated, it is that the test questions require answers of a medical expert as to the matter of insanity, that is, impaired "knowledge" of right and wrong—a legal concept—for which psychiatry as a science provides no means of analysis. Restated again, the test questions put to the psychiatrists are in fact unanswerable from the substance of psychological science. A psychiatrist who accommodates himself to such test questions does not offer expert opinion out of his model of science, but merely functions as an oracle formulating a public issue.

The sharper focus of these alignments has come with the secularization of knowledge. In this, the physician has attained a larger detachment from value judgments traditionally carried by sickness. In point, the physician no longer views sickness and suffering as moral problems with supernatural implications, but as objective phenomena. Not long ago, mental illness was regarded, even by some medical men, as a retributive visitation which balanced sin either in one's own life or in one's ancestors. The psychiatrist as scientist can neither detach himself completely from moral matters, from a culture of which he is a part, nor can he be impartial or indifferent to procedures which are based on faulty evaluations and superstitions.

In recent times, psychiatrists have become restive in their growing awareness of an ambiguity in their function—as experts reporting upon and interpreting medical matters and specialists answering impalpable moral questions. And this restive spirit has carried psychiatry to a reexamination of the basic assumptions which govern its place and define its limitations in public matters of criminal responsibility and mental disease. Science provides no method of determining "knowledge" of right and wrong in another. Such a method is not taught in medical schools or in institutes of psychiatry. Students are merely told that M'Naghten is in the law and to be ready for it. We come belatedly to the discovery that the only person who can *report* "knowledge" of right and wrong is the accused himself. Even so, every psychiatrist knows from experience that the reports from a mentally ill accused, from children and idiots, cannot be conclusive.

In earlier times, physicians more readily acceded to what was naturally expected of them as members of a privileged class and of a learned profession. This motivation arose as well, perhaps, out of the sense of religious duty to take active part in public moral issues. Today, the physician senses more an impropriety on his part to participate in a transaction which carries him beyond his function as reporter of medical events. He may object on the ground that he cannot integrate his science with the abstractions of the law, but his real discomfort lies in the fact that, in the actions of the law, he is a partisan in a moral decision for which, as a medical man, he is not qualified as an expert on morals. No amount of word magic can overcome the inescapable fact that when a moral test is put to him he is *used*. In doing so, he departs from his science and his ethical position in relation to the afflicted. He cannot bring to justice more than a partisan advocacy and, if he goes beyond his proper function as a reporter of sickness of the accused, he becomes a judge of him.

Why should the psychiatrist take this stand? The development of medico-psychological science has come about only in the measure that the psychiatrist has succeeded in removing himself from the moral descriptions of behavioral deviations. The measure of this success has also been the measure of his awareness of the limitations of his discipline. If his science does not provide a means of quantifying moral qualities, of calibrating guilt, then it is conclusive that when a moral test as a matter of law is imposed on him as an expert—a test which is ultimately a matter for the trial advocates of a moral issue —his ethical position is threatened. If this position removes the psychiatrist from the test questions, there remains the need to define his proper role in the trial setting. Should he participate at all in the issue of responsibility and mental illness? Yes, he should, but only to the extent that he brings to the trial process his data of observation, from which he can draw expert conclusions limited by such data. If the psychiatrist goes beyond them, he is not offering an opinion out of the substance but merely out of prestige.

At this point, our thesis may be reduced to this proposal: (1) that M'Naghten or any similar legal test of responsibility should be procedurally restricted to the triers of fact—that the M'Naghten test questions not be directed to the expert, but only to those charged with making the verdict; (2) that the offering of the expert be restricted to a report and opinion that the accused was or was not so changed as to be regarded as mentally ill, and *how* such illness at the time was related to the offense.

Restated, this proposal suggests a procedural but not a substantive change in the criminal law. This is not a radical departure when considered in the light of the long standing procedures of European courts in which, as Judge Biggs concluded, psychiatrists do not control the decision of the courts. Medical experts "do not more than report on the mental condition of the accused, just as physicians examine and report on the physical conditions of a plaintiff who is asking compensation for physical injuries. *Judges or juries make their own decisions as to the mental condition of the defendant.*" [21] (Italics ours). In a recent case in Philadelphia, the M'Naghten test questions were not put to medical experts, but to the jury in the instructions, and the case reached a verdict quickly and without hardship.[22]

This proposal defines the limitations of psychiatry in the public drama of the criminal trial in relation to the issue of responsibility and mental illness. In this position the psychiatrist reports the medical findings, but does not answer questions pertaining to the moral perceptions of the accused; instead, these questions are put to the triers of fact. This was explicit in the recent ruling of the same court which enunciated the Durham Rule, that the psychiatrist's role is limited to furnishing "medical diagnostic testimony as to mental illness, if any, and expert medical opinions as to the relationship, if any, between the disease and the act of which the prisoner is accused." [23]

At this place we may ask, whither we go? Perhaps we should heed the counsel to Alice who asked, "Cheshire Puss . . . would you please tell me which way I ought to go from here?" "That depends a good deal on where you want to get to," said the cat.[24] Where we want to get to is a decision for ourselves and for lawyers who will shape the language of change and the procedural means to bring rational practises into the jurisprudence of insanity. The law may hang on to M'Naghten for some time, but it is clear that its loveless marriage with psychiatry is over. We can urge our courts and legislatures to realize that our practises do not insure the rights of the mentally ill, and to recognize that the traditional ritual and vocabulary of guilt-fastening and condemnation have, far too much, becomes ends in themselves at the expense of constructive social actions and human values. We may then hope to see some foundation for the rational manipulation of mentally ill persons who commit unlawful acts.

In recapitulation, (1) psychiatry has a place in criminal litigation affecting mentally ill defendants, but only within the boundaries of science. (2) While it is with us, the M'Naghten Rule or any variant of it should not be put to the psychiatrist but only to the triers of fact. (3) The M'Naghten Rule should be abandoned as inadequate to meet the standards for maintaining the rights of the mentally ill, and to insure the fullest use of scientific information in the determination of criminal responsibility. (4) The Durham Rule should replace M'Naghten. Durham provides a full range for the introduction of contemporary science in the issue of criminal responsibility of the mentally disabled. After New Hampshire, Durham was the first step to lift psychiatric testimony out of the uncertainties and caprice of M'Naghten. Subsequent decisions in the same jurisdiction have achieved a clearer prescription of the psychiatrist's role in the witness box. Upon him is being imposed a corrective discipline and an improved communication. In Durham, the law is no longer receptive to psychiatric testimony confused with moral judgments; no longer with testimony which is merely a naming and classifying of textbook entities of mental disease or defect. The psychiatrist is now reminded that he is a reporter of his observations from which he draws and shares his inferences. These may enable the triers to make judicious findings of fact which will affect not only the disposition of the accused but the interests of the community and the redemptive interests of the individual.

Furthermore, legislation affected by the Durham decision may clearly set to right the public apprehension that persons found not guilty by reason of mental disease or defect are set free into the community. To the contrary, an acquittal verdict would automatically commit the individual to indeterminate therapeutic custody, thus uniting the operations of Durham into a rational employment of science in criminal law.

The controversy between criminal law and medical science has not abated since the inception of the M'Naghten

Rule in 1843. We have reached a place where psychiatry as a scientific discipline is qualified to articulate its position. It appears that we now have some guide-lines to the end that psychiatry may confirm its position and make a larger contribution to the jurisprudence of insanity. In this connection, some remarks from Alexander Cockburn's address in the defense of Daniel M'Naghten are particularly appropriate. "I think, then, we shall be fully justified in turning to the doctrines of matured science rather than to the maxims put forth in times when neither knowledge, nor philanthropy, nor philosophy, nor common justice, had their full operation in discussions of this nature." [25]

REFERENCES

1. *"Furiosus non intellegit quid agit, et animo, et ratione caret; et non multum distat a brutis."* Bracton lib. 5, 420b. After Clark C. and Finnelly, W., *Reports of Cases Heard and Decided in the House of Lords,* Vol. X (Little, Brown & Co., Boston, 1874), p. 472.

2. Hale's *Pleas of the Crown,* I, 30. After Bousfield, R. M. and Merrett, R., *Report of the Trial of Daniel M'Naghten* (Henry Renshaw, London, 1843), p. 5.

3. Hawkins, *Pleas of the Crown* (1824, I, 1.) After Weihofen, Henry, *Insanity as a Defense in Criminal Law* (Commonwealth Fund, New York, 1933), pp. 19-20.

4. 16 How. St. Tr. 695. Collinson, G. D., *A Treatise on the Law Concerning Idiots, Lunatics, etc.* (W. Reed, London, 1812), pp. 475-6.

5. Collinson, *op. cit.,* p. 477.

6. 27 How. St. Tr. 1312. After Weihofen, *op. cit.,* p. 22.

7. Bousfield & Merrett, *op. cit.,* p. 28.

8. Collinson, *op. cit.,* p. 636.

9. Weihofen, *op. cit.,* p. 23.

10. Rex v. Oxford 9, Car. & P. 525. After Weihofen, *op. cit.,* p. 24.

11. Biggs, John, Jr., *The Guilty Mind* (Harcourt Brace, New York, 1955), pp. 101-102.

12. Reik, Louis E., "The Doe-Ray Correspondence: A

Pioneered Collaboration in the Jurisprudence of Mental Disease," *Yale Law Jour.*, 63: 183-192, Dec. 1953.

13. Bousfield & Merrett, *op. cit.*, 67 et seq.

14. Diamond, Bernard L., "Isaac Ray and the Trial of Daniel M'Naghten." *Jour. A.P.A.*, 112: 651-656, Feb. 1956.

15. Sayres v. Commonwealth, 88 Pa. 291 (1879).

16. Huizinga, J., *The Waning of the Middle Ages* (Doubleday Anchor Books, New York, New York, 1954), p. 237.

17. American Law Institute, *Proceeding of the 32nd Annual Meeting* (May 18-21, 1955), p. 206.

18. Weihofen, Henry, *The Urge to Punish* (Farrar, Straus & Cudahy, New York, 1956), p. 64.

19. United States ex rel. Smith v. Baldi 192 F. 2nd. 566 (C.A. 3 1951).

20. Reik, Louis E., *op. cit.*

21. Biggs, John, Jr., "Procedures for Handling the Mentally Ill Offender in Some European Countries," *Temple Law Quart.*, 29:255, No. 3. 1956.

22. Commonwealth v. Madara. Ct. Oyer & Term. & Q.S. of Philadelphia County, March Term 1956, Nos. 496, 497, 498.

23. Durham v. United States, 214 F. 2nd. 862 (D.C. Cir. 1954).

24. Carroll, Lewis, *Alice in Wonderland* (The Modern Library, New York), p. 86.

25. Bousfield & Merrett, *op. cit.*, p. 26.

Contrary to the popular and ill-founded belief of the 19th and early 20th centuries, the vast majority of our criminal offenders are neither mentally unbalanced nor mentally deficient. On the contrary, most of the recent research evidence which has been compiled, based on the studies of inmate populations of penal institutions, indicates that, for the greater part, offenders do not differ greatly in mental traits from comparable groups in the general population. It should be kept in mind, however, that a proper assessment of the mental traits of the so-called criminal should be based upon samples other than the highly selective inmate populations we find in our prisons.

During the period of 1930 to 1940, Dr. Ralph Banay, then psychiatrist at Sing Sing Prison, estimated in a study conducted in this institution that approximately 38 percent of the inmates suffered from some type of mental disorder. According to his findings, 1 percent could be classified as psychotic, 20 percent as emotionally immature, and 17 percent broadly categorized as falling into some type of psychopathic behavior. More than a decade before, Dr. Bernard Glueck, in a study conducted in the same institution, estimated that 59 per cent of the prison population were either mentally deficient, retarded, or pathological.

Estimates based on a number of recent studies suggest that possibly 25 percent of the inmates of the nation's penal institutions today suffer from some type of either serious or minor mental disorder. Since we have no yardstick for the population as a whole, it is difficult to determine whether this is a high or a low percentage. There is reason to believe, *nevertheless, that the extent of such disorders among the prison population is not excessive, as compared to groups coming from the same or similar socioeconomic backgrounds in the populace at large.*

For the abnormal individual with criminal and violent tendencies, however, special problems are created in handling and treatment. It is also possible that a considerably larger percentage of less serious offenses may be related to the pathological disturbances of certain individuals. Crime may be a symptomatic behavioral expression of certain types of mental disorders, particularly of the paranoidal and compulsive neurotic types, although it is certainly not an expression of diseased mentality for the vast majority of our offenders.

For the pathological offender, difficult problems of custody and treatment are involved. Since the middle of the 19th century, it has been recognized that certain types of prisoners, because of their obvious mental imbalance and derangement, required special forms of supervision and handling, although it was not until the present century that any substantial beginnings were made to bring about such supervision. Indeed, in this century, distinctions were drawn between "the criminally insane" and "insane criminals"—largely based on the period during which the criminality first manifested itself, before or after conviction for a felony.

Dr. Dean C. Tasher, Medical Director of the Maximum Security Division of the Dr. Norman M. Beatty Memorial Hospital in Indiana, indicates the difficult nature of the problems presented in the custody and treatment of mentally disturbed prisoners. His description of the development of the unusual procedures adopted by the Maximum Security Division of the Beatty Memorial Hospital is not only an interesting presentation of the growth of a unique type of institution but, even more significantly, reflects the changes in our social thinking generally concerning the treatment of the emotionally disoriented offender.

Chapter 18

THE CRIMINAL PSYCHOTIC IN AN INSTITUTIONAL SETTING

Dean C. Tasher, M.D.

Medical Director, Maximum Security Division, Dr.
Norman M. Beatty Memorial Hospital, Indiana.

The care and treatment of the criminal psychotic provides
a unique chapter in the history of penal treatment and mental
care. Of particular interest, it appears to me, is the experience
we have had while caring for the male maximum security
patients of the entire state of Indiana at an institution known
as the Dr. Norman M. Beatty Memorial Hospital in Westville,
Indiana. The Maximum Security Division, not yet five years
old, accommodates nearly 400 men whose criminal background or severe behavioral disturbances have led them to
be committed by one route or another to our care, custody
and treatment. The Security Division is a part of the much
larger civil mental hospital at Westville, which has a census
of 1800 men, women and children, and serves the northern
seventeen counties of the state.

Lying in a rural plain area of northern Indiana, about 12
miles south of the shores of Lake Michigan, the grounds of
Beatty Hospital cover 680 acres, of which 230 acres are
occupied by hospital buildings and landscaped grounds. The
Maximum Security Division is built in a figure-eight, two
story, modern, limestone, red brick and glass brick style,
enclosing two courtyards spreading over four and a half acres.
It is joined with the civil division physically by the mutual

sharing of a 1400-seat auditorium and an ultra-modern gymnasium. All of the hospital buildings, sixteen major units in number, are served by a tunnel system, so that patient movement from October through April is entirely underground. The two divisions have separate tunnel systems and the two patient populations do not mix physically at any time. Careful security precautions prevent access of either patient group to the other and the two divisions have separate treatment programs united only at the top echelon of management.

The external security of the Maximum Security Division is provided by a fourteen foot playground type of fence, with a two foot overhang and mercury-vapor floodlights at fifty to seventy-foot intervals. For psychiatric reasons, guard towers, solid walls, foot-or-motor patrols, or observation posts are not used. For the same reason, the psychiatric aides supervising the patients have no physical safeguards other than their knowledge of the handling of mental patients and their own individual initiative in controlling disturbances. Internal security is maintained by locking the aides into the wards without keys as each shift comes on duty. In addition, all aides are "shaken-down" for contraband. Thus, the patient has nothing to gain by overpowering an aide, since there is no key available. Should an aide be tricked into being used by a patient as a hostage, there is still no assurance of escape since a series of electrically-controlled sally ports prevents any hostage attempt. The principle of compartmentalization is carried out, making it impossible for any patient to progress to the outside from within the building without going through from five to eleven locked doors, each of which is controlled by a man on the other side, either visually or from a series of electrical signals. Television control was considered briefly when this system was put into effect, but discarded because of the relatively poor acuity and loss of detailed movement in darkened areas which are characteristic of a closed circuit television control system.

To incorporate these elaborate security measures into a hospital setting with a therapeutic climate has taken the combined thinking of more than a half-century of doctors and advisors. That it is still not adequate is well known to the present administration, who are now planning a sunken-wall type of peripheral security in a new building, scheduled for completion in 1965. By this means, already utilized by the hospital in Waupon, Wisconsin, and the new St. Elizabeth's Hospital in Washington, we hope to reduce the security factor to a minimal role and thus create an atmosphere completely conducive to treatment and one which contrasts even more sharply with penal conceptions.

Background

To best understand the evolution of our present concepts in the management of the criminal psychotic, it will be helpful to recount some of the highlights of the past in Indiana. At first, there was no realization of the possibility that some criminals might be mentally ill. When the records of the Indiana State Prison at Michigan City are consulted, one is struck by the fact that mental illness, as we recognize it today, was unknown during the early years of the prison. Indiana was admitted to the Union in 1816. Six years later, the first prison was completed at Jeffersonville, Indiana, in the form of a stockade. In 1847, the prison was established and the stockade abandoned. Convict labor was an important economic commodity in those days. Because of this and because of an increasing attitude toward more humane treatment of convicts, it was decided to relocate the existing prison into an area more advantageous for these two goals. A third reason was the growing belief that a coeducational prison, as was the one at Jeffersonville, was not exactly proper.

On March 4, 1860, the present Indiana State Prison was established at Michigan City, Indiana, by the direction of Governor Ashbel P. Willard and with the naming of Charles W. Sealey as the first Warden. As one reads the early record, it becomes apparent that the main objective of the prison in those days was to make it self-supporting by means of renting out convict labor, and that the only thought toward rehabilitative measures took the form of spiritual relief. Ministers of Michigan City were invited to conduct services on the seventh day. Since hard work was also considered essential, a typical contract then for prisoners was that of a cooperage firm who hired fifty prisoners at 38c per day for one year. There was a physician, but he was appointed only on a part-time basis.

In 1900 the movement for obtaining some sort of care for the mentally ill prisoner gained momentum. The prison physician, Dr. Alva L. Spinning, reported that he had twenty-nine insane men during the 1898-1900 biennium. He noted that two were discharged by expiration of sentence, one was paroled, five had been transferred back to the prison population, and one had died. This left him with 20 men "still in restraints." The reader is suddenly made aware that apparently the only treatment known at the time was the one of shackles and straight-jackets.

This same year, Warden George A. H. Shideler, who later became known as an early humanitarian in penal circles, made a plea for a special $1250.00 a year to take care of the "criminally insane." His report contains the following statement:

"We are not equipped for the care and keeping of insane men. We have from 17-20 men that are under restraint and almost an equal number that are weak-minded, and the fact that we are not equipped to properly administer to them during their disturbance leads us to believe that these unfortunates are daily growing to be a charge of the State—while, if a proper hospital were provided, many would be brought back from darkness to light of reason and could be discharged at expiration of sentence or on parole, going out to be self-supporting."

The sum requested, $2500.00 for two years, was actually a brave and optimistic request, since the per capita cost of a prisoner in those days was only 32-3/5 cents, of which 9-4/5 cents were allotted for food.

When the Indiana Hospital for Insane Criminals opened in 1912, expecting an eventual total capacity of 145 patients, there were already 132 men awaiting transfer. The hospital experienced the dismal picture of being overcrowded with 149 patients during its first year of existence. Dr. Paul E.

Bowers, the first physician-in-charge, lamented this fact and also commented that food appropriations were inadequate since inflation had brought about a doubling of food costs since 1909. His total payroll including his own salary was $1400 per month.

The building itself cost $65,000, supplemented by prison labor, and consisted of a three-story center building with two-story wings in a "Y" shape. Later, a third central wing was added. All of the original patient population was derived from inmates of the Prison or the State Reformatory with the exception of 24 patients who were committed as lacking comprehension to stand trial. The therapeutic program at that time consisted of gardening, baseball teams, and Sunday concerts.

In 1944, Warden Alfred E. Dowd, the present warden, reviewed the entire history of the prison and its hospital for insane criminals. He came to the following conclusions:

1) The admission rate to the institution was double the death and discharge rate.
2) 340 patients were housed in an expanded hospital providing only 200 bed-space.
3) Civil hospitals throughout the state were housing criminal psychopaths with homicidal tendencies for want of adequate bed space in the Indiana Hospital for Insane Criminals.
4) The prison hospital proper was performing many duties, such as fever-therapy, laboratory workups, hydrotherapy and the treatment of systemic disease which properly should have been performed in the IHIC.
5) Overcrowding had resulted in only the most severe behavioral problems being referred and sometimes transferred to the IHIC.

For these reasons, Warden Dowd recommended a relocation of the institution to a true hospital setting. Although his original suggestion for the erection of such a hospital on one of the Prison Farms was never carried out, the ultimate decision was made to place the new maximum security hospital at a site not far removed from the prison. The present hospital being discussed was constructed during the years of 1952 and 1953 and opened its doors to receive patients on February 22, 1954. The cost of the physical plant was $2,901,027.00, as a part of the greater Beatty Hospital, which cost in excess of twenty million dollars.

Early Development

Upon its opening, the new hospital received, over a period of about eight months, all of the former inmates of the Indiana Hospital for Insane Criminals. In addition, the various civil mental hospitals and state schools throughout Indiana sought to transfer more troublesome patients to the new institution. Each received the benefit of a formal staffing, which included a psychiatric examination, a psychological battery of tests, and a thorough social history obtained by trained social workers.

The first year of operation, when broken down to statistics, is not too impressive. Of 319 patients admitted, only 19 were discharged, including 9 placed on convalescent leave, 5 outright discharges, and 5 deaths. Of the 300 patients remaining, 42 percent were court-controlled cases (meaning committed before trial as lacking comprehension, after trial as being highly probable to commit further acts because of their mental illness, or those committed as being criminal sexual psychopaths); 42 percent were transferred from penal institutions (including the Prison, the Indiana Reformatory, the Indiana State Farm and the Indiana Boys' School); and 16 percent were civil commitments from the other six state mental hospitals and two state schools for mental defectives.

During the next year of February, 1956, to February, 1957, admissions continued to rise, reaching a level of 107, but because of the radical revision of administrative policy, discharges totaled 83. In the course of this year, severe problems arose. Under the leadership of a very permissive administration, Maximum Security found itself finally caught up with a large portion of trouble. Break-outs, hostage deliveries, and walk-aways led to a flood of unfavorable publicity which reached nation-wide proportions via press services and television networks. The mass hysteria of the public exploded to the degree that the farmers of neighboring townships were walking about armed and taking pot-shots at anything that moved. Former Governor Craig was flooded with telegrams and petitions requesting the immediate removal of anything pertaining to the Maximum Security Division. Although lunar probes were unknown then, it would have been a safe conclusion that most of the country-side would have been glad to see all of the Maximum Security Division and its personnel on such a mission.

To quiet and restore order in the administrative chaos, Dr. Clifford L. Williams, Superintendent of Central State Hospital, Indianapolis, was sent to the hospital as Acting Superintendent as an additional duty, and the author was put in charge of Maximum Security. A series of consultants were called in from the Bureau of Prisons, from the Department of Correction of the State of Indiana, and from the outstanding forensic psychiatrists in charge of Washington's own St. Elizabeth's Hospital. After a thorough study of the problem, Doctors Addison Duval and Francis Tartaglino advised several procedures which have been followed through and proved their worth.

Personality conflicts between nursing and security personnel were eliminated by setting up a new type of aide. This employee can function, after training, in any part of the hospital. He can maintain security through his knowledge of locking patterns and give an intramuscular injection in the buttocks with equal ease. He is the product of 250 teaching hours by our security and nursing training school. With this flexibility, the adjustment of posts by each shift supervisor becomes relatively easy. Having realized and given credit to the most important person in the hospital, the aide on the ward or post, our attention was next drawn to the individual characteristics of the professional staff treating the patients. By attrition, the extremes of either end of the spectrum have vanished. The naive and permissibly inclined have found the administrative climate threatening. By the same token, the vindictive and punitive-minded staff members have found their daily life equally uncomfortable and have left.

In the space of two and a half years, there has emerged a somewhat dedicated staff, who do not watch clocks nearly as much as they watch patients. When a difficult situation arises, no one of the administrative personnel puts in a request for overtime, but rather works until the particular problem is solved.

The Current Situation

After considerable deliberation, it seemed advisable to inaugurate a program based upon what would seem, at first glance, to be essentially group practise or child-raising principles. Limits had to be set and they had to be geared to the concept of the average person out in society. There had to be a system of rules, rewards and punishments. The punishments, however, had to be in keeping with accepted psychiatric doctrines. "Togetherness," a popular theme these days, was permitted so long as both employee and patient had common goals. First, a system of evaluation of each patient was set up. By the time this check-and-answer program was completed, it was obvious that the breakouts and riots probably would not have occurred had such a system previously been in effect. By evaluating each person through the observations to his doctor, chief nurse, security supervisor, social worker, charge aide, and psychologist, a definite security rating was obtained for each patient. The patient was then assigned within his classification to a job within the institution, and an individual program outlined. A rigorous system of ward progression was then put into effect, so that each patient progressed or dropped back a notch according to his output and behavioral characteristics. To better communicate this change of the philosophy to the patient body, group psychotherapy was employed, utilizing psychiatric social workers, industrial therapists, a chaplain and the more experienced shift supervisors, as well as the psychology staff and the physicians and other therapists. Frequently, dual therapists were authorized to meet with certain groups with one of the pair being white and the other Negro. Into these groups were placed the psychotic patients with racial conflicts as a major symptom.

Persons unfamiliar with social situations in Indiana may not realize that the Mason-Dixon line takes a sharp bend upward (which does not show on ordinary maps) so that many residents in the southern half of the state have strong feelings about integration. In this respect, it is often said in Indiana that Kentucky captured the half of the State below Indianapolis without a shot being fired. In the hospital we have to point out and resolve the racial conflicts of those persons whose premorbid biases have led to the production of racial hatred as a symptom of psychosis. Others, with religious conflicts, find considerable relief and ventilation opportunity in the group conducted by the Protestant Chaplain.

Other groups have in common the problem of severe aggressive homosexuality. Another deals with the most assaultive, manipulative and dangerous paranoid schizophrenics in the hospital. There is a group composed of those persons who have been found not guilty of their particular crime because of insanity, but who must satisfy the hospital and the committing court that they are not highly likely to commit a similar crime if released to society. A most important group is the ever-changing orientation group composed of newly admitted patients who have not yet been evaluated and formally diagnosed at staff conference. Still another is the group composed of patients who have recently completed either electric-shock therapy or intensive tranquilizer therapy, or a combination of both, and are now ready to move to a different group. A final group is composed of those patients scheduled to leave in four to six weeks to return to society. Patients move from group to group as their legal and psychiatric status changes. All psychotherapy assignment and control of movement is under the scrutiny of a weekly review by the supervising psychiatrist.

As intimated previously, most of the patients are considerably more sick than the average run of civil mental hospital patients. There is a violent or antisocial trend in most of their psychodynamic patterns. Because of this, rather intensive tranquilizing drug and electric-shock therapy is generally employed. This is done to mobilize them into a psychologically receptive state to fully appreciate the direction of the entire hospital staff toward a more productive and conforming mode of life in the future.

This last goal is the hardest one to point out, since our patients do not have the escapism of going home to the family as their main motivation. Instead, they must be prepared to return to prison for a number of years, or back to stand trial for murder, robbery, or other offenses. Some have the dismal prospect of returning to the civil hospital whose staff rejected them because of violence or some unsavory act and know they will meet human resistance, or counter-transference, when they return to await processing for discharge or continued hospitalization.

Preparations for these steps takes a highly developed degree of communication between staff members, ward personnel and patients. We achieve this by the means outlined above and by including many other administrative devices.

1) Each aide on each shift writes weekly progress notes on each patient, outlining what has happened. These are reviewed by the chief nurse and the pertinent findings given to the appropriate department. After one year and a half of practice, aides become so proficient in this that their notes are now copied and initialed by themselves in the official hospital records. The obvious mutual recognition of the aide's effort and management's approval worked wonders in the amount of material which was reported.

2) Special clubs were organized to appeal to the special interests of various patient groups. However, membership was again placed on a competitive basis of production.

a) The patients assigned to the Occupational Therapy Department were given a simple rule of living—if you produce by helping to repair the broken furniture, the radio and TV sets out of order, the torn clothing and shoes that are run-down, and if you make the needed new items such as bookcases, trellises, bulletin boards and all of the other requests that come in from the various parts of the hospital—both Maximum Security and Civil—then, and only then, can you have Hobby Club meetings on Fridays, complete with all the various arts-and-crafts seen in the usual civil hospital occupational therapy divisions. Patients working in other areas of the hospital were also made eligible for membership if their job performances were satisfactory.

The results of this program were rather amazing. Instead of the endless ashtrays, ceramic heads and hands, and fingerpainting displayed in the usual occupational therapy exhibitions, these men began to produce truly useful objects for their relatives—tables, lamps, trays, purses, bill-folds, tablecloths, mats and rugs. To many, this was the first productive act of repayment that they had ever made to their long-suffering families.

b) The Recreational Therapy Department tried many of the usual supportive approaches with only lukewarm interest being generated. After considerable thought, it was decided to appeal once again to the long-lost ego of the patient. Wards were placed on a "must attend" basis, and although initial resistance was met, soon wards developed a keen sense of intramural competition. Teams and spectator cheering sections were organized, patients were elevated to the rank of assistant coaches, and a semblance of normal, healthy competitive sport emerged from a patient body which had laid on its collective back most of the previous years. Weight-lifting classes, bicycle riding, roller skating, punching bag instruction and gymnastic classes helped work off pounds and energy.

c) The school was reorganized with individual assignments being made through a School Advisory Committee. Uneducables (IQ below 70) were discarded, and others whose education had been interrupted by periods of confinement were permitted attendance if they showed proper interest and diligence. Once enrolled for a month, the student may resign but he must stick out the first four weeks. A monthly review by the school committee determined the length of the educational period and the type of subjects taught, as well as suspensions, enrollments and promotions.

d) The group of patients who had sporadically put out a rather nondescript publication were put on a strictly business basis, with control exerted only mildly by the supporting therapists and with their chief control being the competitiveness against other publications. Time after time, various homosexual groups and other pressure groups attempted to gain control of this organization, but staff disapproval prevented any but the able to become editor or a major assistant. The presence of the others was tolerated by the group so long as they continued to make literary and other working contributions. Editors who knew they were soon to leave the institution trained successors so that the general calibre of the publication remained high. Patients were permitted to voice approval or disapproval of various hospital matters and the comments of the "feature writers" were deleted only if they reflected delusional thought or dwelt upon unfortunately true happenings that were best forgotten. Gentle twitting of hospital routine was not only permitted but encouraged.

e) A Patient Committee, with the aim of self-government, had been in operation since early in 1955 and this operation was carefully reviewed. When analyzed, the discussion seemed to break down to a more or less "fencing tournament" between the selected representatives and the staff members. Many of the demands repeatedly made were impossible to grant because of budgetary limitations. Many other comments were about details of ward management which were primarily maintenance problems—e.g., missing lights, non-functioning stools and wash basins, broken windows, etc. Other representatives persisted in bringing up only self-oriented questions, usually based on the subject of "When do I get out?" The Committee was abandoned and individual communications substituted.

f) The previously used Behavior Clinic, which was an outgrowth of the familiar Deputy Warden's hearings used in most prisons, was completely discarded. The patients' desire was to turn this into a type of mock trial, using patient lawyers, verdicts, sentences and the like. The entire procedure which had previously taken the time of five staff members from one to four hours each morning, was changed to the usual hospital procedure of the psychiatrist going over the morning report with the chief nurse and deciding upon the proper actions to take on the basis of the aide's report. These decisions were then explained to the patient by one of the aide supervisors and if resentment remained, the security supervisor would investigate the whole incident until it was certain that no gross injustice had been authorized. As the psychotherapy groups expanded, these patient-staff bickerings nearly disappeared.

g) Music therapy, both individual and group, utilizing vocal and instrumental media is carried on with four or five performances a year, which are attended by the general public, the Maximum Security patients, the civil patients, and the employee population in separate groupings.

h) The individual patient's special or unusual talents are encouraged wherever possible. We have men who make electronic oscillators, those who study philosophy, others who take correspondence courses to complete high school, some who enter artistic competitions, and others whose particular forte is checkers or baseball-score predicting.

i) The patient is never cut off from communication with the appropriate staff member. On each ward, adequate supplies of paper and pencil make it possible for him to inquire or to complain to the staff member whom he knows through his orientation period. This staff member is the man or woman who is charged with providing the correct answer. Each of these queries (written by the aide if the patient is illiterate) is answered, either in writing or in person. This is a rather large correspondence, since many paranoid patients produce five to ten messages a day.

As a result of all of these techniques, the hospital climate becomes one sharply distinguishable from the usual penal atmosphere. True, we have our single special care rooms, complete with the latest security devices, which are promptly used for the deliberately destructive and malignantly assaultive patient. Each such patient represents a bigger challenge, however, and therapy is intensified so that he spends the least possible time in such isolation.

The seasoned convict, accustomed to inmate bosses and "dealing" with employees at various levels, also often finds himself in such a room rather promptly until the realization comes that such techniques have no rewards in a hospital. Instead, he quickly learns that his only reward comes when a total personality change begins to appear. Informers are shocked to learn that no one will "pay" for their information. If they wish to inform, they may, but their information buys them nothing but a tolerant listener. Generally, the aides and supervisors, by their constant vigilance, have already long since been aware of the situation and taken steps to correct it. Only once in eight or ten months does a patient reveal something that has not already been recorded in the reports.

For the statistically-minded, this program is possible because of an attendant ratio of one employee to 2.33 patients and an overall ratio of one employee to 1.96 patients. Because of this relatively high personnel ratio, the overall per capita cost is $5,730, of which $4,195 represents salaries. However, improved administrative procedures and greater patient turnover have shaved this per capita cost from $6,284 two years ago, in the face of mounting costs generally.

Conclusions:

1) The inherent distrust of penal patients and hospital employees toward each other has been broken down by a successful but constantly growing and adapting program.

2) The emergence of a totally unified employee group, sharing a common belief in a mutually emphasized philosophy of *benevolent firmness*, has contributed to this in a large part.

3) The greater recognition should go to members of the patient body, who have found that the criminal code and the law of the jungle do not produce the day-by-day happiness that a constructive, better-living program of recreation, education, and re-orientation to life provides.

4) Intensive electric shock, drug programs, research studies and other somatic therapies have played a large part in this success, but only to the extent of freeing the patient from the bonds of his confusing mental illness. The polishing process necessary for complete social recovery and relative freedom from recidivism is brought about internally in the patient by his positive reaction to the sympathetic yet limiting attitude of the entire hospital team.

For the lawyer as well as the psychiatrist—but especially for the lawyer—the most difficult problems to handle are those dealing with personal morality and sexual behavior. Within homogeneous societies, in which matters of personal morality and ethical choice are clearly defined and stipulated, customary sanctions are frequently sufficiently strong in their operation to obviate the necessity of legislative action. In the modern industrial world, such societies no longer exist. Further, the enormous impact of modern science has drastically altered our views concerning the theological basis of many forms of personal morality. Traditional taboos against the free public discussion of matters of sexual behavior are still so strongly entrenched, nevertheless, that untrammelled research and discussion are still relatively scarce, despite the extensive violations in practise of many of our conventional standards. The recent disclosures of the Kinsey Report, and since the turn of the century, the constant exposure by the Freudian thinkers of our tradition-bound morality, have held up to candid appraisal and public view segments of personal behavior which have more commonly been confined to restricted clinical observation.

It is for these reasons that the recent voluminous findings of the Wolfenden Committee, officially designated in Great Britain as the Report of the Departmental Committee on Homosexual Offenses and Prostitution, is of such signal interest. Despite reluctance to implement many of the findings of this celebrated Committee into legal statutes, and the popular opposition which so commonly emerges in respect to the substance and recommendations of a report of this scope and

*nature, there is considerable agreement concerning the un-
questioned probity and earnestness in pursuit of their task
by this body. Of equal note is the fact that prominent religious leaders of many faiths, including some of our most
orthodox bodies, have had occasion to praise, and even endorse, certain segments of the Report, particularly those embracing the problem of homosexuality.*

*The duplicity in actual sexual morality, which strongly
reproves in its popular ideology many expressions of what it
considers sexual waywardness, and its readiness nevertheless to
acknowledge the extensiveness of the very practises it deplores, creates almost an insuperable obstacle for law enforcement bodies and the courts. As August Vollmer once said, the
police are asked to handle issues which are primarily matters
of concern for medical and religious bodies. The result is an
anarchy of confusion in public attitudes, court adjudications,
and police procedures. Since the laws themselves are essentially behavioristic instruments, as interpreted in terms of our
rules of evidence, the police are impelled to devise a series of
unsavory, if not actual illegal practises, in order to apprehend
certain sexual offenses. Deliberate entrapment is engaged in as
a matter of almost unavoidable procedure under our contradictory and devious sexual codes.*

*Dr. Canio L. Zarrilli, an experienced criminal lawyer and
lecturer in Police Science at the New York Institute of
Criminology and Brooklyn College, has attempted to sift
through the tortuous currents of opinion and prejudice, and
to examine the findings of the Wolfenden Report in terms
of modern medical and scientific concepts. This is no small
undertaking, particularly within the compass of a single chapter. Nevertheless, he has been able to summarize the findings
of the Committee with considerable effectiveness, and even
more significantly from our standpoint, has attempted to indicate how they may be applied to our criminal statutes in the
United States.*

Chapter 19

A CRITICAL ANALYSIS OF THE ROYAL COMMISSION REPORT ON HOMOSEXUALITY AND PROSTITUTION [1]

CANIO LOUIS ZARRILLI, J.S.D.

Senior Instructor in Law, New York Institute of Criminology; Lecturer, Police Science Program, Brooklyn College.

I. *Introductory.*

The recently submitted British "Report of the Departmental Committee on Homosexual Offenses and Prostitution" (also known as The Wolfenden Committee), appointed on August 24, 1954, to consider the law, practise and procedure relating to homosexuality and prostitution in England, Scotland and Wales, and to report any desirable changes therein,[2] brings sharply into focus a wide range of complex problems. These problems involve a variety of scientific, penological, moral, philosophical, theological, sociological, medical, psychiatric and related issues, invariably involved in the formulation of law, particularly in the sphere of sex. The Committee recognized it was "on the difficult borderland between law and morals, and that this is debatable ground." [3]

In dealing with homosexuality, the Committee [4] established a fundamental theory of approach based upon its understanding of the function of the criminal law; [5] examined "homosexuality" and "homosexual offences" from legal, medical, psychiatric, and statistical points of view; [6] summarized the present law and practise;[7] and proposed changes in law and procedures, giving the reasons for such changes as it recommended.[8] It also extensively examined the treatment of offenders and made proposals for preventive measures and research.[9]

With reference to prostitution, consideration was given to the proper domain of the law in respect thereto and a study was made of street offences,[10] living on the earnings of prostitution,[11] premises used for prostitution,[12] procuration,[13] and related laws,[14] and recommendations presented.[15]

The committee met in private on sixty-two days, of which thirty-two were devoted to the oral examination of approximately one hundred and seventy-four witnesses, including police chiefs, educators, sociologists, lawyers, physicians, psychologists, theologians, judges, psychiatrists, penologists, psychoanalysts and representatives of governmental departments. It received written reports from eleven professional bodies, including biological, ethical, legal, medical, and other societies, and from fifteen other witnesses including judges and medical practitioners. In all, forty-six professional and public bodies and governmental departments were represented.[16] The Committee also examined available statistics relating to homosexual offenses and prostitution [17] and compiled a chart of the law on homosexual offenses in European countries.[18]

It is the purpose of this analysis to examine this report, its methodology, findings and salient recommendations from the following points of view: (a) the basic principles to underlie legislation in the fields of homosexuality and prostitution; (b) the relationship of science, medicine and psychiatry to law and to the problem of legislation concerning homosexuality and prostitution; and (c) the problems which arise in the attempt to formulate specific laws dealing with homosexuality and prostitution.

II. *Basic Principles in Considering Legislation in the Fields of Homosexuality and Prostitution.*

Centuries of ignorance, and hardened tradition, make the problem of a satisfactory approach to sex crimes a veritable

Pandora's box. It was therefore inevitable that the recommendation of the Committee, "that homosexual behavior between consenting adults in private be no longer a criminal offense," [19] should produce a storm of controversy in England on the publication of the report.[20] Indeed, despite the support of this recommendation by many prominent medical men, the Archbishop of Canterbury, and the Roman Catholic Lord Pakenham, the British Parliament declined to consider legislation implementing this proposal, Lord Kilmuir, the Lord Chancellor, declaring: "The Government do not think that the general sense of the community is with the Committee in its recommendation, and therefore they think the problem requires further study." [21]

This result is understandable. Sex has traditionally been viewed in Europe and in America as something innately evil and to be curbed. Whether the basis for this attitude is theological, moral, or historical, the bald fact is that it exists, and must be reckoned with by the legislator and social scientist. John Dewey aptly summed up the matter by quoting the proverb, "Give a dog a bad name and hang him!" and declaring that "Human nature has been the dog of the professional moralists." [22] European, English and American culture and law have reflected this view and considered sodomy with particular abhorrence. Dante, in the Middle Ages, conceived the sodomites in hell, tortured by a continual rain of fire, symbolical of unbridled passion.[23]

Gibbon, in the Eighteenth Century, writing of Roman Law in the framework of the current belief in "Natural Law," advised that "a sin, a vice, a crime, are the objects of theology, ethics and jurisprudence," [24] and described the penalty for "unmanly lust" under Justinian, telling us that "a painful death was inflicted by the amputation of the sinful instrument, or the insertion of sharp reeds into the pores and tubes of most exquisite sensibility. . . ." [25] Blackstone comments on sodomy as "the infamous crime against nature, committed with man or beast . . ." and goes on to say:

"I will not act so disagreeable a part, to my readers as well as myself, as to dwell any longer upon a subject, the very mention of which is a disgrace to human nature. It will be more eligible to imitate in this respect the delicacy of our English law, which treats it, in its very indictments, as a crime not fit to be named. . . . Which leads me to add a word concerning its punishment. This the voice of nature and of reason, and the express law of God determined to be capital, of which we have a signal instance, long before the Jewish dispensation, by the destruction of two cities by fire from Heaven; so that this is a universal, not merely a provincial precept; and our ancient law in some degree imitated this punishment, by commanding such miscreants to be burned to death; though Fleta says they should be buried alive; either of which punishments was indifferently used for this crime among the ancient Goths. But now the general punishment of all felonies is the same, namely, by hanging; and this offense (being in time of popery only subject to ecclesiastical censures) was made a felony without benefit of clergy by statute 25 Hen. VIII C. 6 revived and confirmed by 5 Eliz. C. 17, and the rule of law herein is that if both are arrived at years of discretion, *agentes et consentientes pari poenae plectantur.*" [26]

Puritanical American attitudes are well known. The designation of sodomy as the "Crime Against Nature" persists to this day in the New York Penal Law,[27] and in the penal statutes of other states, some two hundred years after Blackstone. Penalties range as high as life imprisonment, even when by mutual consent between adults.[28] The Wolfenden Committee dealt with a situation where buggery was punishable by life imprisonment under the prevailing English statutes.[29]

In view of this history, of which the Committee was vividly conscious,[30] the basic principle on which the controversial recommendation was founded assumes a paramount importance. After stating that its primary duty was to consider the extent to which homosexual behaviour and female prostitution should come under the condemnation of the criminal law, and encountering the difficulty of adequately defining a crime, the Committee stated:

"We have therefore worked with our own formulation of the function of the criminal law so far as it concerns the subjects of this enquiry. In this field, its function, as we see it, is to preserve public order and decency, to protect the citizen from what is offensive or injurious, and to provide sufficient safeguards against exploitation and corruption of others; particularly those who are specially vulnerable because they are young, weak in body or mind, inexperienced, or in a state of special physical, official, or economic dependence.

It is not, in our view, the function of the law to intervene in the private lives of citizens, or to seek to enforce any particular pattern of behavior, further than is necessary to carry out the purposes we have outlined. It follows that we do not believe it to be a function of the law to attempt to cover all the fields of sexual behavior. Certain forms of sexual behavior are regarded by many as sinful, morally wrong, or objectionable for reasons of conscience, or of religious or cultural tradition; and such actions may be reprobated on these grounds. But the criminal law does not cover all such actions at the present time; for instance, adultery and fornication are not offenses for which a person can be punished by the criminal law. Nor indeed is prostitution as such." [31]

After examining the arguments for and against the recommendation, the Committee continued:

". . . There remains one additional counter-argument which we believe to be decisive, namely, the importance which society and the law ought to give to individual freedom of choice and action in matters of private morality. Unless a deliberate attempt is to be made by society, acting through the agency of the law, to equate the sphere of crime with that of sin, there must remain a realm of private morality and immorality which is, in brief and crude terms, not the law's business. To say this is not to condone or encourage private immorality, on the contrary, to emphasize the personal and private nature of moral or immoral conduct is to emphasize the personal and private responsibility of the individual for his own actions; and that is a responsibility which a mature agent can properly be expected to carry for himself without the threat of punishment from the law." [32]

From the standpoint of philosophical jurisprudence the Committee's point of departure is logically loose and arbitrary, since there is admittedly no formulated definition of "public order and decency" nor any definitely deduced standard of what is "offensive or injurious," nor any fixed basis as to what is to be considered "corruption"; [33] nor is there an adequate definition of the terms "sin," or "crime," nor are we told what is meant by "private morality and immorality," and how the sphere of "private morality and immorality which is . . . not the law's business" is to be determined.[34] The dissent of Mr. Adair points out that the criminal law in and of itself carries with it what he terms a "moral" sanction, and that the removal of this sanction "will be regarded as condoning or licensing licentiousness" concerning tendencies which are currently the cause of much "public concern and disgust," and which have been recognized as criminal by English law for 400 years.[35] Enough has been said to indicate on what delicate and borderline realms lie the correct lines of demarcation of the legislative and non-legislative fields with reference to sexual conduct. None the less, the methodology and conclusions of the Committee must be regarded as modern and in accordance with the thinking of our greatest and most progressive jurists and legal philosophers. Mr. Justice Benjamin Cardozo, after examining history, philosophy and custom as forces in our law, stated: "The final cause of law is the welfare of society"; and pointed out that the "method of sociology" is becoming the greatest force of all.[36] He quotes approvingly the statement of Dean Pound that "perhaps the most significant advance in the modern science of law is the change from the analytical to the functional attitude." [37]

Cardozo's "welfare of society" and "method of sociology," and Pound's "functional attitude" are no more capable of exact definition than the terms used by the Wolfenden Committee—yet, they imply the formulation of legal rules on considerations beyond mere philosophy, history and custom. They make imperative that legislators study scientific, economic, and sociological factors and keep abreast of advancing knowledge in all fields, and that existing rules be modified or changed in accordance with this knowledge, even though such modification should conflict with tradition and custom. The truth is to make the law free, and useful to society. It is obvious that the Committee undertook its task within a sociological framework, rather than within a narrow legalism bound to history, examining the most recent medical, psychiatric and scientific sources and statistics as to the nature and etiology of the subject studied. From these sources, in substance, it found that overt homosexuality, where voluntarily engaged in, was essentially a medical, psychiatric, psychological and social problem not properly within the province of the criminal law at this time. Further, it considered that prostitution should not be the concern of the criminal law, but should be dealt with only when publicly injurious or offensive, or where there existed factors of exploitation. However, it is also obvious that where homosexual relations are coercive, or involve the possibility of physical or psychological injury to the young or immature, the weak, or the feeble-minded, or involve annoyance to others, the law should intervene.[38]

It is significant that in the United States, Judge Morris Ploscowe suggested as early as 1951 that "it might be desirable to eliminate the legal prohibitions against adult homosexual behavior in private altogether. Such prohibitions benefit nobody but blackmailers at the present time. The elimination of prohibitions against adult homosexuality in private would not imply social approval of homosexual conduct." [39] And more recently the same proposal has been reiterated by Dr. Benjamin Karpman, an authoritative psychiatrist and student of sex deviations, while insisting on laws against coercive homosexual conduct and for the prevention of the seduction of the immature.[40] In the light of current knowledge, these conclusions are accepted as sound bases for legislation.

III. *Science, Medicine and Psychiatry in Relation to Legislation in These Areas.*

Medical authorities, and psychiatrists in particular, complain with mounting bitterness at what they consider the blind failure of lawyers, judges and legislators to take into consideration their findings concerning criminals and criminal conduct. The conventional test of legal insanity established in the M'Naghten Rule [41]—the intellectual ability to differentiate between right and wrong—and the failure of the law to consider irresistible emotional drives to criminal conduct are examples of the focal attacks constantly made.[42] On the other hand the legal profession, being accustomed to the legal concept of *mens rea* as the fundamental ground of criminal responsibility, is slow to accept changes which it conservatively feels might substitute a claimed emotional irresponsibility for morally and legally deserved punishment. Psychiatry further insists on "psychopathy," a mental disorder marked among other things by "antisocial behavior" [43] and deficiency in "moral" sense,[44] which it is claimed the law does not fully recognize. The theory has been advanced "that criminality, all criminality, is a psychic disease, having definite psychic causation which, when discovered and eliminated, can bring about the cure of criminality." One proposal has even been made to substitute clinics and hospitals for jails and prisons, and psychotherapists for district attorneys.[45] The same prominent authority ascribes current views of society with respect to homosexuality to ancient religious sources and the concept of sin. "Sin," he says, "is a commodity of the Church without which it can no more exist than a chain grocery store can get along without canned soup. The only sins recognized by science are predatory sins, those which result in definite harm to others." [46]

These and other fields of disputation bring into relief dangerous and undesirable conflicts between scientists, lawyers, psychiatrists, moralists and theologians, and indicate a narrow professional provincialism which is inimical to progress. While science and psychiatry have been extremely useful in discovering new knowledge of the mind and emotions, the centuries-old problem of values which occupied Plato and countless thinkers since, remains with us. This is properly the sphere of philosophy, morality, theology, and law, although scientific discovery must be a necessary consideration. The concept of "crime" as a "disease" runs afoul of the legal definitions of crimes, many of which result from normal acts not involving psychotic or psychopathic tendencies, such as statutory rape. While it is popular nowadays to attack the theological concept of "sin," a more balanced approach would scientifically examine the foundations of the religious sense which has been so influential in the history of mankind, in the manner of William James.[47] There is implicit in the search of the psychiatrist for the etiology, treatment, prevention and cure of homosexuality and prostitution, the social, if not the moral and religious, desirability of correcting such tendencies. The psychiatrist who uses the terms "normal pervert," [48] "antisocial behavior," [49] "moral sense" [49] and the like, is obviously dealing in moral values. More broadly, the scientist who seeks new laws to describe the universe presupposes that the quest is desirable and depends on trust in an ultimate order similar to that of the theologians. The atomic physicist, Dr. Polykarp Kusch, recently stated: "Theories in physics are things of beauty, symmetry and great power. . . . Our curiosity is conditioned by the belief, the implicit article of faith, that there is order in the world." [50] At the same time Ernest Nagel, Columbia University professor of philosophy, speaking of science, said: "Philosophically, basic research has important long-range moral implications. Our values must be related to what we discover about the universe. It is the philosopher's job, his obligation, to teach and to think about such things." [51]

Science, psychiatry, law, philosophy, theology and the so-called "social sciences" should therefore be correlatives, not antagonists, in the ultimate purpose of social welfare and control. The effect of this modern interplay and broadening of horizons is no better exemplified than by the support given by the Archbishop of Canterbury and representatives of the

Roman Catholic Church in England to the medically and psychiatrically approved recommendation that homosexual behavior between consenting adults be no longer a criminal offense. It is also noteworthy that adultery, with its origins in the Decalogue, is not within the sphere of English criminal law, and that this crime is largely a dead-letter in the United States, although severely reprehensible theologically and socially. Judges and legal thinkers are obviously adopting a more scientific and medical point of view, dissociating the strict concept of *mens rea* from conduct where it is apparent from scientific findings that the behavior, as in voluntary homosexuality, is largely the result of psychiatric, medical and social factors. Instead, they are adopting the view that such conduct should not be within the ambit of the criminal law or should be excusable. Chief Magistrate John M. Murtagh of New York City has recommended the treatment of prostitution outside the criminal law as a social problem,[52] and has publicly stated that "private morality is not the business of the Government." On the other hand, psychiatrists have approved legal control in the spheres of coercive sexual activity and the seduction of the immature, and infer the social immorality of such conduct. Further, they seem to accept the legal principle of *mens rea* in connection with such acts, although disagreeing with lawyers as to the components of the *mens rea*.[53] The search for "justice"[54] has fascinated the modern scientist, even as it did Plato.

The Wolfenden Committee, in accordance with its sociological approach, while not presuming to make a detailed study of the nature and etiology of homosexuality and prostitution, nevertheless examined the broad current scientific conclusions on these subjects. These conclusions are sometimes in conflict, particularly as to etiology and treatment, and we, as laymen, are not qualified to render competent judgments on them. The following considerations of interest to the lawyer and legislator, as found by the Committee, are supported by claimed scientific evidence.

As to homosexuality (defined as "a sexual propensity for persons of one's own sex"[55]):

1. Homosexual propensities, according to the psychoanalytic school, exist in all persons.[56]
2. Homosexuality is a condition, sometimes latent, sometimes overt, with varying gradations.[57]
3. The concept of homosexuality as a "disease" involving a distinct pathological concomitant does not appear to be supported in fact.[58]
4. A homosexual drive does not always mean uncontrollability and irresponsibility.[59]
5. In some cases homosexual conduct is "compulsive" or "irresistible," and in such cases, even if penal immunity were granted, society should take preventive measures.[60]
6. The concepts of "invert," "pervert," "natural," and "unnatural" have not been found scientifically useful in dealing with homosexuality.[61]
7. Homosexuality exists in all levels of society, and amongst the most intelligent as well as the dullest.[62]
8. There are no adequate statistics covering the extent of homosexuality, but the number of homosexuals, while a small minority, is much greater than is statistically known. The number of exclusive homosexuals may run over 4% of white male adults, while the total number of those having had some form of overt homosexual experience may exceed 37% of the total male population, as estimated by Kinsey.[63] It does not follow that homosexuality is on the increase.[64]
9. Many homosexuals are also heterosexual.[65]
10. Some homosexuals benefit fom psychotherapeutic or other treatment.[66]
11. Often the adolescent and mentally immature may pass through a transitional homosexual phase.[67]
12. Homosexuality exists in many otherwise intact personalities.[68]

As to prostitution:

1. There is no single definite known cause.
2. Economic factors do not contribute to prostitution

to any large decisive extent, although economic pressure may be a factor in individual cases.

3. Early seduction, broken homes, and bad early environment are factors.

4. Most cases are due to psychological factors, inducing a woman to choose this mode of life as easier and more profitable.[68a]

IV. Problems in the Formulation of Specific Laws Dealing with Homosexuality and Prostitution.

It is evident that our sex laws rest on an archaic foundation. With reference to homosexuality, the law, with its traditional failure to readily conform to new thinking and new trends, still bears the imprint of the era of Blackstone, both in England and America. As late as 1949, sodomy, or "the crime against nature," was a felony in every state of the United States, with penalties ranging from one year to life imprisonment at hard labor.[69] The situation was still more monstrous from a scientific point of view because many statutes, like the New York law, made no distinction between voluntary and coercive conduct, and included fellatio and cunillingus between persons of the opposite sex, or even though married—essentially heterosexual conduct. Intercourse with an animal or bird or with a dead body (bestiality and necrophilia) were often joined with the sodomy provisions and punished in the same manner.[70]

The situation remains substantially the same in the United States today except that there has been some modification, as in New York in 1950, where homosexual conduct between consenting adults and youths from 16 to 21 was reduced to a misdemeanor.[71] The law did retain certain features, such as coercive conduct and conduct of adults with the immature under 18 as a felony, and adding the so-called "sexual psychopath" laws permitting a person convicted of sodomy and certain other crimes like rape, to be sentenced to an indeterminate term of one day to life after psychiatric examination.[72] While a statute such as the New York Statute reflects definite recognition of medical and psychiatric knowledge, the insistence on maintaining necrophilia and bestiality in the same statute hardly appears realistic. Such practises do not appear to be related to homosexuality, although necrophilia is said to be associated with extreme sadism,[73] and could be dealt with under the indeterminate sentence provisions of the statute as a psychopathy. Further, some statutes make no distinction between types of homosexual conduct,[74] as anal or oral, passive or active, and as to sex of the partner, so that bisexual conduct involving fellatio or cunillingus may be covered in the same statute as homosexuality.

The Wolfenden Committee was presented with the consideration of typical sex statutes which under English law included buggery,[75] punishable by life imprisonment, even when committed by consenting adults in private; attempted buggery, ten years imprisonment; indecent assault [76] by a male on male, ten years imprisonment; indecent assault by female on female, two years imprisonment; acts of gross indecency [77] between males, procuring acts of gross indecency between males, attempting to procure acts of gross indecency between males, two years imprisonment; assault with intent to commit buggery, ten years imprisonment; soliciting of males by males for immoral purposes, six months to two years; and offenses against bye-laws (involving acts of indecency between persons of the same sex), fine five pounds.[78]

Likewise, it considered the law of Scotland, providing for life imprisonment for sodomy and attempted sodomy.[79] In this unscientific framework of law, the Committee suggested the elimination as a crime of homosexual behavior between consenting adults in private, an adult being defined as a person twenty-one years of age or over. It recommended that buggery, if it was to be retained as a separate offense at all, be classified as a misdemeanor to avoid the legal requirement requiring misprision of felony and thus encourage homosexuals to confide in a doctor who might technically, under English law, be otherwise required to report felonious homosexual conduct.[80] It further suggested that for the protection of the immature, the penalty of life imprisonment be retained for buggery with a boy under sixteen [81] and recommended that the crime of indecent assault embrace all acts of buggery or gross indecency against the will of the partner, whatever his age, providing for ten years' imprisonment. Further provisions included: buggery by a man over 21 with a person above 16 and below 21, not amounting to indecent assault, punishable by five years' imprisonment; buggery or gross indecency committed by a person under twenty-one with consenting partner below that age, punishable by two years imprisonment. However, it was proposed that no prosecution of a child over sixteen and under twenty-one should be instigated except in special circumstances with the sanction of the attorney-general.[82] The proposed scale of penalties, increasing the maximum penalties for acts of gross indecency other than buggery committed by a man over twenty-one with a consenting partner below that age, was because of the increased danger of psychological damage to younger persons.[83] While it might appear illogical to keep homosexual behavior between persons under twenty-one within the sphere of criminal law, while exempting adults, the rationale is the sound medical ground of keeping youths under control for treatment.[84]

Bound up with the nature of the laws is the question of penalties and treatment.[85] Since there is evidence that some homosexuality is transitional, the Committee looked with approval on probationary measures,[86] preferably voluntarily entered into on condition that the convicted person agree to psychiatric treatment.[87] It was pointed out that twenty-four percent of the persons convicted during 1955 in England of homosexual offenses punishable with imprisonment were put on probation.[88] In the work of reorientation, the Committee recognized the place of the clergyman, the psychiatric social worker, the probation officer, the adjusted homosexual, as well as the doctor.[89] The Committee further revealed that in 1955, about 15 percent of imprisoned sexual offenders were found suitable for psychotherapeutic treatment, and further estimated that in the sphere of individual or group treatment that of those selected for treatment, about one-half benefited therefrom.[90] Particular attention was given to treatment of young offenders from fourteen to twenty-one, the usual recommendation being committal to an approved Borstal detention centre or school, or probationary attendance at an attendance centre, to educate boys in the proper use of leisure time.[91]

The Committee recognized the fundamental consideration of punishment as a deterrent and preventive,[92] although there is some evidence that there is as much recidivism among imprisoned homosexuals as among probationers.[93] On the other hand, it recognized a distinct group whom it would be always necessary to submit to compulsory detention for the protection of others.[94] This factor has been clearly recognized in the United States by the adoption of so-called "sexual psychopath laws," although such laws have often been criticized on the ground that there is no scientific way to detect a "psychopath," or any sure form of treatment, besides the difficulty of defining a "psychopath."

A most serious problem in connection with the treatment of offenders—particularly in prisons—is the lack of qualified and experienced psychiatric personnel. This situation is well known in the United States, where there is a shortage of psychiatrists, and the same is true in England.[95] It is also known that such doctors and probationers as are attached to prisons or reformatories perform excellently, but their work is seriously hampered by limitation of time. A justified resentment against society will often result in a prisoner who has been informed on sentence that he is to receive treatment while confined, and then finds no psychiatrist to treat him. It is also well known that others besides sexual offenders are in need of such treatment.[96] The problem of furnishing sufficient medical and psychiatric help is one with which the medical societies and state legislatures should immediately deal. Complete medical and psychiatric reports should be available to a court on sentencing.

Another serious problem is that of gathering satisfactory statistics on the medical as well as criminal aspects of homosexuality and prostitution. Doctors, in examining patients, do not always use the same technique or interrogations. Each case presents so many individual factors that it is difficult to draw conclusions of general validity. However, the type of medical statistics to be gathered and their validity should be determined by a single, unified national or even international medical board, acting in conjunction with state medical and law enforcement agencies. Criminal statistics are notoriously inaccurate for wide divergencies, both as to differences in methods employed, varying in emphases on arrests and convictions, and deficiencies in reporting. Such statistical studies as exist in relation to sex crimes, while painstakingly prepared in certain instances and analyzed,[97] comprise too small a basis on which to draw valid conclusions as to etiology, treatment, nature, recidivism, and other vital factors. There should be adopted a uniform crime reporting system [98] throughout the United States, together with accurate norms of interpretation. The statistics to be gathered in connection with sex crimes should be determined with the cooperation of medical and psychiatric authorities. It is regrettable that adequate statistical approaches, so essential in any social science, have been neglected in dealing with such vital problems as crime and penology.

Prostitution is essentially a social, medical and psychiatric problem, rather than a legal problem. Nevertheless, laws aimed at the procurer, transporter, operator, abducter and "pimp" are properly in the scope of the law, as they involve exploitation. The Wolfenden Committee examined and rejected the concept of legalized prostitution as giving an active legal sanction to a socially undesirable traffic.[99] It considered public solicitation for immoral purposes the proper sphere of legal control, while exempting prostitution in itself from criminal responsibility because the law "is not concerned with private morals or with ethical sanctions." [100]

The focus in any consideration of prostitution must be the prostitute herself. The Committee adequately pointed out the lack of knowledge of etiology as to prostitution.[101] The laws aimed at the prostitutes usually provide for fine or imprisonment on proof of solicitation,[102] often factually difficult to establish and resulting in making deception, chicanery and entrapment common police procedures. Indeed, such procedures are virtually essential in order to procure convictions. The consequence is frequently blackmail, perjury and corruption,[103] similar to that which occurs in connection with the prosecution of homosexual offenses.[104] Another practical factor is that the frequenter or "customer" of the prostitute, although sometimes violating laws aimed at him, is seldom prosecuted or apprehended except to testify against the prostitute. History has shown that no law has ever been able to stamp out the practise, and it has been suggested that legal sanctions against the prostitute be abandoned entirely and that the prostitute be compelled to submit to psychiatric treatment instead. This would still involve a legal determination as to when and under what conditions the courts might compel such treatment. Undoubtedly, the problem is a social rather than a legal one, in which early education, improved economic conditions, and fuller dissemination of sexual information would help. Need for further study of etiology is indicated.[105]

As indicated, the Wolfenden Committee did not attempt to abolish prostitution or to make prostitution illegal—feeling the law ought not to try to do so, and not believing it could be successful even if it tried. The Committee felt that the most the law could do was to free the streets from offensive practises and be made tolerable.[106] It commended the police practise of formal caution and reference to a social worker,[107] and provided for a progressive increase of penalties for street offences running from a maximum fine of forty shillings for a first offense to three months' imprisonment for a third or subsequent offense.[108] It termed the present repeated 40 shillings fine a "farce." The Committee struggled with the difficult requirement of "annoyance" under English law as a basis for the arrest of a common prostitute, and recommended the abolition of this requirement.[109] If the police are to be given power to arrest prostitutes in the streets or elsewhere as common prostitutes or for solicitation, it is difficult to see how any legal method may be devised to reduce the obvious invitation to entrapment, blackmail, and corruption, except by increasing penalties for these activities. There seems to be no adequate solution to this problem.

The recommendation of the Committee for continued research in both homosexuality and prostitution is noteworthy.[110] This should also be done in the United States not only with reference to sex crimes but to all crimes. A uniform code of laws dealing with sex crimes based on a national study is also necessary to put an end to the present patch-quilt of archaic confusion.

In respect to possible application to the United States, and based upon the voluminous findings of the Wolfenden Report, the following summary may be offered in respect to the problem of homosexuality:

1. Homosexual conduct between consenting adults in private should not be a crime. The age of adulthood should be fixed at such age as doctors and psychiatrists establish as the limit of maturity where sex habits are fixed. This may be twenty-one years.

2. Homosexual conduct between consenting persons who are not adults (under 21) should be dealt with by the courts, retaining criminal aspects no higher than misdemeanor in order that jurisdiction may attach, but with provisions for treatment and control of the offender under the alternatives of probation or medical institutionalization. Children under 16 could be dealt with in the same manner as juvenile delinquents.

3. Homosexual conduct between consenting persons, one of whom is adult (over 21) and the other not adult, should be more severely considered against the adult than against the non-adult, with the adult being treated as a felon and the non-adult as a misdemeanant or offender. The age of legal consent should be based on medical opinions, possibly from 16 to 18. Penalties for homosexual conduct with younger and more immature persons should be more severe.

4. All homosexual conduct by persons of legal responsibility (16 or over) by coercion, or with persons incapable of giving consent, such as idiots, imbeciles, or lunatics, or persons under the influence of drugs or intoxicants, should be dealt with feloniously.

5. Courts should have wide latitude in sentencing without fixed minima, and without limitations on suspension of sentence or probation, in order that offenders may be given treatment if advisable.

6. Psychiatric, psychological and medical examinations,

as well as probation reports, should be available to the court in all cases in which they are deemed advisable before sentence. Should such reports indicate a "psychopathic" condition, courts could be empowered to sentence for indeterminate terms up to life.

7. Legislatures and medical societies should make immediate provisions for procurement of sufficient medical and psychiatric personnel for hospitals, prisons, and reformatories.

8. Uniform sex laws, including statutes covering homosexuality, should be adopted, and central research and criminal statistical bureaus established in the United States.

With reference to prostitution:

1. Prostitution as such should not be a crime, but dealt with socially and by education.

2. Transportation, procuring, "pimping," abducting, and acts of commercialization should be crimes of the grade of felony, and severely punished.

3. Solicitation should not be criminal, but at most an offense, and jurisdiction should be given for institutionalization or other treatment.

4. Blackmail, perjury, and bribery should be punished more severely in connection with prostitution and solicitation for immoral purposes than for other crimes.

5. Uniform laws should be adopted for prostitution in the United States, and a central research and statistical bureau established.

V. *Conclusion.*

It has been attempted to discuss the main points of the Wolfenden report, and its practical values to us, on a subject clouded in ignorance and prejudice. The Report opens up a rich and wide variety of fields of exploration. The Report, modern in spirit and thinking, clear and brilliant in exposition, is a monumental example of the sociological and scientific approach to the problem of legislation and justice, no matter what difficulties may be presented in the early adoption of its recommendations.

REFERENCES

1. *Report of the Committee on Homosexual Offenses and Prostitution.* Presented to Parliament by the Secretary of State for the Home Department and the Secretary of State for Scotland by Command of Her Majesty; September, 1957. London, Her Majesty's Stationery Office, 155 pp. (This will hereafter be referred to as the "Report").

2. Report, Par. 1, p. 7.

3. Report, Par. 224, p. 79.

4. The Committee was composed of seventeen members, two of whom resigned prior to the rendition of the final report, and included, among others, lawyers, legislators, physicians and theologians. It was headed by Sir John Wolfenden, C.B.E., as chairman. Report, p. 2.

5. Report, Paragraphs 12-15, p. 9.

6. Report, Paragraphs 17-47, pp. 11-19.

7. Report, Paragraphs 48-77, pp. 20-31.

8. Report, Paragraphs 78-147, pp. 31-53; 115-116.

9. Report, Paragraphs 148-221, pp. 54-78.

10. Report, Paragraphs 222-297, pp. 79-98.

11. Report, Paragraphs 298-307, pp. 98-101.

12. Report, Paragraphs 308-336, pp. 101-109.

13. Report, Paragraphs 337-341, pp. 109-112.

14. Report, Paragraphs 347-354, pp. 112-114.

15. Report, pp. 115-117.

16. Report, pp. 152-155.

17. Report, pp. 130-148.

18. Report, pp. 149-151.

19. Report Page 115. (The Committee fixed the age of legal consent at twenty-one years. Offenses by and against persons under that age, even though voluntary and by con-

sent, should be retained under the jurisdiction of the law for the protection of the immature. Report, Paragraphs 65-72, pp. 25-27. See also Paragraph 62, p. 25).

20. See London Despatch of Thomas P. Ronan, *New York Times*, September 22, 1957.

21. *Time* Magazine, December 16, 1957, pp. 22-25.

22. Dewey, John, *Human Nature and Conduct*, p. 1.

23. Dante Alighieri, *Divina Commedia*, Inferno, Canto XV.

24. Gibbon, Edward, *Decline and Fall of the Roman Empire*, 3 vols., Modern Library Edition, Vol. 2, p. 722.

25. Gibbon, Edward, *op. cit.*, Vol. 2, p. 724.

26. Blackstone, Sir William, *Commentaries*, Part IV, Public Wrongs. Chapter XV, Paragraph IV. (Chitty Edition, Vol. II, pp. 165-166).

27. New York Penal Law, Section 690. (In 1950 this section read: "Crime against Nature; sodomy. Sec. 690. A person who carnally knows in any manner any animal or bird; or carnally knows any male or female person by the anus or by or with the mouth; or voluntarily submits to such carnal knowledge; or attempts sexual intercourse with a dead body is guilty of sodomy and is punishable with imprisonment for not more than twenty years.")

28. Sherwin, Robert Veit, *Sex and the Statutory Law*, Part I, pp. 37, 82.

29. Report, Paragraphs 77, 78, pp. 29-31.

30. Report, Paragraph 60, p. 24.

31. Report, Paragraph 13, 14, p. 10.

32. Report, Paragraph 61, p. 24.

33. Report, Paragraphs 12-16, pp. 9-10.

34. Report, Paragraph 61, p. 24.

35. Report, pp. 118-119.

36. Cardozo, Benjamin, *The Nature of the Judicial Process* (New Haven, Yale University Press), pp. 65-66.

37. Cardozo, Benjamin, *op. cit.*, 73, quoting Pound, Roscoe, *Administrative Application of Legal Standards*, Proceedings of American Bar Association, 1919, pp. 441, 449.

38. Report, Paragraphs 17-47, pp. 11-20.

39. Ploscowe, Morris, *Sex and the Law*, 1951, p. 213.

40. Karpman, Dr. Benjamin, *The Sexual Offender and His Offenses* (The Julian Press, Inc., 1957), p. 328.

41. Snyder, Orvill G., *Who is Wrong about the M'Naghten Rule and Who Cares? Brooklyn Law Review*, Vol. XXIII, No. 1, December 1956.

42. Karpman, Dr. Benjamin, "Psychiatry and the Law," *The Journal of Criminal Law and Criminology*, Vol. 48, No. 2, pp. 164, 169.

43. Karpman, Dr. Benjamin, *Ibid.*, p. 168.

44. Karpman, Dr. Benjamin, *Ibid.*

45. Karpman, Dr. Benjamin, *The Sex Offender and His Offenses*, p. 526.

46. Karpman, Dr. Benjamin, *Ibid.*, p. 328.

47. James, William, *The Varieties of Religious Experience*.

48. Karpman, Dr. Benjamin, *The Sex Offender and His Offenses*, p. 416.

49. Karpman, Dr. Benjamin, "Psychiatry and the Law," *The Journal of Criminal Law and Criminology*, Vol. 48, No. 2, pp. 164, 169.

50. Quoted in *New York Times Magazine*, Sunday, November 24th, 1957, p. 93.

51. Quoted in *New York Times Magazine*, Sunday, November 24th, 1957, p. 98.

52. Murtagh, John M., *Cast the First Stone* (New York, 1957). N. Y. *Daily Mirror*, September 9, 1957.

53. Karpman, Benjamin, *The Sexual Offender and His Offenses*, pp. 327-328.

54. Karpman, Benjamin, "Psychiatry and the Law," *The Journal of Criminal Law and Criminology*, Vol. 48, No. 2, p. 164.

55. Report, Paragraph 18, p. 11.

56. Report, Paragraphs 20, 29, pp. 11, 115.

57. Report, Paragraphs 18, 20, 21, 22, 24; pp. 11, 12, 13.

58. Report, Paragraph 30, p. 15.

59. Report, Paragraph 32, p. 16.

60. Report, Paragraph 33, p. 16.

61. Report, Paragraphs 35, 36, pp. 16-17.

62. Report, Paragraphs 36, p. 17.

63. Report, Paragraphs 37-47, pp. 17-20.

64. Report, Paragraph 42, p. 19.

65. Report, Paragraph 193, p. 66.

66. Report, Paragraphs 194-196, pp. 66-67.

67. Report, Page 73.

68. Report, p. 68.

68A. Report, Paragraph 223, p. 79.

69. Sherwin, Robert Veit, *Sex and the Statutory Law*, Part I, p. 82.

70. See New York Penal Law, Section 690, in effect 1950, and prior thereto. See Reference 27.

71. See New York Penal Law, Section 690, as amended in 1950.

72. New York Penal Law, Sec. 690, 2189 (a), 1944 (a).

73. Karpman, Dr. Benjamin, *The Sexual Offender and His Offenses*, p. 358.

74. Sherwin, Robert Veit, *op. cit.*, pp. 34-38.

75. "Sexual intercourse (a) per anum between man and man; or (b) in the same manner between man and woman, or (c) in any manner between man or woman and beast." Report, p. 30.

76. "An assault accompanied by circumstances of gross indecency on the part of the person assaulting towards the person alleged to have been assaulted." Report, Paragraphs 95, 96, p. 36.

77. "Gross Indecency" is not defined by statute. Report, Par. 104, p. 38. This is often typical of statutes in the United States, which frequently omit specific descriptions of the offense. See New York Penal Law, Sec. 722, Sub. 8.

78. Report, Paragraph 77, p. 30.

79. Report, Paragraph 77, p. 30.

80. Report, Paragraph 94, p. 35.

81. Report, Paragraph 91, p. 34.

82. Report, Paragraph 91, p. 34; Par. 72, p. 27.

83. Report, Paragraph 92, p. 35; and Paragraphs 97-8, p. 37.

84. Report, Paragraph 68, p. 26; Paragraphs 73-4, p. 28.

85. Report, p. 76.

86. Report, Paragraphs 153, 154, p. 55

87. Report, Paragraphs 198-199, p. 68.

88. Report, Paragraph 153, p. 55.

89. Report, Paragraph 196, p. 67.

90. Report, Paragraph 197, p. 67.

91. Report, Paragraphs 159-166, pp. 56-59.

92. Report, Paragraph 201, p. 69; Par. 170, p. 60.

93. Report, Paragraph 200, pp. 68-69.

94. Report, Paragraphs 202-203, p. 69.

95. Report, Paragraph 180, p. 62.

96. Report, Paragraph 183, p. 63.

97. See, for example, Ellis, Dr. Albert, and Brancale, Ralph, M.D., *The Psychology of Sex Offenders*, A Study of Patients at New Jersey Diagnostic Center, 1957.

98. Wallace, Robert, "Crime in the United States," in *Life Magazine*, September 9, 1957, for a discussion of this matter, *inter alia*.

99. Report, Paragraph 292, p. 97; Paragraph 226, p. 80.

100. Report, Paragraph 226, p. 80.

101. Report, Paragraph 297, p. 98.

102. Report, Paragraphs 234-256, pp. 82-84.

103. Murtagh, John M., *Cast the First Stone* (New York, 1957).

104. Report, Paragraphs 109-112, pp. 39-41.

105. Report, Paragraph 297, p. 98.

106. Report, Paragraph 285, p. 95.

107. Report, Paragraph 270, p. 91.

108. Report, Paragraph 275, p. 92.

109. Report, Paragraph 256, p. 87.

110. Report, Paragraphs 213-226, p. 79.

Part IV
Controversial Approaches
to Crime and Criminals

In conjunction with our discussion in Chapter X, note was taken of the significant area of criminology known as criminalistics, which deals with the application of scientific principles in the identification of offenders and the determination of evidence. The examination of handwriting, with a view towards determining the authenticity of documents and signatures, has been employed by the courts since the last century. The documentary specialist has carved for himself a significant niche in the courts as an expert witness. The use of handwriting, however, as a means of probing the individual's mentality has been regarded with considerable suspicion and skepticism by American law enforcement bodies and the courts, and indeed, by academic criminologists as well.

Part of this distrust, it seems, stems from the association of such techniques, in the minds of many American criminologists, with the discredited and pseudo-scientific practises of the so-called occult sciences, phrenology and related practises. There is a deeply ingrained suspicion, amounting almost to a positive aversion, on the part of most accredited students of human behavior to consider points of view and techniques which deviate from institutionalized scientific tradition. The social sciences in America, despite the encouraging progress made in this century, have placed a stamp upon their professional pursuits which is indelibly American and perhaps, for this very reason, quite parochial. Behavioral evidences which are not subject to stipulated forms of comparison and control, and, above all, which do not meet certain standards of measurement, are, more often than not, greeted with considerable reserve.

This partially explains, perhaps, the other reason for the reluctance with which certain concepts and practises have been given an adequate hearing in reputable circles—and that is the popular misgiving concerning the validity of certain forms of psychiatric evidence, particularly of the psychoanalytical variety. European criminology and criminalistics, however, have been far more catholic in their readiness to consider and to use materials from a variety of fields which have been, from the outset, suspect in America. The psychological examination of handwriting, with a view towards assessing the individual's personality and motivational patterns, has not only found an accepted place in European criminalistics, but even more, a respectable place in many of Europe's distinguished institutions of higher learning. Although academic acceptance is not an invariable guarantee of public recognition, it does, frequently, serve as a preliminary indicator of a change in public attitude.

With the recent heightened interest in the use of a variety of projective tests and instruments, not far removed in nature from the interpretation of handwriting, a beginning interest, and possibly a greater degree of acceptance, is being manifested among criminologists and certain behavioral scientists. Within the logico-empirical framework set up by the careful scientific worker, the analytical and comparative study of handwriting specimens may afford significant clues to both overt and covert forms of human expression. Its potential use as a screening device, during a period when we are becoming increasingly concerned with predictive techniques, is not easily to be dismissed.

Klara G. Roman brings to the analysis of handwriting, as a potential tool for the criminologist and the behavioral scientist generally, the true scientist's concern for objectivity and the use of logical inference within carefully stipulated and operationally defined frames of reference. Her skill and integrity are of high professional calibre and her insights have been enriched by her wide clinical knowledge. The development of tools of research, and our need to comprehend more fully the motivations and conditions which facilitate criminal behavior, constitute the most difficult, and at the same time, the most challenging area of criminology. Science in this area, as well as in all others, must retain the resilience and flexibility of view which, without sacrificing its rigid logico-empirical principles, is our only guarantee for wider understanding and insight.

Chapter 20

PSYCHOGRAPHOLOGY IN CRIMINAL INVESTIGATION

Klara G. Roman

The New School for Social Research

Historical Background

Toward the end of the nineteenth century the natural sciences began to turn from a crude empiricism to more scientific methods—a trend shared by modern police science —towards a scientifically based criminology. Where heretofore the investigator relied on experience plus his "sixth sense," he now turned to science for help in the search for and seizure of incriminating evidence. In fact, the tools of field and laboratory work became so sharpened that highly specialized studies were necessary to master them: sometimes a single hair of a person or a single thread of a fabric proved sufficient for tracking down a criminal.

But in the long run, both public and criminologist began to realize that these refined and precise methods, though highly successful in the search for tangible clues, were less effective when it came to exploring the human situation. Such methods proved ineffective in furnishing evidence of certain conflicts, defects, and mental aberrations which appear in criminals more frequently than in the general population.

Indeed, such information is most difficult to obtain through interrogatory procedure, for what a person says or writes about himself is not necessarily valid. There are things he does not want to tell because it might prove embarrassing or incriminating. Other things he cannot reveal because they are repressed and forgotten, or, working deep down in the hidden depths, they escape his awareness.

Nevertheless, police have to know and have to find ways and means of drawing facts from regions closed to *direct* investigation. Here, modern psychology offers assistance through *indirect* methods such as through the use of projective techniques. Among these, Rorschach, Thematic Apperception, Figure Drawing, and the Szondi Tests, and many others, help induce unselfconscious revelations, turning the subject into an "informer" on himself.

Criminologists soon became appreciative of the practical use of these personality tests. L. K. Frank, in fact, likened them to the indirect methods of analysis that have been developed in other sciences, such as the use of X-rays and electrical measurements.

French and German criminologists include graphology as another valuable *indirect* method of personality study. Though akin in many respects to the projective techniques, graphology has a broader scope. More flexible in its modes of application, it is based not merely on the interpretation of imaginative projection, but, more significantly, upon the interpretation of expressive movements as seen in handwriting.

Graphology, the analysis and interpretation of handwriting, is a widely employed psychological tool. It has quite a venerable lineage in Europe, where it has been taught for decades at leading universities and medical schools as an "applied science." European criminologists early recognized the value of identifying information afforded by graphology. The distinctive nature of the handwriting process, together with the fact that every handwriting is unique and never naturally duplicated by any other, led clinical and forensic psychologists to conclude that analysis of handwriting is valuable in penetrating to the *inner ego* of the writer.

This is clearly recognized in Hans Gross' classic work on *Criminal Investigation*, first published in 1904, and republished many times since, the latest edition being that of 1950. Gross states that we can usually tell at first sight whether a specific handwriting is that of a scholar or a laborer, of a glamorous socialite or a compulsive accountant. "In fact," he adds, "once we admit this much, we are in a sense already practising graphology." He even went so far as to say that "the most important thing which an investigating officer can extract from a writing is the *character* of an individual."

A definite contribution to the recognition of graphology was Binet's famous experiment in correlating character traits with handwriting features. It attempted to establish conclusively that *honesty* and *intelligence* clearly show up in the graphic indices of handwriting. French findings were soon taken up by German scientists who carried on further experimental investigations and clinical work with customary thoroughness. Among the host of neurologists, psychologists, and psychiatrists, we need only mention Kraepelin, who devised a scale for measuring writing pressure and speed in the handwriting of the normal and mentally disturbed. The *Kraepelin* scale is still used for clinical purposes—by Kretschmer and Enke, for instance, and many others.

This line of experimental work, and the development of tools for psychometric and statistical research, were further advanced by the graphodyne devised by myself over twenty-five years ago and more recently refined along electronic lines by one of my former students, C. A. Tripp.

Of more recent vintage is the work of the Swiss graphologist, Max Pulver, who discussed the dynamics revealed in the script of notorious criminals in his book, *Trieb und Verbrechen in der Handschrift (Drive and Crime in Handwriting)*. A more extensive study along similar lines has been undertaken by R. Wieser, handwriting examiner and graphologist to the Courts and Police of Austria. Wieser studied the handwriting and case histories of about nine hundred criminals and compared them with nondelinquents equated for age, sex, and socioeconomic status. She found that there is *one* characteristic—an abnormality common to every criminal handwriting, known as "gestörter Grundrhythmus," i.e., disturbance and weakness of the basic rhythm. This seems to provide a clue in handwriting to *general criminal disposition*.

In addition, Wieser noted that the *disposition to certain specific types* of crime is also expressed in handwriting by a corresponding specific constellation of graphic indicators. Thus, according to this researcher, one can differentiate the script of a murderer, a safebreaker, a confidence man, an embezzler, and others. Wieser's findings are approved in German-speaking countries, and put to use in criminal investigation.

Pulver and Wieser are only a few of the many significant contributors to this field. One should also mention Professors of Graphology R. Pophal of the University of Hamburg; H. Muller of the University of Berlin; H. Knobloch of the University of Mainz; L. Wagner of the University of Munich; and R. Rau of the University of Bonn. All have published standard works in this field. Further, there are specific reference books such as Dr. O. Deitigsmann's *Textbook of Handwriting Identification*, H. Peter's *Studies of Homosexual Handwritings before and after Psychotherapy*, and Dr. G. Grünewald's various experimental studies of psychomotor phenomena.

Application of Graphological Methods

Recently, I have had the occasion of examining the handwritings of three adolescents from the toughest group in a state school, each showing his inability to follow instructions and conform to norms. It was clearly noted that the personal impulses and expressive movements intruded upon and broke down the conventional graphic symbols. The first handwriting examined, according to this analysis, revealed the boy who tends to commit petty larceny and who tries his hand at safecracking. Evidences were revealed of the imaginative projection of a jimmy, most likely the tool he wanted to feel in his hand. The second writing displayed the graphic characteristics of a weakling, a boy who yields to every whim and demand because he has no power of resistance. His aberrant tendencies were clearly expressed in the contortions and lack of resilience of the spineless body of the letter forms he traced. Analysis of the third writing disclosed a potential killer. Ferocious, even violent, gestures in the lower parts of the capital *S* in certain word patterns could be readily observed. The easiest way to catch the meaning of this slashing tension is to imitate the gesture implied so that the expressive forces behind it may work in and through one's own body. In other words, the meaning of the projected image can almost be experienced and understood through *empathy*.

These specimens clearly revealed how handwriting can tell us something about the ominous trends inherent in potential criminals. Here were three clearly anti-social dispositions, each expressed in its own way, revealing how certain personality types fit certain types of crime.

Regrettably enough, American criminology, though willing to avail itself of help given by the projective techniques, has been reluctant, *up to this point*, to apply *graphology* to the same problems. Here, graphology seems to be relegated to a strange corner of psychology; and the study of handwriting, as such, is resorted to only in cases of handwriting identification.

But even in handwriting identification, the more thorough and fully-rounded training of a scientific graphologist is preferable. This is nowhere better illustrated than by Captain Arthur J. Quirke, Handwriting Analyst to the Department of Justice of the Irish Free State, and author of *Forged, Anonymous and Suspect Documents*. Taking an analogy from medical practise, he maintains that a handwriting analyst who works upon a calligraphic basis only, and has no knowledge of the fundamental principles of graphology, bears the same relation to the graphologically trained analyst as the ordinary midwife to a skilled obstetric surgeon.

In illustration, let us examine an extraordinary case that might deceive anyone but a skilled graphological dissector. We frequently have occasion to examine two handwritings so apparently different from one another that mere calligraphic comparison of formal characteristics would not suffice to identify them as written by the same hand. But as a matter of fact they actually are. Let us point out a few of the clues which may lead a clinically experienced graphologist to disclose the psychological relationship between the two. Both may be identified as having been written by a lefthander, and with the left hand. Both may reveal superior intelligence, plus a similar high level of educational and social background. Both may suggest similar age and sex, though neither chronological age nor sex can be ascertained from handwriting.

In the examination of such dual handwritings, it was shown that one specimen was that of a French convent school hand—coined Sacré-Coeur style—with an English twist to it, suggesting a French-Canadian college background. Extremes of restriction were noted, while the other script seemed poles apart in its attempt at extreme release. Such polarities suggest reaction formation, or that which is apt to take place when repressed impulses are substituted for by opposite or contrasting impulses.

In fact, this is precisely what happened. The radical change from restriction to release occurred with remission from a psychotic episode—predisposition to which was clearly evident in the earlier restricted hand. The later, spread-out writing, with its excessive release, constituted a kind of self-defense of the writer against the former restriction which she was now rejecting.

A decisive step toward the introduction of *objective methods* in graphology was taken in this country by Lewinson and Zubin, who devised a method of presenting in graph form the dynamics in handwriting, by differentiating normal scripts from the abnormal. Dr. Rose Wolfson, clinical psychologist, made a statistically validated study of delinquent and non-delinquent adolescents based on the Lewinson-Zubin method in which the statistical distribution of the delinquents shows significant deviations from that of the non-delinquent group.

Principles of Graphology

At this point it would be well to explain briefly the method and procedure of graphology and state the three empirical pillars which give credence to its overall concept and theory:

1.) *Each handwriting is unique and never duplicated.* The physiognomy of handwriting, just like a person's face, retains its essential and identifiable characteristics throughout the years.

2.) But handwriting like personality *is continually in the process of change*, inevitably reflecting the growth, maturation, and aging of the writer, as well as the effects of crucial events, cathartic or traumatic as they may be. In spite of these changes, a man's handwriting remains forever and uniquely his. Thus, in response to the challenging question—Is a man one person from birth to death?—we may say that, as judged by his handwriting, he certainly is.

3.) Moreover, there is also *consistency of expression*. The mode of execution, one's style—guided by lasting personal dispositions—is similar in speech, voice, gesture, general behavior, *and* handwriting. But, unlike the fleeting patterns of speech, voice and gesture, handwriting has the peculiar advantage of fossilizing that expression, leaving a visible record for leisurely, minute analysis.

Graphological procedures involve a number of basic elements, such as: (a) viewing the writing pattern as a whole in order to grasp its overall expression; (b) analyzing the graphic characteristics and correlating them with the personality factors they stand for; and (c) relating the graphic indicators into syndromes and synthesizing them in the context of the whole, enabling the graphologist thereby to draw an integrated, dynamic personality picture. It should be emphasized that it is never the form of single letters alone, nor any particular characteristic, but the combination and interaction of all parts of the writing pattern that reveal the personality of the writer.

Modern graphology is concerned with the problem of objectifying its procedure, on the one hand, and, on the other, of charting these results in an appropriately visual way, comprehensive to non-graphologist and graphologist alike. Such developments as the electrographodyne have given further range to *experimental* and *statistical* procedure.

In respect to graphical recording, various charts have been devised. One of the latest—which seems to stand up to other practical tests—is the graphological psychogram recently devised by George W. Staempfli and myself. Here the basic structure of a personality is rendered pictorially through the shape and distribution of solid areas on a so-called "profile map."

Clinical and Forensic Uses of Graphology

Perhaps graphology's most practical asset is the way it lends itself equally well to group screening and individual case study. The intensive research of the past few decades has equipped the well-trained and clinically oriented graphologist with short-cuts to the quick recognition of key syndromes. Thus, with a practised eye, one can screen case loads of writing in a relatively short time, whereas other approaches might require innumerable hours both for obtaining the material and interpreting the results.

In group screening, the grossly normal can be rapidly separated from the potentially delinquent, thus immediately narrowing the range of probable suspects. Further, through indications of particular behavior disorders in the handwriting, one is able quickly to classify clinical groups (e.g., functional psychosis, organic conditions and other psychopathology), and also pick out, just as in a police line-up, those whose specific personality type fits a specific crime.

Moreover, distinguishing traits, such as lefthandedness, speech or voice disorders, ethnic gestural patterns, occupational habits or skills—even the country where handwriting was first learned—can be easily discerned.

Screening becomes particularly valuable in handling juvenile delinquency. The scripts of two firebugs taken from the screening service at the Treatment Clinic of the New York Domestic Relations Court were recently examined. Both severely disturbed boys needed quick psychiatric help. The handwriting of the first promptly suggested some psychophysical disorder—most likely epilepsy—a condition known neither by the father, a prizefighter, nor divulged by earlier routine neurological examinations. Intensive case study, in joint collaboration with psychiatric and psychological personnel, confirmed the graphological diagnosis as epilepsy. The second handwriting was clinically classified as a typical schizophrenic script. The handwritings of these two delinquent arsonists illustrated the important point that similar delinquent manifestations may stem from quite different roots.

Screening becomes particularly valuable in discovering potential juvenile delinquency as well, by using ordinary class assignments as the handwriting material. What better contribution to mental hygiene than this means of detecting ominous trends before behavior difficulties arise? In this way, graphology might conceivably become an effective tool in preventive therapy.

If adequate handwriting material is available, complete individual personality studies can be made, either of a cross-sectional or longitudinal nature. The cross-sectional individual case study provides a practical description of the individual, his attitudes and his pattern of behavior *at the time the writing was produced*. The longitudinal study uses consecutive handwriting samples for serial study and provides information about the changes in personality occurring *over an extended period of time*. It may also pinpoint crucial or possibly traumatic moments in a life history through marked, dramatic changes in the handwriting.

Despite the validity of graphological techniques, the accumulation of scientific standards, and its acceptance abroad, relatively little interest has been displayed in its adoption in the United States. Outside of lectures at The New School for Social Research in New York City, there is virtually no other course of graphology given as part of the curriculum of an accredited college or university anywhere in the United States. Moreover, there is no set of academic standards to attest the background and reliability of the handwriting analyst. As for sorely needed scientific research opportunities, these are practically nil. Surely if we are to progress, we must revise the *status quo*.

Yet it is encouraging to note that there is a healthy increase in interest which may well lead to a better understanding of the potential value of graphology, and that this in turn will no doubt promote and stimulate research. Indeed, the day may not be far distant when the fully-trained graphologist will work side by side with the clinical and forensic psychologist all over this country.

Among the several criteria which are considered basic in the development of an adequate scientific explanation, including the validity of the basic assumptions being employed and the logical coherence of the explanation as confirmed by tested experience, is the capacity to predict and control the data being studied. Indeed, to most scientists, the capacity to predict and control comprises the summum bonum *of all scientific research. Within the field of the physical sciences, this predictive capacity largely serves the function of reinforcing the interpretation of the phenomenon being analyzed. In extension, however, a knowledge of this principle enables the scientist to apply his findings to conditions and situations which may be put to practical use. Technology, thus, becomes the means whereby the predictive insight may be put to productive use.*

In the behavioral sciences, a knowledge of causal factors and conditions which contribute to the human problem being studied implies the very nature of the controls which are being sought. In brief, our understanding as to why a given situation is brought about in the human field suggests ways and means by which it may be controlled, provided (1) we are sufficiently concerned about securing its control, and (2) that a knowledge of the causes may be efficiently and effectively translated into workable policy.

For some time, criminologists and other students of human behavior have been interested in developing predictive devices which will enable us to determine, with some reasonable assurance when and under what conditions delinquency and criminality are most apt to occur. Since 1923, efforts to anticipate the probability of success or failure of parole through the establishment of measurable statistical criteria have been attempted by E. W. Burgess, Clark Tibbitts, and Ferris Laune. More recently, studies within the same broad area have been conducted by George Vold, and the celebrated husband and wife team of Sheldon and Eleanor Glueck.

Although frequently in the center of considerable controversy among behavioral scientists, and especially sociologists, concerning the soundness of their hypotheses and the effectiveness of their methods, the Gluecks, nevertheless, have performed a prodigious task in carrying out a monumental series of widely cited studies of young offenders and delinquents. From these studies have emerged a number of promising predictive instruments. Significant in the work of this illustrious couple has been the painstaking and continuous effort through the years of constant improvement of the instruments they have devised. Among their works which have left a lasting imprint upon the entire field of delinquency and criminology are Five Hundred Criminal Careers, One Thousand Juvenile Delinquents, *and the recent impressive* Unraveling Juvenile Delinquency, *based upon a carefully controlled research design drawn from samples of 500 delinquents and 500 non-delinquents. From this latter work, which has stirred up considerable interest as well as controversy among professional criminologists, have emerged two significant recent volumes*—Physique and Delinquency *and* Predicting Delinquency and Crime.

In response to professional criticism that the validity of the Glueck prediction tables applied largely, if at all, to the samples from which the research data was drawn, the Gluecks, in true scientific spirit, have attempted to test their criteria in other contexts and among groups whose background and socio-cultural characteristics differed from their original Boston samples. In this chapter, Maude M. Craig, Director of Research of the New York City Youth Board, describes the procedures and results obtained thus far in the attempt to indicate whether the predictive table devised by the Gluecks has validity beyond the range of the initial group studied. The organization of this project and its execu-

tion, carried on in close concert with the Gluecks, is to a considerable degree due to her sustained efforts and the interest of the New York City Youth Board in probing the roots of delinquent disorder.

Of special interest is the fact that, unlike most such efforts at validation of predictive instruments, where data is sought in retrospect in order to establish the validity of the instrument, the Youth Board study is projective in character. In this study, the predictive criteria were applied to the children studied long before they gave evidence of the sustained delinquent behavior which the instrument attempts to uncover.

Chapter 21

AN EXPERIMENT IN THE PREDICTION OF DELINQUENCY: AN APPLICATION OF THE GLUECK PREDICTION SCALE

Maude M. Craig

Director of Research, New York City Youth Board

Introductory Note

It seems particularly appropriate at this time to refer to certain remarks made before the International Congress on Criminology at the London meeting three years ago by Dr. Eleanor Glueck in her presentation on the "Status of Glueck Prediction Studies":

"Ever since the publication of 'Unraveling Juvenile Delinquency' there has been considerable discussion about the applicability of these (prediction) tables to groups differing in composition from those on whom they were initially constructed; and most particularly to boys as young as six. We see only one definitive way of resolving these questions, and that is by applying the tables to various samples of cases differing from the group on whom they were initially constructed. The possibly relevant differences involve ethnic origins, age distribution, socioeconomic status, types of neighborhood and intelligence level. It is important, also, to apply the tables experimentally to a large group of boys at the point of school entrance, and to follow these youngsters for several years in order to determine to what extent the predictions made at this early stage in their lives prove to be accurate." [1]

Six years ago, at the start of the 1952-53 school year, the New York City Youth Board undertook the kind of validation study envisioned by the Gluecks. This presentation will summarize the methodology employed by the Gluecks to develop the delinquency predictive instrument which is under scrutiny. It will also describe the Youth Board's validation experiment, with particular emphasis on how the group selected for study compares with 1,000 delinquent and non-delinquent boys comprising the Glueck sample population. And, finally, it will present the most recent findings available from the continuing Youth Board experiment.

The Predictive Instrument

The Gluecks selected five hundred persistently delinquent boys from among those committed to correctional institutions in Massachusetts. A group of five hundred non-delinquents, chosen from the general public school population in Boston, was matched as closely as possible on the basis of age, intelligence, ethnic derivation, and neighborhood conditions. During a ten-year study period the 500 matched pairs were compared for 402 potentially "causal factors" relating to social and ecological conditions, physique, and personality traits. The inter-disciplinary nature of the researches was emphasized by the composition of the staff working with the Gluecks; it included social investigators, psychologists, a psychiatrist, Rorschach analysts, physical anthropologists, and statisticians. The results of these intensive investigations have been published in detail in their book entitled *Unraveling Juvenile Delinquency*.

With the data at their disposal, the Gluecks proceeded to construct three predictive instruments composed of factors which not only differentiated between delinquents and non-delinquents, but could also be "applied to children at the point of school entrance, without waiting for the actual appearance of serious and persistent antisociality." [2] The three tables each constructed with five factors, were based on the differences in certain character traits derived from the Rorschach Test; on personality differences available from the psychiatric interview; and on intra-family social factors. The last-named, the Social Factors Table, was the one selected by the New York City Youth Board for its validation experiment (See Table I). As the Gluecks noted:

"From a practical point of view, the five factors in the social background can be more easily and widely obtained than the factors of the other two prediction tables, simply because there are many more persons skillful in gathering social data than there are in securing and interpreting Rorschach and psychiatric material." [3]

Table 1

GLUECK SOCIAL FACTORS PREDICTION CLASSIFICATIONS *

Social Factor and Sub-class	Weighted Failure Score
1. Discipline of Boy by Father	
Overstrict or erratic	71.8
Lax	59.8
Firm but kindly	9.3
2. Supervision of Boy by Mother	
Unsuitable	83.2
Fair	57.5
Close or suitable	9.9
3. Affection of Father for Boy	
Indifferent or hostile	75.9
Warm (including overprotective)	33.8
4. Affection of Mother for Boy	
Indifferent or hostile	86.2
Warm (including overprotective)	43.1
5. Cohesiveness of Family	
Unintegrated	96.9
Some elements of cohesion	61.3
Cohesive	20.6

* Source: Glueck, Sheldon and Eleanor T., *Unraveling Juvenile Delinquency* (The Commonwealth Fund, New York, 1950), p. 261.

The five elements comprising the Social Factors Prediction Table are indicative of the parent-child relationships and the extent of family cohesiveness. The weighted failure scores, calculated by the Gluecks in constructing this table, represent the scores used in rating a youngster. For example, among the five social factors in the table is the factor "Discipline of Boy by Father." A total of 433 boys in the original study had paternal discipline which was described as "overstrict or erratic"; of these 433 boys, 311, or 71.8 percent were delinquents. Thus, the percentage of incidence of delinquency among boys whose fathers were "overstrict or erratic"; i.e., 71.8 percent, is termed the weighted failure score. Similarly, it was found that 59.8 percent of the boys whose paternal discipline was "lax" had become delinquents, whereas only 9.3 percent of the boys with "firm but kindly" fathers developed into delinquents. The same method of calculation was used to develop the weighted failure scores shown in the table for the several sub-classes under the other four social factors.

The summation of the lowest and highest scores possible on each of the five factors resulted in a range of 116.7 through 414, which was originally divided into seven class intervals and subsequently reduced to four classes.

Table 2

CONSTRUCTION OF FOUR-CLASS PREDICTION TABLE FROM FIVE FACTORS OF SOCIAL BACKGROUND

A. Number of Boys in Each of Four Score Classes

Weighted Failure Score Class	Total Delinquents and Non-Delinquents	Number of Delinquents	Number of Non-Delinquents
Total	890	451	439
Under 200	293	24	269
200-249	108	40	68
250-299	192	122	70
300 and over	297	265	32

B. Percentage Distribution or Chances for Delinquency or Non-Delinquency

Weighted Failure Score Class	Total Chances	Chances of Delinquency	Chances of Non-Delinquency
Under 200	100.0	8.2	91.8
200-249	100.0	37.0	63.0
250-299	100.0	63.5	36.5
300 and over	100.0	89.2	10.8

Source: Glueck, Sheldon and Eleanor T., *Unraveling Juvenile Delinquency*, (The Commonwealth Fund, New York, 1950), from Tables XX-2 and XX-3, pp. 261-262.

Table 3

COMPARATIVE ETHNIC DISTRIBUTIONS OF WHITE (NON-PUERTO RICAN) BOYS INCLUDED IN YOUTH BOARD SAMPLE AND GLUECK STUDY

Ethnic Origin [1]	Number in Youth Board Sample	Percentage Distribution Youth Board Sample	1,000 Glueck Cases [2]
Total	127	100.0	100.0
Italian (Including Maltese)	29	22.8	24.6
Jewish	25	19.7	2.0
Irish	20	15.7	19.0
Slavic	11	8.7	6.4
German, Austrian, Scandinavian, Dutch	11	8.7	3.2
Native U.S.	10	7.9	7.8
Near Eastern	6	4.7	3.4
English	5	3.9	25.6
Spanish, Portuguese	5	3.9	2.4
French	3	2.4	5.4
South and Central American	2	1.6	0
Chinese	0	0	0.2

1. Ethnic origin as defined in Glueck study, *Unraveling Juvenile Delinquency,* p. 33.

2. Data on 1000 Glueck cases taken from Table IV-6, p. 38, of the same study.

Each of the 451 delinquents and 439 non-delinquents, on whom data were available on all five factors, was assigned appropriate failure scores for each of these factors. The failure scores were then added together to produce a total score for each boy, after which the cases were distributed into the appropriate score classes. Thus, out of the 293 boys whose total scores were less than 200, a total of 24, or 8.2 percent, proved to be delinquent and the remaining 269 (91.8 percent) were not delinquents. At the other extreme, in the group of cases with total scores exceeding 300, there were 265 delinquents among the 297 boys falling into that classification, or 89.2 percent of the group. The Gluecks refer to the percentage of delinquents or non-delinquents in each category as the chances of delinquency or non-delinquency.

The Youth Board's Experiment

The New York City Youth Board viewed these investigations with considerable interest because the findings are so intimately related to its philosophy and goals. The Board has been established on a two-point basis for its operations in addition to extending traditional preventive and treatment facilities. Its first concern is to develop ways to reach potentially delinquent children at a time when treatment can be most effective, and before their problems have resulted in overt anti-social behavior. Secondly, the Youth Board is seeking to develop effective skills in providing treatment for children and their families. The prognostic instrument developed by the Gluecks can be of inestimable value in further focusing and refining the Youth Board's program. If the Social Factors Prediction Table proves valid, it would make it possible to select those children most in need of community services at a very early age; it would also pave the way for further development of effective treatment techniques in dealing with such children and their families.

Earlier attempts to apply the Social Factors Prediction Table yielded results which were suggestive of the value of working further with this instrument.[4] However, all of these studies were "after the fact," that is, they applied the table to children who had already exhibited delinquent behavior. The New York City Youth Board, in its current experiment, was the first to initiate a study where the table was applied to a group of children prior to the onset of overt symptoms of delinquency. The study initiated in the Fall of 1952, with the financial aid of the Ford Foundation, has been under way for six years. At the present time a total of 303 boys is included in the research; of this total, 224 were brought into the study during the academic year of 1952-53, another 32 came in during the succeeding two years, and the remaining 47 were added in the Spring of 1956.

Two points of particular significance emerge when our sample is compared with the sample used by the Gluecks in constructing the Table.[5] First, all of the 303 boys were selected for study by the Youth Board when they were entering the first grade or kindergarten, so that their ages *at selection* ranged from 5½ to 6½ years. In sharp contrast, the 500 pairs of delinquents and non-delinquents were selected by the Gluecks when their ages ranged from eleven to seventeen years. Secondly, whereas nearly three out of five boys in the Youth study were of Negro or Puerto Rican origin (58.1 percent), not one Negro or Puerto Rican is to be found among the Glueck selections. Additional disparities are to be found when the comparison is restricted to the respective white (non-Puerto Rican) populations of the two studies. While only 2 percent of the Glueck cases were of

Table 4

DISTRIBUTION OF BOYS IN TOTAL YOUTH BOARD SAMPLE BY PREDICTION SCORE CLASS

A. Four-Class Table

Prediction Score Class (Chances of Delinquency)	Number	Percent
Total	303	100.0
8.2	156	51.5
37.0	57	18.8
63.5	65	21.5
89.2	25	8.2

B. Two-Class Table

Chances of Delinquency	Number	Percent
Total	303	100.0
Less than 50 Chances out of 100	213	70.3
More than 50 Chances out of 100	90	29.7

Jewish parentage, one-fifth of the Youth Board boys were so classified. Also, a quarter of the Glueck sample were English by descent, whereas only 4 percent of the Youth Board group had such origin.

Although age at selection and ethnic origin provided significant differences between the two study groups, data relating to neighborhood conditions suggest basic similarities in this variable. The two samples were drawn from areas generally characterized by an incidence of high delinquency and low economic and social status.

Study Procedure

The details on how the 303 boys in the Youth Board experiment were selected and assigned delinquency prediction scores have been described in an earlier report.[6] To obtain the data on the five social factors needed to calculate the chances for delinquency for each boy in the study, interviews with parents (mostly mothers) were conducted in the homes; and additional information was obtained from those official and unofficial agencies who had served the families. A structured form was used to guide the more than thirty case workers who made the home interviews; it indicated the kind of factual material needed to score the five social factors. The agency reports were a valuable addition to the family picture provided by the home interview. In some instances the agency reports served to correct misleading impressions created by family respondents during home interviews.

After all of these materials had been assembled for each child, two persons were assigned to rate the boys in accordance with the Glueck Social Factors Prediction Table. The two raters worked independently in scoring each case. The lack of any previous experience of this nature apparently did not affect the reliability of the ratings. In 90 percent of the Sample 1 cases, for example, the two raters independently placed the boys in the same delinquency prediction class.

The results of the rating procedure on the 303 boys in the three samples have been suggestive. Slightly more than *half* of the youngsters received the lowest of the four ratings, approximately one-fifth fell into each of the next two rating categories, while slightly less than ten percent of the boys were assigned the rating with the highest chances of delinquency. When the four rating classes were reduced to two, a total of 90 boys were shown as "likely" to become delinquents, that is to have more than a 50-50 chance of delinquency.

Problems Encountered

In an experimental study of this kind, involving, as it does, so many aspects of human behavior and communication, various difficulties were presented. We have already noted, for example, deliberate attempts to mislead the home interviewer which were disclosed through reports from social agencies which had served the families. The implication is that among families *not known* to social agencies, there may be similar instances of erroneous information which remained uncorrected and which may have affected the assigned ratings.

Without attempting to evaluate their significance, the following are some of the other problems encountered in the course of the Youth Board's experiment. In general, only the mother was interviewed. Thus, the very vital role of the father, directly related to two of the five predictive factors, was left to the mother's interpretation primarily. Cultural differences between the interviewer and the respondent may have served to increase the source of error. The skill of the interviewer was important. In addition, many mothers tended to offer data more characteristic of the *total* family situation, rather than focusing their observations on the particular child being studied. It is also important to note that a large part of the information used in scoring was secured from *one* home interview.

The geographical mobility of the families proved to be an additional and expensive complication. The families all resided in four school districts in one borough of New York City when the boys were first selected for study. Now they attend 90 different schools. The majority (90%) of the families have remained in the city. Some have left New York State and now live as far away as Michigan and Puerto Rico. Despite this far-flung dispersal, it has been possible to obtain follow-up school data in all but one instance.

Results to Date

For the past six years the teachers of the boys who comprise *Sample 1* have been interviewed to ascertain the boy's behavior in terms of conduct, relationships with teacher and other children, personality patterns, as well as attitudes and achievement. Concurrently, police records were checked to determine which boys had been known to the police and/or courts, and the nature of the offenses. They also were cleared through the Social Service Exchange for additional official and unofficial agency data. The outcome of these investigations has been determined within the framework of the four delinquency predictions classes.

Delinquency was defined as persistent delinquent behavior in accordance with the Gluecks' definition and not merely as isolated delinquent acts. Youngsters so classified may or may not have had a police contact. Those boys termed predelinquent or anti-social were those exhibiting seriously hostile and disruptive behavior. Many are serious attendance problems.

The 39 boys classified under "disruptive behavior" were

those who are doing little or no school work, were inattentive, hyperactive, pesty, attention-getting, non-conforming and mischievous in their behavior. We call them our "suspended judgment" group.

The majority of the 157 boys classified as "no serious problem" included those youngsters who appeared to the teacher as basically well adjusted, even though they might present some type of mildly deviant behavior. We have also included in this group those boys showing neurotic symptoms, such as shyness and timidity.

Of the 156 boys whose prediction score classes indicated they were "not likely" to become delinquents (8.2 and 37.0), 3 boys, or 2 percent of this group, have failed so far to bear out the prediction. At the same time, 13, or 19.4 percent of the 67 boys who scored as "likely" to become delinquents (63.5 and 89.2), have actually fulfilled that prediction. If, in addition to the 16 confirmed delinquents, the 11 youngsters who are currently exhibiting serious pre-delinquent traits also turn delinquent, the combination would yield the following results:

Three percent (3%) of the group predicted "unlikely" to become delinquent, (five out of 156) would have failed; and nearly one-third (32.8 percent) of the group predicted as "likely" to achieve delinquency would have borne out that prediction (22 of the 67).

In general, the results so far suggest that this prediction table may select future delinquents at the time children are entering school. It is still much too soon to reach any definitive conclusions on the validity of this instrument, since boys have not yet attained the age level characteristic of many juvenile delinquents. The Glueck investigations disclosed that 41 percent of the delinquents were from 13 to 16 years of age at the time of their first court appearance. None of the boys in the Youth Board experiment have reached that age bracket. It is the Youth Board's intention to continue to follow-up and study the progress of the 303 boys until it can reasonably be determined that they have either become, or are not likely to become, delinquent.

REFERENCES

1. Glueck, Eleanor T., "Status of Glueck Prediction Studies," *Journal of Criminal Law, Criminology and Police Science*, Vol. 47 (1), May-June 1956, p. 23.

2. Glueck, Sheldon and Eleanor T., *Unraveling Juvenile Delinquency* (The Commonwealth Fund, New York, 1950).

3. *Ibid.*, pp. 258, 269.

4. Black, Bertram J., and Glick, Selma J., "Recidivism at Hawthorne-Cedar Knolls School—Predicted Versus Actual Outcome for Delinquent Boys," *Research Monograph No. 2* (Jewish Board of Guardians, New York, 1952).

5. Glueck, Eleanor T., "Status of Glueck Prediction Studies," *Journal of Criminal Law, Criminology and Police Science*, Vol. 47 (1), May-June 1956.

6. Craig, Maude M., "An Experiment in the Validation of the Glueck Prediction Scale Progress Report from November 1952 to December 1956," Research Department, New York City Youth Board, July 1957.

As far back as the Fifth Century B.C., the Greek thinkers had already developed a typology of bodily types, based upon the belief that linkages existed between the gross forms of bodily constitution and certain broad temperamental qualities. This question has recurrently emerged in man's thinking concerning the reasons for the differences in human behavior and the quality of response, and the manifestations of physical appearance which appeared so striking to the uncritical eye. With the more refined insights of the scientific view of the 19th century, and the sophistication derived from the growth of Linnean classification and the empirical method, the search for such crude associations was transmuted into a more basic consideration—the attempt to distinguish between the influences of heredity and environment.

In the development of this historic controversy of nature vs. nurture, the criminologists have played a conspicuous role. Indeed, one of the gratifying aspects of the development of criminology as a science has been the light it has frequently shed upon problems which extend far beyond the restricted interests of criminology itself. By virtue of the fact that the central problem of criminology, despite recent exceptions made upon occasion by certain modern criminologists, has been the issue as to how men acquire criminal and anti-social traits, the criminologist has been forced into a variety of adjacent areas of scholarship, ranging from physiology to cultural organization. While criminologists have often repeated their age-long plea, that a science of criminology could not be established until adequate, systematic and empirically-grounded theories of personality and society were developed, *the fact remains that, in the absence of such formulations, the criminologist has had to establish such views for himself.*

In this continuous quest for principles of causation, the periodic return to a consideration of bodily and constitutional factors as contributing to criminality has been impressive. Lombroso, considered by many students the father of modern criminology, in focussing attention upon physical characteristics as basic in the determination of criminal behavior, has provided a constant point of departure for both environmental and biological studies. In the course of this development, however, American criminologists have tended to veer away sharply from the neo-Lombrosian views which so frequently characterize the research and theoretical interests of their European counterparts. There is very likely a sound sociological reason for this divergence. Subject to the powerful "cultural imperatives" which operate within their respective cultural milieux, American sociologists have very likely been profoundly affected by the rapidity of social change in America and a social and political ideology which stresses the adaptability and potential of the human personality. In the older, more class-controlled societies of Europe, where traditional status positions have maintained some hold upon current thinking, it is understandable that antisocial and criminal traits were more readily identified with segments of the class-structured social system.

Of late, the works of Hooton and Sheldon in America, and particularly the recent work of Sheldon and Eleanor Glueck, have inspired considerable interest, and even concern, in certain scholarly circles, about the renewed emphasis upon physical characteristics as contributing to crime. Professor Peter P. Lejins traces the development of the divergent schools of interest in the nature-nurture controversy and, more significantly, attempts to establish a basis upon which the controversy may be tentatively reconciled in the interests of advancing research. The editor finds it difficult to accept some of the propositions suggested by Professor Lejins as a basis for this type of reconciliation but welcomes his searching and scholarly effort to devise a workable modus operandi.

The primary reason for this view is the crudity with

which basic categories of distinctions have been devised, even in the case of the superior and improved efforts which have been made by the recent researchers. The lack of commitment to an etiological point of view, which Professor Lejins holds to be a virtue, simply becomes, in many instances, the inability to ask the proper hypothetical questions. Far from a virtue, it may become a serious defect in the undertaking of the entire research design. The problem of bodily types, physiological processes, hereditary traits, and impulsive trends towards behavior can, in the long run, only be established, it appears to the editor, in the light of a refurbished set of concepts. These concepts would set up a framework for what the editor has so frequently referred to as a "sociology of biology," work upon which has already begun.

Nevertheless, it must be readily granted that any progress that may eventually be made in this field can only be accomplished by such initial attempts as represented by the kinds of queries posed by Professor Lejins in the next chapter.

Chapter 22

HEREDITARY ENDOWMENT, ENVIRONMENTAL
INFLUENCES AND CRIMINALITY

PETER P. LEJINS

Professor of Sociology
University of Maryland

The specific controversial area which I am to discuss—hereditary endowment, environmental influences and criminality—revolves around two conflicting propositions in criminological theory. The first proposition asserts that criminal behavior is to a significant degree determined by the physical characteristics of the offender. The second states that criminal behavior is determined by the environmental factors, primarily the social environment, and the role of the physical characteristics is relatively unimportant. It should be noted that these two contradictory propositions are stated at this point in their least controversial form. In reality, they are often phrased much more dogmatically and imply much more of an exclusion of each other than the above formulation might suggest. For instance, the one is sometimes stated as the concept of the "born criminal," which implies that a person is biologically predestined to commit crimes; the other is on occasion dramatically formulated in the dictum that "society deserves its criminals," implying that the conditions which society tolerates make criminals of its children.

To give an impressionistic illustration of the controversy, let me relate two instances. One consists in the publication of an article by Alfred Lindesmith and Yale Levin, "The

Lombrosian Myth in Criminology," appearing in 1937, in which the authors express and undertake to substantiate the prevailing opinion of the American criminologists of that period that the Lombrosian, and by that token the biological or hereditary explanation of crime, not only has failed to make a contribution toward our understanding of crime, but actually has delayed our understanding of criminal behavior by steering our thinking onto the wrong track, i.e., away from social-environmental interpretations. The other instance is a proposal made at the Second International Congress on Criminology in Paris in 1950, which consisted in the suggestion that the seat of the International Criminological Society be moved to Rome in order to pay proper honor to the contribution of Lombroso, the founder of our science. The spirit of the above-mentioned article and of the proposal to which I just referred seems to indicate the scope of the controversy very well.

This controversy in criminological etiology is but a repercussion of a much more general controversy in the social sciences, or even the science of man, between nature and nurture. Here, in brief review, are the salient issues for the criminologist involved in this controversy.

This problem clearly transcends the limits of criminological discussion. Some therefore point out that it is not up to the criminologist to solve it but that, rather than wasting time on this age-long and presumably sterile discussion, he should by-pass it and go on with more fruitful immediate research considerations. Sometimes this point is pushed further to the extent of denying the very possibility of scientific criminology at the present time, because of its dependence on the more general disciplines of psychology and sociology, which themselves have not yet been developed fully as empirical sciences.[1] The opposite point, however, is also made upon occasion; namely, that the criminologist should not wait for some more general science to provide him with a general theory, but that he himself should be working on the development of that general theory through the media available to him in his own specific discipline. This, it is held, is the proper way for general theory to be developed. Still another objection to the criminologists staying away "in disgust" from the nature-nurture controversy is the contention that the stand on this controversy, if avoided explicitly, usually still remains implicitly and *has* to be present. Any practical handling of the crime problem, it is maintained, implies one etiological theory or another, leaning either toward nurture or toward nature.

Another consideration within the same complex of problems is the solution offered by the pragmatic theory of causality; namely, that a cause means a manipulable necessary antecedent rather than just a necessary antecedent. The solution, therefore, of the nature-nurture problem should be sought by the criminologist in the very process of developing the methods of handling the crime problem. "To bring about, to produce, to make, to generate, is to effect, and that which serves this purpose is a cause in the only legitimate existential sense of the word," as John Dewey put it.[2]

Another complex of issues closely allied with the problem of the criminal bodily type is that of determining precisely what the bodily type means. Are the characteristics involved here what we call the constitution, or do they involve also what is often referred to as acquired characteristics? As we all know, criminal etiology is often subdivided into constitutional as distinct from environmental theories. Is the bodily type or the constitution something passed on *via* biological heredity only, or is this bodily type or constitution made up of more or less permanent characteristics which are, however, not necessarily biologically inherited and can also be acquired? For instance, the constitutional inferiority of the criminal might perhaps be due to the consequences of poverty. The writers and researchers in this area vary on this point, the present tendency, at least among major contributors, seemingly being that of recognizing the criminologically relevant constitution as a complex of both relatively permanent and predominantly inherited traits. The writers at present seem to be very cautious about committing themselves to the absolute permanency and complete biological inheritance of the criminologically significant constitution, allowing their stand to remain somewhat vague "on the fringes." In this sense, the statement by William H. Sheldon in *The Varieties of Human Physique,* in the footnote on page 2, is very typical:

"Although by constitution we refer to the relatively stable aspects of a person's endowment, we do not mean to insist, and indeed do not believe, that the human constitution is an altogether fixed and unalterable hereditary entity. We mean by constitution the basic, underlying pattern of the living individual, as it is at the time when the individual is studied. That constitution is closely determined by heredity is highly probable, but we do not know that it is entirely so determined." [3]

To what extent the ultimate relationships between biologically inherited and environmentally produced characteristics still lack necessary distinctive clarity can readily be seen from one simple proposition, *viz.,* the possibility of personality traits which are inherited but which were produced in the parental stock by certain environmental conditions such as, for example, the dietary deprivations of a specific social group. What the exclusive meanings of the terms *constitution, heredity,* and *environment* may be in a situation of this type has not been clarified for the purposes of criminological theory.

Still another sequence of issues is involved in the exact meaning of the term constitution or bodily type. These terms may be limited to the anatomical or morphological aspects of the human organism only, or they may be interpreted to include human physiology; or, finally, they might be used to denote also the traits commonly referred to as psychological. Lombroso, especially in his earlier works, limited the meaning of his criminal type to a large extent to the anatomical characteristics. The Neo-Lombrosians sought to improve upon Lombroso by including within their criminological types the physiological processes. Especially typical in this respect is the stand of the so-called endocrinological school, which focuses its attention essentially on the functions rather than on the static characteristics of the human body. More recent investigators such as, for instance, Sheldon, readily recognize all of these aspects of the human constitution—the anatomy or morphology, physiology and psychology—but sometimes limit themselves to just one of these. Unlike the early investigators, who frequently lacked awareness and appreciation of related factors, modern investigators restrict themselves as the result of a deliberate limitation of the field of inquiry.[4]

Presumably any discussion of the relationship between the bodily traits and the criminality of the behavior should operate with terms which are defined with sufficient precision along the lines indicated above, in order to arrive at statements which may be afforded the status of scientific propositions or in order to permit the conducting of research which may produce scientifically relevant results. It is encouraging to see that some of the more modern writings do make a definite effort at a precise definition of terms. See, for instance, the chapter entitled "General Orientation" in *Physique and Delinquency* by Sheldon and Eleanor Glueck, especially the incorporated "Notes" in this volume.[5]

Now that I have very briefly catalogued the major concepts involved in this discussion, let me equally briefly characterize the major schools of criminological inquiry in this area.

The attempts to clarify the relationship between the bodily characteristics and the criminality of behavior fall into two rather distinct historical developments. One of these, for speedy reference, can be identified with the following: Lombroso, Goring, the Neo-Lombrosians, and Hooton. The other, similarly, can also be identified by a few key references: the ancient Greek classification of temperaments, Kretschmer's work, William H. Sheldon's somatotyping, and the studies of Sheldon and Eleanor Glueck on the physique of delinquents. Let us briefly trace these two historical developments.

Cesare Lombroso is justly considered the originator of the first-mentioned development. He should be exonerated, as Earnest A. Hooton points out, of having continued the earlier, even less scientific, interpretations by the phrenologists.[6] Lombroso's proposal, when reduced to the simplest terms, was that criminal behavior is the result of a special physical constitution of man, which is due to atavism and degeneracy. Especially in his later writings, Lombroso stressed that the social environment may contribute to the manifestation of the innate criminalistic tendencies of his born criminal, so that these, under certain conditions, may remain unrealized. Lombroso's weakest point was the methodology he employed to establish an empirical basis for his theory. This methodology was at times so naive, from our present point of view, that even such a champion of the intrinsic quality of Lombroso's quest as Earnest Hooton readily acknowledges this weakness.[7] Because of the faulty methodology and faulty assumptions (e.g., the "savage" nature of primitive man), Lombroso's findings were shown to be erroneous in subsequent decades by many researchers who, while not themselves using superior methodology, managed to obtain results different from those of Lombroso. In general, their findings were that there are as many anatomical and physiological deviates among non-criminals as there are among the criminals.

This type of research, not all of which debunked Lombroso but which, in certain instances, actually supported his findings, culminated in the monumental work by Charles Goring, *The English Convict*, published in 1913. Goring, under the guidance of Professor Karl Pearson, used modern statistical methods for comparing samples of criminals and non-criminals to test Lombroso's theory and emerged with findings which actually denied the validity of Lombroso's contentions. For a long time, these results sealed the fate of Lombroso's theories—at least in the English-speaking countries. It was not until Hooton's arrival on the scene that anyone seriously doubted the conclusiveness of Goring's attack.[8] Goring's view was interpreted by Hooton as a preconceived plan to disprove Lombroso's theory of criminality, the weaknesses of which he carefully points out. Hooton lists some five "methods of distorting evidence" employed by Goring.[9]

A very interesting criticism of Lombroso's theories, which is less widely known and of a different non-empirical type, was voiced very early by Gabriel Tarde, a well-known French sociologist and a distinguished criminologist in his own right. Summarized briefly, this criticism can be formulated as follows: Lombroso's theory is from the very outset a hopeless endeavor, since it attempts to interpret criminal behavior, a function of such a changing variable as criminal law, in terms of such a stable variable as the almost immutable biological heredity of man.

While the safely-buried corpse of Lombrosian theory lay dormant in the United States and other English-speaking countries for decades, the Neo-Lombrosians carried on the teachings of their master in Italy, Spain, and in the Latin-American countries, specializing primarily in the presumable refinements of the theory by exploring the physiology, the endocrine glands, and other bodily factors.

Hooton's research instituted a revival of the issues raised by Lombroso. Touching only upon the major issues, one should point out the following new elements introduced by Hooton into this discussion. He attacked the practice of comparing the physique of the criminal with that of the non-criminal outside of the context of a specific racial or nationality group.[10] He never attempted to find significant differences between a criminal and a non-criminal individual, but attempted to establish differences between the averages of the samples of criminal and non-criminal groups. Hooton's own drawings of funny little men, in his *Crime and the Man*, are supposed to depict average traits of groups and not individual offenders.

In addition to these two methodological innovations, which are important in themselves, Hooton reached the following three major conclusions:

1. there exists a measurable difference between the criminal and the non-criminal population with regard to anthropological measurements and morphological observations;
2. this difference means, among other things, constitutional inferiority of the criminals as compared with the non-criminals;
3. criminals, when classified according to their offenses, present measurable differences between the offender groups in terms of physique.

From the avalanche of criticism which Hooton's study provoked, the following may be singled out: the faulty definition of the criminal, which was limited in Hooton's usage to imprisoned offenders only; the poor non-criminal sample used in his study; the lack of clear definition of the key concept of physical inferiority; the lack of appreciation of the fact that the offenders identified by Hooton with a specific kind of offense, for which they were serving a term when studied, had in reality committed a variety of offenses; and criticisms of a similar character. As a result of these and other criticisms, Hooton's study has had very little impact on American criminology and has not directly stimulated any further research or inquiry. Its results were held by many American criminologists to be a sad mistake, and by others a big puzzling question mark, in need of considerable additional research before any use could be made of Hooton's work. It is only in the countries with predominant Neo-Lombrosian tendencies that Hooton's work has been acclaimed as a major contribution of American criminology. When in 1942, about three years after the appearance of Hooton's work, I was discussing with one of our foremost American criminologists a course the latter was teaching, in reply to the question as to how much time he allowed for the discussion of Hooton's research, the answer I received was: "None; I would not waste the time of my students on that sort of thing."

The second of the two developments dealing with the relationship of physique and human behavior is the one which received its early impetus with the ancient Greeks, who, as is commonly reported, distinguished four kinds of temperament: choleric, melancholic, phlegmatic, and sanguine. These temperamental qualities were believed, in some way, to be anchored in the elements of the human body. As far as can be determined, no implications for criminality, as we understand it today, were made during this early period. At the same time the Greeks differentiated between two types of human physique: one dominated by the vertical dimension, and the other by the horizontal dimension.[11] Without going into the niceties of the exact meaning of the term, *temperament*, it should suffice to say for the purpose of the present discussion, that by temperament is meant the relatively permanent basic response pattern characteristic of a particular individual. It was Ernst Kretschmer (1921) who related the concept of temperament with the physical build of the individual. According to Kretschmer, the three types of physique—pyknic, athletic, and asthenic—are indicative of three different basic types of temperament, or character. Kretschmer related these types to certain major types of mental disorder.

It was William H. Sheldon who attempted to connect body type and the corresponding total personality with criminal behavior. Sheldon's somatotyping has been sufficiently popularized in this country so that no detailed listing and explanation of his more general terms are required here. The essence of Sheldon's contribution is not the distinction of the three basic somatotypes, i.e., the endomorph, mesomorph, and ectomorph, which are pretty much the same as Kretschmer's types, but rather the introduction and careful definition of many other, and what one might call, subsidiary concepts. Above all, Sheldon's work is characterized by an effort to develop a precise scientific methodology for the observation and description of the bodily types.

As far as criminological theory is concerned, Sheldon's main contribution was the bombshell-like finding which appears in his *Varieties of Delinquent Youth*, published in 1949. This finding was that all sixteen of the youths whom he identified among the 200 residents of the Hayden Goodwill Inn, a South Boston social agency, as endowed with residual or primary criminality, happen to be, without exception, endomorphic mesomorphs. By primary criminality, Sheldon means law violations which are not due to mental deficiency or psychiatric reasons. It should be noted that Sheldon did not make exaggerated claims for his findings, readily recognizing that the somatotyping alone, in spite of the very high correlation in his study, has virtually no predictive value for delinquency. Sheldon recognized that there are many endomorphic mesomorphs who do not show any criminalistic tendencies, and, also, that there are many criminals, probably also of the residual-criminality type, who are not endomorphic mesomorphs. Nevertheless his finding was sufficiently dramatic to merit attention. For the first time in the history of the social sciences, it appeared that a scholar, thoroughly aware of the requirements of the scientific method and in a study systematically described in a voluminous work, revealed a very high correlation between a certain type of criminality and the physical build.

An interesting observation, which immediately comes to mind, is the apparent contradiction between the findings of Hooton and Sheldon. Hooton's comparisons of criminals and non-criminals within their respective racial and national groups suggested that criminals are characterized by constitutional inferiority; in Sheldon's Hayden Inn series, the primary criminals are mesomorphs with high indices for this component in the cases of all subjects studied, with the exception of one. They were, in other words, athletically-built individuals. Sheldon himself was aware of the discrepancy and attempted to explain it through the fact that while Hooton dealt with the total population of prisons, his group of sixteen boys represented a carefully selected group of primary criminals. Sheldon volunteers the statement that if he had taken the total Hayden Inn population, he would probably have seen the same picture of inferiority as Hooton and Lombroso did in their observed criminal populations.[12]

One might speculate whether the Sheldon findings would have had a similar reception as Hooton's among American sociological criminologists if it were not for another event which took place a year after the appearance of the *Varieties of Delinquent Youth*. That was the appearance of *Unraveling Juvenile Delinquency* by Sheldon and Eleanor Glueck in 1950. In this study, as is now well known, the authors, among their detailed procedures, made use of Sheldon's method of somatotyping and applied it to both delinquent and nondelinquent boys. Their results were almost as spectacular as that of Sheldon's: 60.1 percent of the delinquents turned out to be mesomorphs, while only 30.7 percent of the non-delinquents fell into this category. The Gluecks' findings appear to have had a much wider impact than did the work of Sheldon. The Gluecks were not only widely known and respected as careful researchers in criminology, thoroughly familiar with the requirements of the scientific method, but probably more important, were not identified as committed to any particular etiological theory of criminality. If some critics appear to have taken Sheldon's sixteen boys with a certain degree of skepticism because of Sheldon's known partiality to somatotyping, a similar result, appearing as one of the aspects of the Gluecks' study, did not warrant any such reservation. The importance of their findings was, of course, appreciated by the Gluecks themselves. The implications of these findings were examined in detailed statistical analysis in a still later volume, published in 1956, entitled *Physique and Delinquency*. The challenging implications involved in the established correlation between the physical type and delinquency was already indicated in the *Unraveling*. Many additional significant relationships are disclosed in this new work.

Perhaps the most important contribution of the Gluecks' studies consists not in the reaffirmation of the discovery made by Sheldon of the high correlation between one of the somatotypes (mesomorphy) and delinquent behavior, but in the light shed on the nature of this correlation. One of the main difficulties of anthropological or biological criminology from the beginning has been the problem as to the *nature* of the relationship between the physique and criminality. Lombroso and other early anthropological criminologists assumed that there was a direct tendency to commit offenses on the part of those characterized by a certain physique. This was soon questioned as a highly unlikely proposition, frequently by using an argument similar to the one advanced by Tarde. It was difficult to conceive the nature of inmate tendencies which might be transmitted through biological heredity, directed towards the violation of laws which vary greatly with time and place. To overcome this difficulty, the early criminologists postulated the existence of certain general biologically-anchored tendencies, such as cruelty, dishonesty, and similar traits, which in themselves were not necessarily directed against specific legal norms. This modification, however, was equally unsatisfactory. Later advocates of the biological type, thus, began to speak about certain predispositions or general "moral" weaknesses which, given appropriate adverse circumstances, might manifest themselves in criminal behavior. All such propositions were invariably general and vague, without any specific explanation as to how, from some kind of general predisposition or tendency, the criminal behavior results.

The findings of Sheldon and the Gluecks for the first time suggest a very plausible mechanism, which connects a specific kind of physique with a specific kind of criminal behavior. The mesomorph, in general, is a man of action. Placed in a problem-situation, he acts to get out of it. If his actions are against the law, he is automatically identified as a delinquent. An ectomorph is not a man of action. He is the thinker and the brooder. Rather than doing something about his problems, he "suffers them out." A neurotic, or even a psychotic, condition is more likely to result than delinquent behavior. The endomorph is more apt not to take his problems too seriously, to put up with them, and to go on enjoying life in his own way. The likelihood of his becoming delinquent is not far beyond the average chance.

These are, of course, only very crude general interpretations. The Gluecks provide more refined specific insights into the relationship between the somatotypes and their characteristic patterns of response to the various circumstances in which children find themselves. A detailed presentation is not in order here. It should suffice to state that the Gluecks have found *both*, certain "traits" *and* "sociocultural factors" to be significantly associated with delinquent rather than with non-delinquent boys, regardless of the somatotype. On the other hand, they have found certain "traits" and certain "sociocultural factors" to be highly correlated with delinquency in certain bodily types and not in others. It is perhaps well to quote their three major conclusions:

"1. The basic morphologic differentiation of the physique types is accompanied by differences in the incidence among them of certain traits, some of which are actually associated with delinquency, others potentially so.

2. Differences in the physical and temperamental structure of body types bring about some variation in their response to environmental pressures.

3. Differences in the incidence of certain traits among the physique types, as well as divergences in their reactions to the environment, are reflected in certain differences in the etiology of delinquency among the body types." [13]

Thus, it seems that for the first time a plausible suggestion for a way out of the longstanding controversy between the role of the hereditary endowment expressed in the physique of the individual and the role of the environmental influences has been found, or at least a definite step toward its solution in the interpretation of criminal behavior. Surely only a rabid environmentalist could object today to a hypothetical proposition that the different types of physique may have correspondingly different basic patterns of response related to them. The fervent plea by Earnest Hooton [14] to recognize this possibility might now safely be granted by the environmentalists in the form suggested by the researches of the Gluecks. On the other hand, a modern criminological anthropologist should be willing to admit that the hereditary tendencies alone are not likely to be sufficient to account for the majority of criminal acts; and that the conditions of the social environment must be visualized as instrumental in guiding these impulses into acceptable or unacceptable channels.

It is perhaps a fitting symbol that Sheldon and Eleanor Glueck have dedicated their volume on *Physique and Delinquency* to Professor Earnest A. Hooton. The two distinct movements discerned in this chapter, both of which attempt to link physique and criminal behavior, are thus themselves joined in this latest and most illuminating work. However, much more research and interpretation are still needed to make the hypotheses and the findings of these two powerful streams of thought meaningful for each other and, in turn, compatible with the environmentalist point of view and the established beginnings of scientific knowledge. We are still only in the merest beginning stages of the gradual solution of the nature-nurture dilemma. In the field of criminology, however, promising steps by means of empirical research seem to have been made. The current status of the nature-nurture controversy in the interpretation of criminal behavior could, it appears, be formulated as follows: differentiated physique is connected with different basic response patterns to environmental pressures which, accordingly, sometimes do and sometimes do not lead to criminal behavior. This is the etiological theory of the moment, and a research assignment at the same time.

1. This frequently-made point is presented especially forcefully by Jerome Michael and Mortimer J. Adler in their *Crime, Law and Social Science*, 1933; see, e.g., pp. 390 and 391.

2. John Dewey, *Logic* (Henry Holt and Co., New York, 1938), p. 461. See also Peter P. Lejins, "Pragmatic Etiology of Delinquent Behavior," *Social Forces*, Vol. 29, No. 3, March 1951.

3. Wm. H. Sheldon, *The Varieties of Human Physique* (Harper & Bros., New York, 1940).

4. See, for instance, William Sheldon's deliberate limitation of his study to morphological aspects. Wm. H. Sheldon, *op. cit.*, p. 4.

5. Sheldon and Eleanor Glueck, *Physique and Delinquency* (Harper and Bros., New York, 1956), pp. 1-25, especially pp. 15 ff.

6. Earnest A. Hooton, *The American Criminal*, Vol. I (Harvard University Press, Cambridge, Mass., 1939), p. 17.

7. *Ibid.*

8. See, e.g., E. H. Sutherland's statement in 1947: "Hooton, an American anthropologist, attempted in opposition to the almost unanimous opinion of other scholars, to revive the Lombrosian theory." E. H. Sutherland, *Principles of Criminology* (J. B. Lippincott, New York, 1947), p. 91.

9. Earnest A. Hooton, *The American Criminal*, Vol. I (Harvard University Press, Cambridge, Mass.), pp. 18-20 and ff.

10. *Ibid.*, p. 10.

11. Wm. H. Sheldon, *op. cit.*, pp. 10-11.

12. Wm. H. Sheldon, *Varieties of Delinquent Youth* (Harper and Bros., New York, 1949), p. 758.

13. Sheldon and Eleanor Glueck, *Physique and Delinquency*, p. 249.

14. E. A. Hooton, *Crime and the Man* (Harvard University Press, Cambridge, Mass., 1939), pp. 3-12.

Patterns of behavior—whether licit or illicit, socially acceptable or antisocial—are forms of adaptation to the social structure. It was in this light that the late dean of American criminologists, E. H. Sutherland, proposed that criminal behavior be examined. Different types of criminal behavior, he suggested, may be scrutinized as if each type comprised an integrated behavioral complex, focussing upon certain socially acquired needs and reinforced by a variety of institutional patterns whose historic development emerged from conditions within the social system. Thus, he maintained, there is an unmistakable aura of professionalism which characterizes the behavioral practise of the habitual or professional offender. The professional thief, the embezzler, the blackmailer, the confidence man, the circus grifter, and other forms of professional lawbreakers operate within their own orbits, circumscribed by the peculiar occupational and behavioral patterns which distinguish their special criminal occupational callings. This insight by Sutherland, and the illustrative examples he provided as to how crime might be profitably studied in this way, opens up a promising vista for the further scientific study of crime, although there are as yet relatively few operational research studies which build upon this view.

There are, however, vast patterns of institutional behavior regarded with varying degrees of moral dubiousness. These widely practised social forms are not characteristic only of certain social groups but are virtually coextensive with the entire social structure. Gambling is such a form of social adaptation. A singular problem in the determination of criminal or antisocial behavior, and for law enforcement generally, arises when the attitude towards such a widely prevalent practise is, at the same time, profoundly ambivalent. In a sense, this problem is somewhat akin to the confused and ofttimes contradictory social attitudes towards personal morality, of which indeed gambling is sometimes considered a part, and sexual behavior, touched upon in Chapter 19.

This issue of social ambivalence towards a given form of behavior, whether it be gambling, alcoholism, or sexual conduct, poses an extremely interesting problem for the criminologist for two reasons. In the first place, it engages his interest because it is closely related to the behavioral patterns of the entire society. As a form of social behavior which reflects many deep-seated aspects of the social scene, it provides more than an index of a debatable form of social behavior. It provides, as well, a significant commentary upon the kinds of values the given social order tends to foster and encourage. Seen in this light, studies of such marginally normative patterns of behavior open up broad horizons, indicating with painful clarity the kind of people we are and the type of social values we tend to accept, if not to honor, if only in the breach. Such studies in mass self-deception—the willingness to accept in practise what we deny in principle—may be deeply revealing of the trends in public morality and, indeed, social change. Studies in this marginal phase of criminology, in addition to shedding light upon nascent processes of deviant behavior, can provide profound insights into the character of the social structure and the mechanisms of social change.

There is a further problem, however, provided in the form of the ethical choices we are compelled to face and acknowledge as a result of our previously mentioned ambivalent attitudes to such a practise as gambling. The problem is confounded by the fact that in a complex social order such as ours, the multiplicity of traditional practises and permissive standards of different groups vary in their public attitudes towards such a problem. To add to the confusion, agencies which traditionally are identified with moral and ethical problems are frequently impelled to accept or endorse a socially dubious practise because of the pressures of expedience.

In the last resort, however, enduring institutional values are ultimately determined by behavioral practise rather than by professions of intent or faith. The commitment to such practises have far-reaching effects upon the entire social system in their cumulative impact. Nor can difficult ethical choices be easily resolved by mere acknowledgement of an existent practise. Acknowledgement, in itself, hardly constitutes a justification for a given practise, irrespective of how wide its following.

The problem of gambling is particularly interesting and sensitive when examined in the light of the above considerations. It is quite likely that there are certain profoundly rooted and "built-in" compulsions within the social structure itself which encourage, facilitate, and may even make virtually inevitable, certain forms of gambling. To attempt to legislate against such a practise, thus, may represent an effort, in a sense, to legislate against deeply-inlaid values. Holding up the mirror of opprobrium and public condemnation through legislative practise may constitute an equivalent of the periodic cleansing ceremonies characteristic of certain forms of primitive ritual. To examine ourselves in the light of our social compulsions, if nothing else, may compel us, in paraphrase of Matthew Arnold, "to see ourselves clearly and to see ourselves whole."

Chapter 23

THE DILEMMA OF AMERICAN GAMBLING: CRIME OR PASTIME?

HERBERT A. BLOCH, PH.D.

Professor of Sociology and Anthropology, Brooklyn College; Coordinator, Police Science Program, Brooklyn College; Graduate School, New York University.

Gambling and Social Pathology

Despite moral and legal strictures of long standing placed against it by religious bodies and other groups concerned with human ethical welfare, gambling has continually presented an extremely difficult practise to modify, no less to extirpate from the human scene. The reasons for this lie, partially in the deep recesses of man's instinctual nature, but far more likely in the kinds of social compulsions which our highly complex and organized social living itself creates. It is this latter aspect which raises some particularly pertinent issues—first, in respect to the character of our social life which tends to make various forms of gambling almost inevitable and, secondly, in the kind of widespread moral dubiousness which, while professing to recognize it as an evil, will nevertheless tend to accept it. To further confound the problem, we have the rather remarkable spectacle of religious bodies which, in recognizing some of the inherent evils implicit in gambling, are either oblivious of or indifferent to its deeply imbedded social nature and are willing, nevertheless, to capitalize upon it.

This contradictory and ambivalent attitude should not be construed as typical of only certain groups and certain religious bodies. It is a pervasive symptomatic condition of the dual and conflicting attitudes with which we regard many other problems in modern American social life as well. It has not been entirely an exaggeration or a mere figure of speech to regard our society as having a "schizoid" culture. What is significant here is the fact that we fail to recognize the profound roots with which such a problem as gambling has sunk its tentacles into the subsoil of everyday American life and how deeply it has pervaded, in subtle and overt form, so many aspects of American social life. In our well-intentioned efforts to remove a problem from the American scene—*any* problem —we fail to take cognizance of the well-known sociological fact that a "problem" is merely a symptom of a type of social organization and partially a reflection of the kind of leisure which a society provides for its people. In a particularly perceptive phrase used by Lawrence K. Frank a few years ago in referring to the indissoluble unity of American social life and its problem manifestations, we frequently fail to take heed of the fact that "society (itself) is the patient." [1]

The ways in which a society learns to enjoy its leisure is invariably a manifestation of some of its most basic values, its aspirations and its hopes. Gambling, in its diversified forms, is consequently deeply revealing of the kind of people we are and reflective of many of the values generated by the American social system. This may be a difficult fact to apprehend and an even more unpalatable fact to accept. Although virtually all known societies have indulged in gambling to a greater or lesser degree, the extensiveness of American gambling practise, and the degree with which it has permeated our personal and family living patterns, would appear to constitute an unmistakable earmark of some of the major orientations of our form of social life. To understand this properly, one has simply to examine the record of the American people in respect to the long-sustained interest in speculation and games of chance, as well as the history of gambling itself as a social art and a form of human behavior.

Some conception of the hold which games of chance have

exercised upon the American people can be gained from the various estimates which were made at the time of the Kefauver Senatorial Hearings on crime a few years ago and before the current crackdown on organized gambling ventures. It should be recognized that the full extent of gambling is impossible to estimate with any degree of precision, especially if one takes into account such activities as card games played at home, bingo parties of various description, bridge playing among women's groups, and the like. However, the numbers of individuals and amounts of money involved in the various forms of institutionalized gambling, such as horse racing, the "numbers and policy" games, sporting events, and professional card games have provided us with some rough estimates. It was generally assumed at the time of the Kefauver hearings that approximately 50,000,000 adult Americans participated in some form of professional gambling, involving an annual sum of approximately $30,000,000,000 and yielding an annual profit to the gambling syndicates and entrepreneurs of about $6,000,000,000.[2] This annual profit was reputed to be greater than the combined annual profits of our largest industrial enterprises, including such organizations as the United States Steel Corporation, General Motors, and the General Electric Corporation. Indeed, one estimate actually placed the annual volume of profits from gambling ventures as greater than the total profits of the hundred largest manufacturing companies in the United States.

Although it is difficult to determine at this time how much of this gambling is still going on, because of variations in state and local regulations and varying degrees of stringency in law enforcement, there is little direct evidence to indicate that the preoccupation of the public with gambling has altered substantially for the country as a whole. Although fluctuations in the volume of gambling may be seen in relation to crisis periods and periodic tightening of legal restrictions brought about by a temporarily aroused citizenry, the general volume of gambling has remained at a relatively high level during the entire century. The sociologist, Mowrer, in a study of widely varying problem conditions, has shown that gambling tends to increase during periods of war, post-war years, and during periods of rising prosperity.³ Certainly, an examination of the record during this century would afford little evidence of the fact that the American public's interest in gambling as a form of diversion or as a means of sudden wealth has revealed any indication of a declining trend. Indeed, a sober reading of the record would tend to indicate the very contrary.

As we examine this enormous popular interest in an activity which is regarded by many thoughtful citizens as wrong, and by some as completely reprehensible, we should recognize that gambling has an extremely ancient history. As an institutionalized and informal pastime, it is not necessarily an evil and may, in fact, as it has in the past, serve as an important form of recreation. Artifacts and relics pertaining to various games of chance, such as paired cubes, throwing stones, drawing sticks, gaming boards, and similar contrivances, have been found in the archeological remains of the Sumerian, Egyptian, and Chinese cultures. The Greeks were particularly familiar with games of chance, and the casting of paired and multiple cubes was an especially favored pastime among the Romans. Primitive cultures, from the ancient Peruvian to the Bantu in Africa and the Eskimo in North America, have regaled themselves with such amusements as matching fingers or rolling pebbles or other objects, in which the element of chance constituted one of the principal attractions. Early magic and religious rituals relied heavily upon chance, as in the study of the entrails of sacrificial animals among the Romans, although divine intervention was employed as an explanatory device in order to impose some sense of order upon the unknown and the unpredictable. Card-playing has a lengthy history, many of the forms of our modern games predating the medieval era in European history.

Gambling emerges as a form of social pathology only when there is widespread resentment against it because of the psychological and social problems which it creates. In the first place, in the inveterate gambler it frequently becomes an addiction, as in the celebrated character of Dostoevski's minor classic, *The Gambler*, who neglected personal, family, and social responsibilities. Historically, the gambler has been condemned largely for his failure to perform the normal productive functions ordinarily expected of him rather than because of the nature of the gambling itself.

As previously mentioned, gambling is inextricably interwoven with the traditions and patterns of leisure which a people have learned to enjoy. Leisure as such is invariably appraised by any people in relation to the time which is freed as a consequence of the performance of primary responsibilities and productive activity. In most societies, thus, leisure may be respectably enjoyed only when work is put first. Furthermore, the recreation must not be considered socially destructive or unproductive in itself. This latter consideration, while not a universal characteristic of "antisocial" recreation, may nevertheless become so in a culture like our own, which places a high value upon economic activity and material achievement. How strong the condemnation of unproductive leisure becomes depends largely upon the person's social and economic class position in society. In underprivileged economic groups, such non-utilitarian activity may be strongly condemned, but in wealthier middle-class groups, however, it is significant to realize that gambling, though "wasteful," does not carry the same stigma.[4]

Unlike excessive drinking, drug addiction, or sex demoralization, gambling produces no directly deteriorating effects upon the human organism or the social group. Its danger lies in the fact that it interferes with the normal assumption of responsibility which organized society compels. Second, gambling, as any other form of widely accepted and extensively practised, although tabooed form of social behavior, may become a social problem because of its intimate association with unscrupulous and lawless elements. Despite public strictures against it, particularly in the United States, gambling in its various institutionalized forms, ranging from card games for low or high stakes, horse-racing, bingo, betting on the outcome of various forms of athletic competition, and pinball and other mechanical gambling contrivances to the vast "numbers and policy" games which prey upon small-income groups in our large cities, has become a significant element in modern recreational life. Even before it became associated with underworld and vice elements, however, gambling had been viewed with profound suspicion because of the peculiar psychological, cultural and familial disabilities it was believed to produce. In fact, certain religious bodies, such as the Methodists, have fought gambling almost as strenuously as the directly deteriorating vices.

Nevertheless, because of the ambivalence of the public, which upon occasion condemns gambling as socially destructive while regarding with indifference or approval bingo games played in church parlors, gambling has become extremely difficult to control. Because of this, many modern European and Latin-American countries have capitalized upon what is conceived as an ineradicable "human weakness" by diverting the profits from gambling to public revenues in the form of vast governmentally controlled national lotteries.

The Social Reasons for Gambling

Why do people gamble? The essential basis for all gambling seems to inhere in the chance factor of success for its participants, irrespective of the type of device or game which is employed. The *aleatory* (or chance) element, however, always varies. Gambling may call for skill, as in certain card games and athletic competitions, or it may simply depend upon the chance throw of a pair of dice or the draw of a card, as in stud poker. In any event, the element of chance is always present. It is an indispensable aspect of its universal appeal.

Certain social and cultural systems seem to foster and exploit the chance element in human life, particularly those societies where status largely depends upon competitive pecuniary standards. This is notably true in the United States, where rapid commercial expansion and industrial development conspire to spur the individual to economic success through sharp competitive practise, and where industrial expansion has upon occasion depended to a considerable degree upon precarious and speculative enterprise. In the United States, for example, the distinction between certain forms of approved and legitimate stock-market speculation and the cultivation of the gambling interest is largely a matter of degree, yet one is approved and the other condemned. An illustration of this may be seen in the sharp rise of speculation among basic commodities, at perilous expense to the American economic structure and the national security, which occurred at the beginning of the Korean crisis early in the summer of 1950. Operating almost entirely on credit, speculators at the very start of the Korean war began to buy up "futures" of soybeans, wheat, lard, and other necessities. According to an analysis by the Commodity Exchange Authority of the United States Department of Agriculture, up to 85 or 90 percent of the dealings in soybeans for July 21, 1950, was pure speculation—betting that the market would go up as a result of the crisis. An interpretation of the report of the Commodity Exchange Authority reveals the following:

A speculator who purchased just before the Korean episode and deposited the minimum margin could have "cashed in" five weeks later, on July 28, with an approximate 450 percent profit on lard, 300 percent on cottonseed oil, 300 percent on soybeans, 150 percent on cotton or wool tops, and a comparatively modest 100 percent on the relatively sluggish wheat futures.[5]

Operating against chance, however, are the stabilizing and routinized mechanisms which are the bases of the social order. In order to achieve any type of security, every society strives to reduce ignorance and the unpredictable, as a means of insuring its own continuance. Nevertheless, a certain degree of ignorance concerning the operation of both physical and human events must, of necessity, always exist. Ignorance of events, therefore, and of their outcome serves as a dynamic function in all societies.[6] Where knowledge of the outcome of a given series of human events is certain, there is no incentive toward competition and other forms of social striving. Von Neumann and Morgenstern have demonstrated this point of view in their analysis of economic behavior as compared to the "sporting" chance present in playing games.[7]

For a society such as our own—complex, impersonal, and

yet highly competitive—a great premium is placed upon conformity and the need for routine. At the same time there is great pressure to break the routine—to initiate, to promote, and to experiment in order to bring about the dynamic growth of a continuously expanding social economy. For large masses of individuals, this is difficult, if not impossible. Hedged in by stereotyped employment which is ever becoming increasingly regularized, the fear of insecurity, the pressures of family, and the opinion of others, the average individual fears to "take a chance" that may mean riches and prestige, despite the traditional assurance that the country's growth and expansion have depended upon people who *did* exactly that. Moreover, as Allison Davis, E. W. Bakke and the Lynds have shown in their studies of working-class families, lower socioeconomic class members frequently feel that they are trapped and that there exists neither opportunity nor incentive for further advancement.[8] For many, however, the opportunity of making a "killing," whether by betting on the Irish Sweepstakes or by winning the giant jackpot on some television "giveaway" program or by answering the "$64,000 question," appears a genuine possibility; the odds are hardly ever taken into consideration. Further, the rewards are immediate; there is no lengthy and painful deferment with the risks of achievement uncertain.[9] Gambling serves a contemporary function strongly reminiscent of the practise of magic and ritualistic formulas among primitives, who entertain the notion that the unpredictable contains for them among its infinite possibilities the chance of good fortune. It is probably no accident that inveterate gamblers are the most superstitious of men. This uncertainty is played upon by all people in all cultures and is the source of the perennial folk proverb, "While there's life, there's hope." In a highly complex and impersonal industrial society such as our own, where the rewards and the risks are proportionately greater, the problematical risks of uncertainty are even more challenging and, in a sense, while more ominous are also more alluring.

Gambling is an escape from the routine and boredom characteristic of much of modern industrial life in which the sense of creation and the "instinct of workmanship" have been lost. "Taking a chance" destroys routine and hence is pleasurable, particularly in a culture where the unchanging and predictable routines of employment are sharply separated from "leisure"—the time when the individual *really* "lives." The desire for thrills through new experience, so much a part of American life and sharpened so keenly by the huckstering quality of American advertising, makes the public readily open to exploitation by a wide variety of gambling interests, as the sociologists, Moore and Tumin, have pointed out:

> Certainly the attractiveness of many games of chance, as well as those games and sports where chance may equalize or offset known differences in skill and performance, rests in large measure on their unpredictable outcome. In fact, there is some rough evidence that ignorance of the future in recreational activities assumes an especially significant role where routine and boredom are characteristic of work assignments and where there is a sharp break between working time and leisure time.[10]

There remain, finally, the conditions of the individual's characteristic class and cultural associations, opportunity, and the large blocks of unplanned leisure, which our modern and highly mobile society permits. Games of chance are traditionally found, and even encouraged, in the play of children in modern society, ranging from traditional children's guessing and matching games to the early imitation of adult gambling and card games. In many families, on all class levels, card-playing and other forms of gambling, even when the stakes are low, have become deeply entrenched. There are ethnic, class, and even sex differentials in these common forms of recreation. Bridge-playing is largely a middle-class diversion, while poker is traditionally considered a "man's game," and the casting of dice, aside from professional gambling interest, is common among Negroes. For many young men of the lower economic and middle classes, learning to play cards is part of the process of growing up and becoming identified with adults and their standards. For the individual with few inner resources, whose employment offers little opportunity for progressive challenge and advancement, and is tedious and boring, and in whose early experience gambling in some form has played a part, to learn to gamble is as commonplace and natural as to become an ardent baseball fan or a television addict.

In summary, gambling provides a function in well-organized societies where the stress of competition (with its lack of predictability) is great, and where, in contrast, the regimen of economic and social life is rigorous. Such a society, placing a premium upon "risk" and "taking a chance," provides through gambling an outlet for many individuals who, hedged in by social restrictions and limited or no opportunity, would otherwise find little satisfaction for the need for new experience and pecuniary success. This penchant for taking a chance is expressed in the popular cliché: "Why not? What have you got to lose?" The implications are twofold.

In the first place, the probability of being the winner or the loser in a gaming enterprise provides suspense, insecurity, new experience, and hope, serving important emotional needs in individuals whose lives are increasingly regularized. Other historical periods and other cultural groups have provided us with similar examples. Although the unique conditions which existed at the time must also be taken into consideration, this may account in part for the heavy gambling in cards in certain classes, such as the landed English gentry of the seventeenth and eighteenth centuries.[11] Although highly stable and securely ensconced in the social structure through special favor and privilege, "life in the country," as judged by descriptive accounts, diaries, and letters of the period, was extremely boring. Gambling provided a precarious diversion, as did the risks of fox-hunting: a man would risk his entire estate upon the turn of a card. This aristocratic tradition had its counterpart in this country in the ante-bellum South among wealthy plantation owners. The suave and aristocratic riverboat gambler has become a stereotype in American folklore, if not an American folk hero, as any viewer of television may testify.

In the second place, the belief that chance works equally in favor of each one of the contestants in a gambling venture sustains the hope for status or rewards, which the individual feels may *not* be achieved through conventional and acceptable channels. (Who hasn't dreamed of what he would do if he had a million dollars?) Further, in American life, the "get-something-for-nothing" philosophy is expressed in a wide range of activities from saving box-tops for premiums to the enormous prizes of the television "giveaway" programs. This incentive, ironically, operates even when what is given away—as, for example, a thousand cans of dog food—may have very little or no value to the contestant. The antics of a fictional "Get-Rich-Quick Wallingford" or his realistic counterpart, "Bet-a-Million" Gates, the financial tycoon, excited the admiration, envy, and emulation of an earlier generation of Americans at the beginning of the century, just as the giant radio and television "jackpot" contests entice their present-day children and grandchildren. The "built-in" compulsions of the social system are still there. In fact, in view of the nature of the present social order, they have become intensified and well-nigh inevitable.

The Gambler As A Personality Type

Since gambling is so extensive, gamblers, unlike alcoholics, do not fall into any specific typological classifications. Nevertheless, certain common characteristics may be found in their personalities. Gambling, as a form of addiction, occurs when the individual consistently and continuously neglects his important primary duties and obligations to his family, employer, and community for the sake of gambling. The life-histories of inveterate gamblers indicate a transitional period in their careers when their regular routines are seriously jeopardized and it becomes increasingly common for them to stay away from home and job for lengthy periods. The inveterate gambler becomes as unpredictable and undependable as the alcoholic, as far as his home and his work are concerned. Aside from horse-racing and other spectacles which encourage gambling, most forms of professional gambling may be indulged in at any time of the day or night, and night-long sessions, disrupting the routine of normal life, are quite common. For the gambler who consistently pursues his gambling interests, therefore, the discipline and orderliness which to some degree characterize the lives of most individuals are gone.

It is not uncommon to find occasional evidences of neglect of diet and sleep. Neglect of personal appearance, a matter of great importance in a highly competitive society, is another characteristic; although not very common, this is a revelation of class. In fact, some gamblers sedulously cultivate a dapper appearance as a means of indicating affluence and respectability and betokening, among other things, solvency as a gambling partner or adversary. The interesting psychological feature of gambling is the enormous hold it finally comes to exert upon the personality, comparable in a sense to the grip of alcohol, without its adverse physical effects. Once addicted, even though the gambler may recognize the harm his practise is causing his family, business associates, and others, he will nevertheless continue to follow his bent, living in the hope of making up in one final sweep of winnings an amount sufficient to compensate for his previous losses and, consequently, to make restitution to his family and friends. The motive to gamble, when once it has achieved a "functional autonomy" of its own, may dominate other primary considerations of the personality.[12] This impetus is so strong that the individual may transgress against law in order to accomplish his purpose. Embezzlement is a common offense of gamblers.

The continual suspense in which the gambler lives engenders an emotional tension. He is frequently taut, the hypertension being sustained for lengthy periods of time. He cannot afford to relax since he is invariably either raising funds for his gambling forays or planning for or making his bets. He devotes considerable time and energy to his enterprises. The amount of time spent in working over his "dope sheets" in horse-racing, for example, and the degree of concentration required, are impressive.

Subjected to the tension involved in continuous risk-taking, the gambler learns to affect characteristic expressive behavior. His inner turmoil and anxiety are frequently repressed through an assumption of stoical calm, evidenced in the well-known "poker face" of the inveterate card-player

Moreover, just as the alcoholic secretes liquor and funds for a potential drinking bout, the gambler will retain a reservoir of funds—his "betting money"—which he will not use even for pressing personal needs or the needs of his family. Finally, there is interesting evidence of the mechanisms of compensation and other characteristic forms of psychological tension-reducing devices: for example, he frequently boasts about his winnings, real or fictitious, to nongamblers, while he bemoans the exaggerated extent of his losses to his fellow-gamblers.

The specialized humor of gambling and the jokes which gamblers exchange among themselves reflect their tensions and their underlying cynicism, the latter an evidence that they are aware of the futility of gambling. Striking is the paradox between the gambler's perennial hope that he can "beat the game" and his realistic knowledge that it is virtually impossible to do so.

Gambling: A Dilemma of Modern Society

The practise and organization of gambling seem to follow a cycle. So well entrenched is it as a form of recreation, and so propitious are the various cultural elements in modern society which promote it, that, as in the case of the prohibition of alcohol, legislation and other forms of arbitrary social control are frequently considered an infringement upon personal prerogative and privilege. Consequently, it remains a widespread practise which, in its disorganizing effects upon groups and personalities and the possibilities for exploitation it offers to lawless elements, may continue to go largely uncontrolled, despite periodic soul-searching and the temporary checks of public indignation. And when control *is* attempted, it is virtually impossible to maintain because of the secure place which gambling enjoys in the institutional patterns of folkways. As a result, legislation and other controls can at best, in the long run, be only partially successful. The public outcry and consternation in the wake of the disclosures of the Kefauver Committee ushered in what will very likely prove a continuing although a temporary pressure for such partial control. Such measures do not deter but actually provide an incentive toward the opening-up of forms of gambling still proscribed, paving the way once more toward eventual irresponsible control by lawless and corrupt elements. As the cycle gains momentum, this invites further legal control, again difficult or impossible to enforce and leading to further corruption, with the result that eventually considerable popular pressure is exerted to legalize all forms of gambling. When this occurs, the dangers of widespread legalized gambling invite hazards for the entire society, reintroducing the need for partial control; and the cycle begins again.[13] In a subtle and unrecognized way, the pressure is already upon us. The dilatory attitude of both public officials and private bodies towards the question of such an innocuous pastime as bingo, irrespective of the commendable purposes for which the proceeds of such an activity are to be used, may already constitute the first thin opening of the wedge. This is apparently the phase of the cycle which we have presently reached.

Gambling: Social Dilemma and Moral Problem

It is at this point that Americans must ask themselves some profoundly disturbing and realistic questions. There is a peculiar philosophic doctrine known as "solipsism" which holds as its fundamental premise the denial of the existence of outside reality. This evasive quality of the American mentality is well-known in respect to certain public issues. Certainly, Americans can no longer engage in such solipsism in respect to the matter of gambling, nor can they any longer regard the intrusion into their public life of such issues as to whether bingo should or should not be played in public places as an issue provoked largely by cantankerous groups or publicity-seeking politicians. The path of least resistance is not as innocuous as it would appear, even though many of our citizens have tended to cultivate the attitude that they would rather not be bothered. It is at this point that the heated adversaries for and against public tolerance and legal approval of gambling raise some agitating questions. Unfortunately for us, the questions are not easy, nor do they permit of facile solutions. They are subtle and have far-reaching implications. In presenting such arguments, it is not merely an arbitrary matter of "you 'pays' your money and you 'takes' your choice."

The proponent of a tolerant view towards gambling would state, as a matter of course, that since gambling is always a matter of degree, at what point do we attempt to control it, no less stop it. At the present time, he would hold, if we reduce the argument to its ultimate conclusion, it is largely a matter of the kind of premises in many instances in which the gambling is being carried on that is being objected to. Hardly any one would recommend the invasion of the privacy of the home, irrespective of how high the stakes might be in a neighborhood card game. Certainly, he would stipulate, when the argument is reduced to this level, it appears completely absurd and ridiculous.

His adversary, at this point, however, would state that the problem is not as simple as this. While recognizing that the "private" gambling practises of Americans can hardly be controlled by law—no more than a friendly bet between associates on the outcome of the World Series can be regulated—the approval of "public" gambling, whether in the form of gambling casinos, state-controlled slot machines, bingo, or public lotteries, is an entirely different matter. The tolerance of such activities intensifies an unwholesome practise already deeply inherent in American folkways and serves as a goad and incitement to many others, particularly the young, who might ordinarily not be inclined to gamble. We hardly resolve an issue by acknowledging its existence—a fallacy which, incidentally, the Kinsey Report in respect to sex-behavior may likewise have done so much to encourage.

At this point, however, the hardheaded protagonist of a more enlightened attitude towards gambling would enter the following demurrer: the tolerance of certain forms of gambling (such as horse racing) and betting on sporting events, while disapproving other forms, is nothing but a type of moral and legal hypocrisy. On the basis of what type of lucid argument, he would say, can it be stated that one type is less "immoral" or more "immoral" than another type? Let us be consistent, he would argue—if gambling is socially dangerous and morally wrong, then it's wrong all the way down the line. His reform-seeking antagonist, however, is not discouraged by this line of argument. There are, he would argue, no absolute dichotomies in modern life, no clearcut blacks and whites or mutually exclusive choices, but a series of painfully weighted decisions consisting of many complex elements. While sporting events, such as horse racing and athletic competitions, invariably introduce the element of chance and hence invite betting on their outcomes, this is a different matter than advocating and encouraging "pure" gambling, where the hazard is primarily based upon luck. Vast sums of money expended in this way are demoralizing to the individual, socially wasteful, and economically unproductive.

Such arguments, states the more permissive proponent of gambling, overlook the fact that gambling will very likely continue anyway. Only a long process of reeducation and retraining of the American people, beginning in the home and the grade school, may have any appreciable effect, and even then, the outcome is dubious. Why not, accordingly, capitalize on gambling? It is only a matter of time before lawless elements will once more begin to gain control of the public's unwhetted appetite for gaming, inviting all of the unsavory accompanying conditions of vice and crime with which we have become all too familiar. After all, in the state of Nevada where gambling is legal, an estimated 15.5 percent of the total state revenue is derived from gambling, as well as 8.5 percent and 22.4 percent of the revenues collected by counties and municipalities respectively. Further, under such auspices, the gambling-minded citizen is given something resembling a fair break, something he doesn't get under the uncontrolled conditions of clandestine gambling. After all, many citizens also object to the sale of alcoholic beverages; nevertheless, a considerable source of our national revenue is obtained from the sale of liquor. Further, European governments have sponsored national lotteries for a half-century without, as far as we can tell, any appreciable weakening of the moral fibre from this source.

Indeed, a British Royal Commission, appointed in 1949 to

examine the problem of gambling, made the following statement after an exhaustive two year survey: "We can find no
support for the belief that gambling, provided that it is kept
within reasonable bounds, does serious harm either to the
character of those who take part . . . their family circle (or)
the community generally." As a result of its survey, the Commission actually recommended that the person of modest
circumstances with a little money to gamble be afforded the
same opportunity for placing bets as his more affluent fellow
citizen. It would be presumptuous to assert that the British
character has degenerated since that famous pronouncement
and, even if it had, to attribute such a decline to a more
tolerant public view of gambling.

Here the argument becomes vitriolic and bitter. Aside
from the unwholesome spectacle of mothers with shopping-
bags accompanied by their offspring playing the ubiquitous
"one arm bandits" in the shopping emporia of such a state as
Nevada, and any moral enervation which such a practise may
induce, the overt acceptance of such a human weakness invariably paves the way for further corrosive impact upon the
already precarious human personality. Vice breeds vice, as
we have painfully learned in the course of human affairs, and
any government, national or local, loses in the long run when
it tolerates such an abuse, irrespective of the weaknesses and
demoralized demands of the population. And so the argument runs.

From the standpoint of control, gambling thus presents
two major problems: that of the disorganized individual gambler and that of widespread effective control. The extreme
gambler, whose disorganization constitutes a serious problem
to himself, his family and to society, requires concerted
therapeutic and psychiatric care. This does not concern us
here.

The social control of gambling, however, for the protection of the public at large, presents two alternatives: (1)
Gambling may be diminished or removed only to the degree
that other leisure-time practises and recreational choices are
cultivated—a problem involving widespread social reappraisal
and social reconstruction. (2) As a more expedient solution,

gambling may be regulated in accordance with conventional social practise within localized areas on the basis of "local option," through adequate permissive and controlling legislation. For the present, both courses may be profitably followed.

If, ultimately, the first course is to be pursued—and it may be by far the more commendable and salutary—it means a slow and steady appraisal of many intricate phases of our total social mechanism, attempting through immediate and long-range efforts to ameliorate the sources of tension and stultification that provide many of the superficial goals in American life. In its outreach, and in its accompanying by-product of an invigorating recreational life in the deepest sense, such a course must touch upon all the major institutions in American life, acknowledging the total interrelatedness that binds all institutions together. Nevertheless, its primary focus of attack must be based upon those aspects of our institutional life which limit the capacity of the individual for full self-expression and which would deny to him the limitless range of his creative possibilities.

A rigid and uncompromising adherence to the formula of material success at the expense of other avenues of self-expression, irrespective of how much we may deny this in our public pronouncements and credos, will do little to alter the substantive nature of this problem. Nor can we continue our penchant for resolving many of our lesser problems by ignoring them. For the fact remains that many of our "lesser" problems, so-called, constitute the real basis for the major problems we face. The consequent enrichment of America's spiritual and social life is a goal worth striving for, irrespective of how arduous and agonizing the effort, and one upon which all Americans would agree.

REFERENCES

1. Lawrence K. Frank, *Society as the Patient* (New Brunswick, N. J., 1948), pp. 1-20.

2. See, for example, some of these disclosures in the

Second Interim Report of the Kefauver Committee (Washington, D. C.: U. S. Government Printing Office, 1951).

3. Ernest R. Mowrer, "Social Crises & Social Disorganization," *American Sociological Review*, XV (February 1950), p. 64.

4. For an analysis of social conceptions of value and their relation to the use of leisure, see the author's *Disorganization: Personal and Social* (Alfred A. Knopf, Inc., New York City, 1952), pp. 423-427.

5. U. S. Department of Agriculture, *Report of the Commodity Exchange Authority* (Washington, D. C., August 1950).

6. See Robert K. Merton, "The Unanticipated Consequences of Purposive Social Action," *American Sociological Review*, I (December 1936), pp. 894-904.

7. Cf. John von Neumann & Oskar Morgenstern, *Theory of Games and Economic Behavior* (2nd ed.; Princeton, Princeton University Press, 1947). See also Oskar Morgenstern, "The Theory of Games," *Scientific American*, CLXXX, No. 5 (May 1949), pp. 22-25.

8. See, e.g., Allison Davis, "The Motivation of the Underprivileged Worker," ETC: *A Review of General Semantics*, III, No. 4 (Summer, 1946), pp. 243-53. Also, E. Wright Bakke, *The Unemployed Worker* (New Haven, 1940).

9. For an analysis of such a value-structure in which immediate gratification is prized and deferment of gratification appears meaningless, see Albert K. Cohen, *Delinquent Boys: The Culture of the Gang* (Glencoe, Illinois, 1955).

10. Wilbert E. Moore & Melvin M. Tumin, "Some Social Functions of Ignorance," *American Sociological Review*, XIV, No. 6 (December 1949), esp. pp. 794 and 795.

11. Cf., e.g., David Matthew, *The Social Structure of Caroline England* (London, Oxford University Press, 1948).

12. Cf. Gordon W. Allport, *Personality: A Psychological Interpretation* (New York: Henry Holt & Co., 1937), chap. vii.

13. An examination of attempts to impose legislative curbs upon gambling in the United States suggests very strongly that the cycle described occurs with impressive regularity in relation to restrictive legislation.

NAME INDEX